Internet Ex...
For Windows®

Cheat Sheet

Internet Explorer Toolbar Buttons

Toolbar Button	What It Does
	Goes back to the previously displayed page
	Returns to the page where you were before you went back
	Stops downloading the current page
	Downloads a fresh copy of the current page
	Goes to your designated start page
	Calls up the Search bar
	Calls up the Favorites bar
	Calls up the History bar
	Summons Outlook Express for Internet e-mail or news
	Prints the current page
	Summons FrontPage Express to edit the Web page
	Starts a Web discussion
	Calls up the Real.com home page
	Summons the MSN Messenger Service

Outlook Express Buttons

Outlook Express Button	What It Does
New Mail	Composes a new e-mail message
Send/Recv	Delivers any pending e-mail and checks for new e-mail
Addresses	Summons the Address Book
Print	Prints the message
Delete	Deletes the message
Reply	Sends a message back to the author of an incoming message
Reply All	Sends a message to everyone to whom the original message was addressed
Forward	Forwards a message to another user
Previous	Retrieves the previous message from your Inbox
Next	Retrieves the next message from your Inbox
Newsgroups	Lets you choose a newsgroup

Internet Explorer 5.5 For Windows For Dummies

Cheat Sheet

Web Addresses to Remember

URL	What It Is
www.microsoft.com/ie/ie5	Internet Explorer 5.5 home page
msdn.microsoft.com/ie	The home page for Microsoft's Internet Explorer Developer Center, where you will find lots of good information about creating Web pages for Internet Explorer 5.5
www.msn.com	The Microsoft Network home page
www.hotmail.com	The Hotmail home page
www.yahoo.com	The Yahoo! search service
www.lycos.com	The Lycos search service
www.altavista.com	The AltaVista search service

Internet Explorer Keyboard Shortcuts

Keyboard Shortcut	What It Does
Backspace	Back (previous page)
Shift+Backspace	Forward (next page)
Shift+F10	Displays the pop-up menu for a link
Ctrl+Shift+Tab	Moves to the next frame
F5	Refreshes the current page
Esc	Stops downloading
Ctrl+O	Goes to a new page
Ctrl+N	Opens a new window
Ctrl+S	Saves the current page
Ctrl+P	Prints the current page

Essential Connection Information

If you don't know what to put in the following blanks, call your Internet service provider for help:

My user ID: _____

My password: *(No! Don't Write It Here!)*

Phone number I dial to access the Internet:
_____

My e-mail address: _____

Customer service phone number: _____

DNS Server IP Address: ____.____.____.____

E-mail SMTP Server Address: _____

E-mail POP3 Server Address: _____

News Server Name: _____

MSN Messenger Buttons

MSN Messenger Button	What It Does
Add	Adds someone to your contact list
Send	Sends an instant message
Status	Changes your online status
Mail	Calls up your Hotmail Inbox
Block	Blocks the sender

IDG BOOKS WORLDWIDE

Copyright © 2000 IDG Books Worldwide, Inc. All rights reserved.
Cheat Sheet $2.95 value. Item 0738-9.
For more information about IDG Books, call 1-800-762-2974.

For Dummies®: Bestselling Book Series for Beginners

TM

References for the Rest of Us! ®

BESTSELLING BOOK SERIES

Are you intimidated and confused by computers? Do you find that traditional manuals are overloaded with technical details you'll never use? Do your friends and family always call you to fix simple problems on their PCs? Then the *...For Dummies*® computer book series from IDG Books Worldwide is for you.

...For Dummies books are written for those frustrated computer users who know they aren't really dumb but find that PC hardware, software, and indeed the unique vocabulary of computing make them feel helpless. *...For Dummies* books use a lighthearted approach, a down-to-earth style, and even cartoons and humorous icons to dispel computer novices' fears and build their confidence. Lighthearted but not lightweight, these books are a perfect survival guide for anyone forced to use a computer.

> *"I like my copy so much I told friends; now they bought copies."*
>
> — Irene C., Orwell, Ohio

> *"Quick, concise, nontechnical, and humorous."*
>
> — Jay A., Elburn, Illinois

> *"Thanks, I needed this book. Now I can sleep at night."*
>
> — Robin F., British Columbia, Canada

Already, millions of satisfied readers agree. They have made *...For Dummies* books the #1 introductory level computer book series and have written asking for more. So, if you're looking for the most fun and easy way to learn about computers, look to *...For Dummies* books to give you a helping hand.

IDG BOOKS WORLDWIDE ®

Internet Explorer 5.5 For Windows®

FOR DUMMIES®

Internet Explorer 5.5 For Windows® FOR DUMMIES®

by Doug Lowe

IDG Books Worldwide, Inc.
An International Data Group Company

Foster City, CA ◆ Chicago, IL ◆ Indianapolis, IN ◆ New York, NY

Internet Explorer 5.5 For Windows® For Dummies®

Published by
IDG Books Worldwide, Inc.
An International Data Group Company
919 E. Hillsdale Blvd.
Suite 400
Foster City, CA 94404
www.idgbooks.com (IDG Books Worldwide Web site)
www.dummies.com (Dummies Press Web site)

Library of Congress Control Number: 00-102507

ISBN: 0-7645-0738-9

Printed in the United States of America

10 9 8 7 6 5 4 3 2 1

1B/QS/QY/QQ/IN

Distributed in the United States by IDG Books Worldwide, Inc.

Distributed by CDG Books Canada Inc. for Canada; by Transworld Publishers Limited in the United Kingdom; by IDG Norge Books for Norway; by IDG Sweden Books for Sweden; by IDG Books Australia Publishing Corporation Pty. Ltd. for Australia and New Zealand; by TransQuest Publishers Pte Ltd. for Singapore, Malaysia, Thailand, Indonesia, and Hong Kong; by Gotop Information Inc. for Taiwan; by ICG Muse, Inc. for Japan; by Intersoft for South Africa; by Eyrolles for France; by International Thomson Publishing for Germany, Austria and Switzerland; by Distribuidora Cuspide for Argentina; by LR International for Brazil; by Galileo Libros for Chile; by Ediciones ZETA S.C.R. Ltda. for Peru; by WS Computer Publishing Corporation, Inc., for the Philippines; by Contemporanea de Ediciones for Venezuela; by Express Computer Distributors for the Caribbean and West Indies; by Micronesia Media Distributor, Inc. for Micronesia; by Chips Computadoras S.A. de C.V. for Mexico; by Editorial Norma de Panama S.A. for Panama; by American Bookshops for Finland.

For general information on IDG Books Worldwide's books in the U.S., please call our Consumer Customer Service department at 800-762-2974. For reseller information, including discounts and premium sales, please call our Reseller Customer Service department at 800-434-3422.

For information on where to purchase IDG Books Worldwide's books outside the U.S., please contact our International Sales department at 317-596-5530 or fax 317-572-4002.

For consumer information on foreign language translations, please contact our Customer Service department at 1-800-434-3422, fax 317-572-4002, or e-mail rights@idgbooks.com.

For information on licensing foreign or domestic rights, please phone +1-650-653-7098.

For sales inquiries and special prices for bulk quantities, please contact our Order Services department at 800-434-3422 or write to the address above.

For information on using IDG Books Worldwide's books in the classroom or for ordering examination copies, please contact our Educational Sales department at 800-434-2086 or fax 317-572-4005.

For press review copies, author interviews, or other publicity information, please contact our Public Relations department at 650-653-7000 or fax 650-653-7500.

For authorization to photocopy items for corporate, personal, or educational use, please contact Copyright Clearance Center, 222 Rosewood Drive, Danvers, MA 01923, or fax 978-750-4470.

is a registered trademark under exclusive license to IDG Books Worldwide, Inc. from International Data Group, Inc.

About the Author

Doug Lowe lives in sunny Fresno, California (where the motto is "At least it's a *dry* heat"), with his wife, Debbie; daughters, Rebecca, Sarah, and Bethany; and female golden retrievers, Nutmeg and Ginger. He works full-time creating outstanding literary works, such as *Internet Explorer 5.5 For Windows For Dummies,* and wonders why he hasn't yet won a Pulitzer Prize or had one of his books made into a movie starring Harrison Ford so that he can retire. Doug really thinks that Harrison Ford would be excellent as the Dummies Man and thinks that John Kilcullen's people should call Harrison real soon before someone else steals the idea.

If Harrison isn't available, Jar Jar Binks could do a credible job. Doug's working title for the screenplay is *Net Wars 5.5: The Dummy Menace.*

Doug spends most of his spare time (which amounts to about three full hours per month) following his daughters to their various sports events and Improv performances. Hiking is also a favorite hobby, so much so that Doug really would like to write *Hiking For Dummies* or *Backpacking For Dummies* but hasn't had the time to write a proposal yet because these computer books just keep coming up. Maybe someday.

ABOUT IDG BOOKS WORLDWIDE

Welcome to the world of IDG Books Worldwide.

IDG Books Worldwide, Inc., is a subsidiary of International Data Group, the world's largest publisher of computer-related information and the leading global provider of information services on information technology. IDG was founded more than 30 years ago by Patrick J. McGovern and now employs more than 9,000 people worldwide. IDG publishes more than 290 computer publications in over 75 countries. More than 90 million people read one or more IDG publications each month.

Launched in 1990, IDG Books Worldwide is today the #1 publisher of best-selling computer books in the United States. We are proud to have received eight awards from the Computer Press Association in recognition of editorial excellence and three from Computer Currents' First Annual Readers' Choice Awards. Our best-selling ...*For Dummies*® series has more than 50 million copies in print with translations in 31 languages. IDG Books Worldwide, through a joint venture with IDG's Hi-Tech Beijing, became the first U.S. publisher to publish a computer book in the People's Republic of China. In record time, IDG Books Worldwide has become the first choice for millions of readers around the world who want to learn how to better manage their businesses.

Our mission is simple: Every one of our books is designed to bring extra value and skill-building instructions to the reader. Our books are written by experts who understand and care about our readers. The knowledge base of our editorial staff comes from years of experience in publishing, education, and journalism — experience we use to produce books to carry us into the new millennium. In short, we care about books, so we attract the best people. We devote special attention to details such as audience, interior design, use of icons, and illustrations. And because we use an efficient process of authoring, editing, and desktop publishing our books electronically, we can spend more time ensuring superior content and less time on the technicalities of making books.

You can count on our commitment to deliver high-quality books at competitive prices on topics you want to read about. At IDG Books Worldwide, we continue in the IDG tradition of delivering quality for more than 30 years. You'll find no better book on a subject than one from IDG Books Worldwide.

John J. Kilcullen

John Kilcullen
Chairman and CEO
IDG Books Worldwide, Inc.

Eighth Annual Computer Press Awards ≥1992

Ninth Annual Computer Press Awards ≥1993

Tenth Annual Computer Press Awards ≥1994

Eleventh Annual Computer Press Awards ≥1995

Dedication

This book is dedicated to Bethany. May all your explorations be fruitful.

Author's Acknowledgments

One of the things I like best about writing a book like this comes when the book is on the verge of being finished and I have the pleasure of taking a few moments to thank the many people who helped along the way. I'll start with project editor Dana Lesh, who did a great job of seeing this entire project through from start to finish and demonstrated uncalled-for patience as deadlines came and went and manuscript didn't. Dana is responsible for turning my hapless prose into the finished book you now hold in your hand.

Thanks also to Allen Wyatt for his excellent technical review and copy editors Beth Parlon and Rebekah Mancilla for correcting all my spelling errors and other silly mistakes.

I'd also like to thank my good friends Jerry and Dianne McKneely for helping out with the MSN Messenger and NetMeeting material.

This book borrows heavily from the previous edition, *Internet Explorer 5 For Dummies*, so I'd like to thank the crew that helped with that one, too: project editor Kyle Looper, copy editor Stephanie Koutek, and the ubiquitous Allen Wyatt.

Publisher's Acknowledgments

We're proud of this book; please register your comments through our IDG Books Worldwide Online Registration Form located at http://my2cents.dummies.com.

Some of the people who helped bring this book to market include the following:

Acquisitions, Editorial, and Media Development

Project Editor: Dana Rhodes Lesh

    (Previous Edition: Kyle Looper)

Acquisitions Editor: Steven H. Hayes

Copy Editor: Beth Parlon

    (Previous Edition: Stephanie Koutek)

Proof Editor: Dwight Ramsey

Technical Editor: Allen Wyatt

Editorial Manager: Rev Mengle

Editorial Assistant: Candace Nicholson

Production

Project Coordinator: Emily Wichlinski

Layout and Graphics: Amy Adrian, Jason Guy, Barry Offringa, Jill Piscatelli, Brent Savage, Jacque Schneider

Proofreaders: Corey Bowen, John Greenough, Susan Moritz, Marianne Santy, Charles Spencer, York Production Services, Inc.

Indexer: York Production Services, Inc.

Special Help

Ted Cains, Amanda M. Foxworth, Donna S. Frederick, Rebekah Mancilla

---

General and Administrative

IDG Books Worldwide, Inc.: John Kilcullen, CEO

IDG Books Technology Publishing Group: Richard Swadley, Senior Vice President and Publisher; Walter R. Bruce III, Vice President and Publisher; Joseph Wikert, Vice President and Publisher; Mary Bednarek, Vice President and Director, Product Development; Andy Cummings, Publishing Director, General User Group; Mary C. Corder, Editorial Director; Barry Pruett, Publishing Director

IDG Books Consumer Publishing Group: Roland Elgey, Senior Vice President and Publisher; Kathleen A. Welton, Vice President and Publisher; Kevin Thornton, Acquisitions Manager; Kristin A. Cocks, Editorial Director

IDG Books Internet Publishing Group: Brenda McLaughlin, Senior Vice President and Publisher; Sofia Marchant, Online Marketing Manager

IDG Books Production for Branded Press: Debbie Stailey, Director of Production; Cindy L. Phipps, Manager of Project Coordination, Production Proofreading, and Indexing; Tony Augsburger, Manager of Prepress, Reprints, and Systems; Laura Carpenter, Production Control Manager; Shelley Lea, Supervisor of Graphics and Design; Debbie J. Gates, Production Systems Specialist; Robert Springer, Supervisor of Proofreading; Trudy Coler, Page Layout Manager; Troy Barnes, Page Layout Supervisor, Kathie Schutte, Senior Page Layout Supervisor; Michael Sullivan, Production Supervisor

Packaging and Book Design: Patty Page, Manager, Promotions Marketing

◆

The publisher would like to give special thanks to Patrick J. McGovern, without whom this book would not have been possible.

◆

Contents at a Glance

Introduction *1*

Part I: Preparing for an Internet Exploration *7*
Chapter 1: Welcome to the Internet 9
Chapter 2: Getting Connected with Internet Explorer 19

Part II: Embarking on a World Wide Web Adventure *37*
Chapter 3: Pushing Off 39
Chapter 4: Searching the Web 63
Chapter 5: Getting around the Web Quickly 77
Chapter 6: Working Offline 89
Chapter 7: Getting Help While You Explore 95

Part III: Getting Connected with Outlook Express *105*
Chapter 8: E-mailing with Outlook Express 107
Chapter 9: E-mail Shortcuts and Tricks 127
Chapter 10: Using Outlook Express with Hotmail 151
Chapter 11: The Instant Message Connection 167
Chapter 12: Accessing Newsgroups with Outlook Express 185

Part IV: Customizing Your Explorations *199*
Chapter 13: Doing It Your Way: Personalizing Internet Explorer 201
Chapter 14: Using the Content Advisor to Make Sure
   That Your Kids Surf Safely 221
Chapter 15: Lowering the Cone of Silence: Using Internet Explorer's
   Security Features 231
Chapter 16: Creating a Login Script 239

Part V: Grow Your Own Web Pages *251*
Chapter 17: So You Want Your Own Web Site 253
Chapter 18: Creating Web Pages with FrontPage Express 261
Chapter 19: Publishing Your Web Pages 283
Chapter 20: Ain't Misbehavin' (Or, Creating and Using DHTML Behaviors) 293
Chapter 21: Still More New DHTML Features for Web Developers 319

Part VI: The Part of Tens **329**

Chapter 22: Ten Tips for Using Internet Explorer Efficiently 331

Chapter 23: Ten Things That Sometimes Go Wrong 337

Chapter 24: Ten Safety Tips for Kids on the Net 343

Appendix A: Glossary **347**

Index **361**

Book Registration Information......................**Back of Book**

Cartoons at a Glance

By Rich Tennant

page 7

page 37

page 105

page 199

page 251

page 329

Fax: 978-546-7747
E-mail: richtennant@the5thwave.com
World Wide Web: www.the5thwave.com

Table of Contents

Introduction *1*
    Why Another Internet Book? 1
    How to Use This Book 2
    Foolish Assumptions 3
    How This Book Is Organized 4
        Part I: Preparing for an Internet Exploration 4
        Part II: Embarking on a World Wide Web Adventure 4
        Part III: Getting Connected with Outlook Express 5
        Part IV: Customizing Your Explorations 5
        Part V: Grow Your Own Web Pages 5
        Part VI: The Part of Tens 5
        Glossary 5
    Icons Used in This Book 6
    Where to Go from Here 6

Part I: Preparing for an Internet Exploration *7*

Chapter 1: Welcome to the Internet **9**
    What Is This Internet Thing? 9
    The Internet: A Network of Networks 11
    Who Invented the Internet? 11
    The Many Faces of the Internet 12
        The World Wide Web 12
        Electronic mail 14
        Newsgroups 15
        File Transfer Protocol 17
        Instant messages 17

Chapter 2: Getting Connected with Internet Explorer **19**
    You May Already Be on the Internet. 19
    But If You're Not Already on the Internet 20
    First, You Need a Modem 21
    Or . . . You Can Take the Cable or DSL Plunge 22
    Next, You Need a Service Provider 23
        Online services 24
        Basic Internet service providers 26
    Finally, You Need Internet Explorer 28
    Now You Can Set Up Your Internet Connection 30

Part II: Embarking on a World Wide Web Adventure 37

Chapter 3: Pushing Off 39
Starting Internet Explorer 39
Making Sense of the Internet Explorer Screen 42
Oh, the Places You'll Go! 45
Understanding Web addresses 45
Going to a specific page 47
Following the links 48
Yes, you can go back 50
It's all history now 50
Refreshing a Page 52
Stop! Enough Already! 53
Working in Full-Screen View 53
Printing a Web Page 54
Changing the Font Size 56
Saving a Web Page 57
Saving a Picture 58
Downloading a File 59
Finding Text 61
Exiting Internet Explorer 61

Chapter 4: Searching the Web 63
Finding Stuff Fast 63
Customizing the Search Bar 66
Searching from the Address Bar 67
Using Popular Search Services 68
AltaVista 69
EuroSeek 70
Excite 70
GoTo.com 71
Infoseek (GO.com) 71
Lycos 72
MSN Search 74
Northern Light 74
Yahoo! 75

Chapter 5: Getting around the Web Quickly 77
Playing Favorites 77
Adding a Web page to the Favorites menu 78
Going to one of your favorite places 79
Using Favorites folders 80
Organizing your Favorites 81
Using the Favorites button on the Standard toolbar 82

Using the Links Toolbar 83
    Accessing the Links toolbar 84
    Adding a link 86
    Removing a link 86

Chapter 6: Working Offline ....**.89**
Making a Page Available Offline 90
Viewing Web Pages Offline 91
Synchronizing Your Offline Pages 92

Chapter 7: Getting Help While You Explore ....**.95**
Summoning Help 95
Getting to Know the Help Window 96
Scanning the Contents 97
Scanning the Index 98
Searching for Help Topics 99
Listing Your Favorite Help Topics 99
Troubleshooting at Your Fingertips 101
Getting Help Online 102

Part III: Getting Connected with Outlook Express *105*

Chapter 8: E-mailing with Outlook Express ....**.107**
Starting Outlook Express 108
Sending E-mail 109
Checking Your Message for Spelling Errors 112
Sending Attachments 113
Using HTML Formatting 115
Receiving E-mail 117
Saving an Attachment as a File 118
Using the Address Book 119
    Adding a name to the Address Book 119
    Sending a message to someone in the Address Book ...122
    Changing or deleting Address Book entries 123
    Working with Address Book folders 123

Chapter 9: E-mail Shortcuts and Tricks ....**.127**
Using Outlook Express Folders 127
    Creating a new folder 128
    Moving messages to another folder 129
Filtering Your Mail 130
    Using message rules 130
    Blocking senders 134

Using Stationery 135
    Creating a message with stationery 135
    Setting the default stationery 137
    Creating new stationery 138
Signing Off with Signatures 142
Looking Up an E-mail Address 143
Creating and Using Mailing Groups 144
Changing Identities 147
Reading Mail Offline 149
Sending and Receiving Secure Messages 149

Chapter 10: Using Outlook Express with Hotmail **151**
Why Bother with Hotmail? 151
Signing Up for a Hotmail Account 152
Configuring Outlook Express to Use an Existing Hotmail Account 160
Using Outlook Express to Access Your Hotmail Account 163
Using Hotmail from the Web 163

Chapter 11: The Instant Message Connection **167**
Using MSN Messenger 167
    Setting up MSN Messenger 168
    Running MSN Messenger 169
    Adding contacts 170
    Sending an instant message 173
    Receiving an instant message 174
    Gone fishing: Letting your friends know that you're offline 175
Using NetMeeting 176
    Placing a NetMeeting call 177
    Using the NetMeeting chat feature 179
    Drawing on the Whiteboard 180
    Sending a file 182
    Sharing an application 184

Chapter 12: Accessing Newsgroups with Outlook Express **185**
Introducing Newsgroups 185
Using Usenet 186
The Microsoft Public Newsgroups 188
Accessing Newsgroups 188
Subscribing to a Newsgroup 191
Reading Threads 192
Reading an Article 193
Replying to an Article 194
Writing a New Article 195
Using Stationery and HTML Formatting 195
Dealing with Attachments 196
Working Offline 197

Part IV: Customizing Your Explorations 199

Chapter 13: Doing It Your Way: Personalizing Internet Explorer ...201

Toiling with the Toolbars 201
    Playing hide and seek with the toolbars 202
    Customizing the Standard Buttons toolbar 204
Tweaking Internet Explorer's Options 206
    Saluting the General options 207
    Serenading the Security options 209
    Cruising with the Content options 210
    Cajoling the Connections options 211
    Perusing the Programs options 211
    Achieving Advanced options 212
Changing Your Home Page 214
Customizing msn.com 215
    Information you can add 215
    Customizing your home page 217

**Chapter 14: Using the Content Advisor to Make Sure
That Your Kids Surf Safely 221**

About Internet Ratings 221
Limitations of Internet Ratings 224
Activating the Content Advisor 224
Dealing with Unrated Sites 228
Banning or Allowing Specific Sites 229

**Chapter 15: Lowering the Cone of Silence: Using
Internet Explorer's Security Features 231**

Security Issues to Worry About 232
    Sending information over the Internet 232
    Downloading programs over the Internet 232
    Viewing Web pages that do more than meets the eye 233
Scrambling: It's Not Just for Breakfast Anymore 233
Zoning Out 235
Certifying Your Security 237
Security Options You Should Leave Alone 238

Chapter 16: Creating a Login Script 239

What Is a Dial-up Networking Script? 239
Planning a Script 240
Creating a Script 241
Working with Script Commands 242
    Beginning and ending with proc main and endproc 244
    Waiting for stuff: waitfor 244
    Typing text: transmit 245
Attaching the Script to a Dial-Up Connection 246

Part V: Grow Your Own Web Pages *251*

Chapter 17: So You Want Your Own Web Site **253**

Clarifying Some Familiar Terminology 253
Deciding What to Put on Your Web Site 254
Personal home pages 254
Special interest Web sites 254
Business Web sites 255
Finding a Home for Your Web Site 255
Internet service providers 256
Web hosting services 256
Getting a free site 257
Software for Creating Web Sites 258

Chapter 18: Creating Web Pages with FrontPage Express **261**

Installing FrontPage Express 261
Starting FrontPage Express 266
Using the Personal Home Page Wizard 267
Formatting Text in a Web Document 271
Applying a style 271
Applying text formatting 271
Aligning and indenting text 273
Creating bulleted and numbered lists 274
Creating a Hyperlink 275
Spicing Up Your Page with Graphics 276
Inserting a horizontal line 276
Inserting a picture 277
Inserting a marquee 279
Adding a background image 280
Viewing HTML Source Code 281

Chapter 19: Publishing Your Web Pages **283**

Using the Web Publishing Wizard 283
Using the Web Publishing Wizard for the first time 284
Updating your Web files 289
Serving It Up with Personal Web Server 289
Starting Personal Web Server 290
Publishing a Web page to Personal Web Server 291
Accessing a Web page on Personal Web Server 291

Chapter 20: Ain't Misbehavin' (Or, Creating and Using DHTML Behaviors) **293**

Understanding DHTML Behaviors 294
Scripts, Styles, and Custom Tags: A Little Review (Yuck!) 295
Scripts 295
Style sheets 299
Custom tags 303

Creating a DHTML Behavior 304
  Creating an HTC file 304
  Applying a behavior 306
Creating Custom Tags with Behaviors 307
Using Behavior Properties, Methods, and Events 309
  Exposing properties 309
  Exposing methods 312
  Exposing events 316
But Wait, There's More 318

**Chapter 21: Still More New DHTML Features
for Web Developers** **319**
Creating ViewLink Components 319
Edit This! 323
Writing Sideways with the writing mode Attribute 324
Creating Drop Caps and Other Effects 326
Zooming In 327
But Wait, There's More! 328

Part VI: The Part of Tens **329**

Chapter 22: Ten Tips for Using Internet Explorer Efficiently **331**
Customizing Your Start Page 331
Stashing Goodies in the Favorites Menu 332
Customizing Your Links Toolbar 332
Creating Desktop Shortcuts 333
Discovering Weird Places to Click 334
Searching Tips 334
Dealing with Those Annoying Ad Windows 335
Typing Web Addresses the Easy Way 335
Using Other Software to Improve Internet Explorer 336

Chapter 23: Ten Things That Sometimes Go Wrong **337**
I Don't Have Internet Explorer! 337
I Can't Connect to the Internet! 338
I Forgot My Password! 339
I Got an Unexpected Error Message! 339
The Internet Explorer Window Disappeared! 340
I Can't Find a File I Downloaded! 341
I Was Disconnected in the Middle of a Two-Hour Download! 342
I Can't Find That Cool Web Page I Saw Yesterday! 342
I've Started a Nuclear War! 342

Chapter 24: Ten Safety Tips for Kids on the Net 343

Don't Believe That People Really Are Who They Say They Are 343
Never Give Out Your Address, Phone Number,
    Real Last Name, or Credit Card Number 344
Never Pretend to Be Someone You're Not 344
Save Inappropriate Postings to a File So That
    You Can Show Them to an Adult 344
If Someone Says Something Inappropriate to You
    in a Chat, Save the Chat Log 344
Watch Your Language 345
Don't Obsess 345
Report Inappropriate Behavior to an Adult 345
If You Feel Uncomfortable, Leave 345
Parents, Be Involved with Your Kids' Online Activities 346

Appendix A: Glossary *347*

Index *361*

Book Registration Information ....*Back of Book*

Introduction

Will it never end? Just when you thought you had your computer and the Internet all figured out, Microsoft has the nerve to throw a new version of your trusted friend Internet Explorer at you. Ready or not, watch out because here comes Internet Explorer 5.5!

This book can direct your attention toward Internet Explorer's landing spot so that you can get out of the way. Or, if you can't move with the speed of cyberspace, you can at least hold the book over your head like a helmet.

I have good news: Internet Explorer 5.5 is what we in the computer business like to call a "dot" upgrade, which means that it is but a minor upgrade from the previous version. It's as if Internet Explorer 5 dropped in to the barbershop for a trim and out came Internet Explorer 5.5. Not a radical transformation, just a snip here and there.

But there's still a lot to figure out with Internet Explorer 5.5: features such as streaming media, instant messaging, and Outlook Express . . . the list goes on and on. If you're a Web developer or an aspiring HTML author, there are FrontPage Express and new Dynamic HTML features to contend with.

This book tackles all these subjects and more, in plain English and with no pretense. No lofty prose here. The language is friendly. You don't need a graduate degree in computer science to get through it. I have no Pulitzer ambitions for this book, but it would be cool if it were made into a movie starring Harrison Ford.

I even occasionally take a carefully aimed potshot at the hallowed and sacred traditions of Internetdom, just to bring a bit of fun to an otherwise dry and tasteless subject. If that doesn't work, I throw in an occasional lawyer joke.

Why Another Internet Book?

Unfortunately, when it comes right down to it, Internet Explorer — like the Internet itself — isn't as easy to use as *they* would have you believe. Alas, Internet Explorer is nothing more than a computer program, and like any computer program, it has its own commands to master, menus to traverse, icons to decipher, nuances to discover, and quirks to work around. Bother.

Oh, and then take the Internet itself. Frankly, the Internet is a sprawling mess. It's filled with klutzy interfaces, programs that don't work the way they should, and systems that were designed decades ago. Finding the information you need on the Internet can be like the proverbial search for a needle in a haystack. The Internet is everything they say it is — except easy to use.

That's why you need this book to take you by the hand and walk you step-by-step through all the details of using Internet Explorer 5.5. This book doesn't bog you down with a bunch of puffed-up techno-jargon that makes you feel like your head is about to explode. Instead, this book spells out what you need to know in language that promises not to rap your urge to know more.

Sure, plenty of books about the Internet already crowd the computer section of your local bookstore. IDG Books Worldwide, Inc. even has several excellent books available: *The Internet For Dummies,* 7th Edition, is an especially good general introduction to the Internet. But if you are using — or are planning to use — Internet Explorer, you need to know more than generic Internet stuff. You need to know specifically how to use the features of Internet Explorer 5.5. Many of these features are unique to Internet Explorer 5.5 and are not found in any other Web browser.

How to Use This Book

The beauty of this book is that you don't have to read it through from start to finish. You wouldn't dare pick up the latest Clancy or Grisham novel and skip straight to page 173. But with this book, you can. That's because this book works like a reference. You can read as much or as little of it as you need. You can turn to any part of the book, start reading, and then put the book down after finding the information you need and get on with your life.

On occasion, this book directs you to use specific keyboard shortcuts to get things done. I indicate such key combinations like this:

Ctrl+Z

This means to hold down the Ctrl key while pressing the Z key, and then release both together. Don't type the plus sign.

Sometimes, I tell you to use a menu command. For example, you may see something like this:

File➪Open

This means to use the keyboard or mouse to open the File menu and then choose the Open command. (The underlined letters are the keyboard hot keys for the command. To use them, first press the Alt key. In the preceding example, you press and release the Alt key, press and release the F key, and then press and release the O key.) Whenever I describe a message or information you see on-screen, it looks like this:

```
Are we having fun yet?
```

Anything you are instructed to type appears in bold, like so: Type **puns** in the field. You type exactly what you see, with or without spaces.

Internet links are shown <u>underlined</u>, the way they appear on-screen in Internet Explorer. Internet addresses (technically known as *URLs*) appear like this: www.whatever.com.

Another little nicety about this book is that when I tell you to click one of those little toolbar buttons on Internet Explorer's screen, a picture of the button appears in the margin. Seeing what the button looks like helps you find it on-screen.

This book rarely directs you elsewhere for information — just about everything you need to know about using Internet Explorer is in here. However, two other books may come in handy from time to time. The first is *Windows 98 For Dummies,* by Andy Rathbone (published by IDG Books Worldwide, Inc.), which is helpful if you're not sure how to perform a Windows 98 task such as copying a file or creating a new folder. The second book is *The Internet For Dummies,* 7th Edition, by John R. Levine, Carol Baroudi, and Margaret Levine Young (also published by IDG Books Worldwide), which is helpful if you decide to venture into the dark recesses of the Internet.

Foolish Assumptions

I'm making only three assumptions about you:

- ✔ You use a computer.
- ✔ You use Windows Millennium or one of its predecessors, Windows 98 or Windows 95.
- ✔ You access (or are thinking about accessing) the Internet with Internet Explorer 5.5.

Nothing else. I don't assume that you're a computer guru who knows how to change a controller card or configure memory for optimal usage. Such technical chores are best handled by people who like computers. Hopefully, you are on speaking terms with such a person. Do your best to keep it that way.

How This Book Is Organized

Inside this book are ample chapters arranged into seven parts. Each chapter is broken down into sections that cover various aspects of the chapter's main subject. The chapters have a logical sequence, so reading them in order makes sense (if you're crazy enough to read this entire book). But you don't have to read them that way. You can flip open the book to any page and start reading.

The following sections give you the lowdown on what's in each of the seven parts.

Part I: Preparing for an Internet Exploration

The two chapters in this part deal with really introductory stuff: what the Internet is and how to get connected to it. Part I is the place to start if you haven't visited the Internet before and you're not sure what the World Wide Web is, what www.microsoft.com means, or how to connect your computer to the Internet.

Part II: Embarking on a World Wide Web Adventure

This part is the heart and soul of the book. Its chapters show you how to use the basic features of Internet Explorer to untangle the World Wide Web. You find out how to surf the Web like a pro using the Internet Explorer 5.5 Web browsing features, how to look up information on the Web, how to build a library of your favorite Web sites so that you don't always have to hunt them down, and how to get help when you're stuck. You can also read about setting up your computer to download the Web pages you're most interested in while you sleep by using offline synchronization.

Part III: Getting Connected with Outlook Express

The chapters in this part show you how to use Outlook Express, the e-mail program that comes with Internet Explorer. With Outlook Express, you can send and receive e-mail, set up an address book, and participate in Internet newsgroups. You also find out how to use MSN Messenger, Microsoft's instant message program that lets you talk online with your friends.

Part IV: Customizing Your Explorations

The four chapters in this part show you how to configure Internet Explorer by tweaking its options so that it suits your working style. This stuff is best read by people who like to show their computers who's the boss.

Part V: Grow Your Own Web Pages

If you're someone who enjoys creating your own Web pages, check out the five chapters in this part. Here, you find out how to create your own Web pages using Microsoft FrontPage Express, which you can download for free from the Internet or which may already be on your computer. Then you find out how to post your HTML documents to a Web site using the new Web Publishing Wizard. And for the technically inclined, you learn how to incorporate the new Dynamic HTML features into your Web pages.

Part VI: The Part of Tens

This wouldn't be a *For Dummies* book if it didn't include a collection of chapters with lists of interesting snippets: Ten Tips for Using Internet Explorer Efficiently, Ten Things That Sometimes Go Wrong, and so on.

Glossary

People use so much techno-babble when they discuss the Internet that I decided to include an extensive glossary of online terms, free of charge. With this glossary in hand, you can beat the silicon-heads at their own game.

Icons Used in This Book

As you read all this wonderful prose, you occasionally encounter the following icons. They appear in the margins to draw your attention to important information.

Uh-oh, some technical drivel is about to come your way. Cover your eyes if you find technical information offensive.

This icon points out traps you may fall into if you're not careful. Heed these warnings and all shall go well with you, with your children, and with your children's children.

Pay special attention to this icon — it points to some particularly useful tidbit, perhaps a shortcut or a way of using a command that you may not have considered.

This icon points out important information to definitely remember as you use the Internet Explorer features being discussed. The information may not be totally new to you; it may just remind you of something you've temporarily forgotten.

This icon points out a new feature of Internet Explorer 5.5 for those Internet Explorer 5 veterans in the audience.

Where to Go from Here

The Internet is an exciting new computer frontier, and Internet Explorer is hands-down the best way to experience the Internet. So where do you go from here? Online, of course. With this book at your side, you can visit the world from your desktop. Happy exploring!

Part I
Preparing for an Internet Exploration

The 5th Wave   By Rich Tennant

INTERNET ACCESS
.50¢ - Min.

In this part . . .

*T*he Internet is one of the best things to happen to computers since the invention of the On button. Everyone and his uncle are going online these days. Even television commercials are in on the act — it's amazing how many ads flash Internet addresses at the end. The Internet promises to revolutionize the way we do business, the way we buy cars, the way kids learn at school, even the way we shop for groceries.

The two chapters in this part give you a gentle introduction to the Internet. In Chapter 1, you get a crash course on what the Internet is and why everyone is so excited about it. Then, in Chapter 2, you find out how to get yourself connected so that you don't miss out on all the excitement.

Chapter 1

Welcome to the Internet

In This Chapter

▶ A mercifully brief description of the Internet

▶ A rational explanation of why you should give a hoot about the Internet

▶ An overview of the different faces of the Internet

*O*nce upon a time, there were seven stranded castaways lost on a desert isle somewhere in the Pacific. They were completely cut off from civilization: no television, no newspapers, and worst of all — gasp — no Internet access! What would they do?

Fortunately, they had a genius among them: a professor, who figured out a way to access the Internet by using an old radio, a few coconut shells, and electricity generated by a makeshift stationary bicycle. The professor set up a Web page announcing the location of the island, but the hapless first mate, Gilligan, somehow managed to crash the server only moments before a Coast Guard sailor was about to access their home page.

So what's the point of this story? Simply that just about everyone — even the crew of the *S.S. Minnow* — is cruising the Internet these days. If you want to join the tour but you're afraid you know even less about the Internet than Gilligan, this chapter is for you. It provides a brief introduction to what the Internet is and why you would want to use it. So grab your pith helmet and start exploring!

What Is This Internet Thing?

The *Internet* is an enormous computer network that links tens of millions of computers all across the planet. The Internet lets you, while sitting at your own private computer in a small town in Iowa, access computers in Moscow or Geneva or Tokyo or Washington, D.C. The Internet is the most exciting thing to happen to computers since the invention of the mouse.

Is the Internet really as big as they say it is?

The simple fact is, no one really knows just how big the Internet actually is. That's because no one really owns the Internet. But several organizations make it their business to try periodically to find out how big the Internet is. The science is far from exact, but these organizations are able to come up with pretty reasonable estimates.

One of the best known Internet surveys is the Internet Domain Survey, conducted twice a year by a company called Network Wizards. In January 2000, Network Wizards found that more than 72 million computers were connected to the Internet. When compared with the January 1999 survey, the 2000 survey shows that the Internet has grown by 28 percent over the past year. In that one-year period, more than 16 million computers were added to the Internet.

That's about one every two seconds. Surveys, such as those of Network Wizards, count only those computers that have registered a *host name,* such as www.mycomputer.com. Thus, the Network Wizards survey doesn't even factor in the millions of home computers that access the Internet without having their own host names.

Truth is, no one really knows how many people use the Internet. The only indisputable point is that the Internet is big — and getting bigger every day.

If you find these figures interesting, you can check the results of the latest Internet Domain Survey by visiting the Network Wizards Web site at www.nw.com.

Most people are actually referring to the Internet when they talk about the *Information Superhighway*. The Information Superhighway is supposed to enable every man, woman, and child in the United States — indeed, on the entire planet — to access instantly and without error every conceivable bit of information that has ever been discovered.

Unfortunately, the Information Superhighway is, at best, only a promise of what the future holds. Currently, the Internet still requires a fairly major investment in computer equipment. (A decent computer for accessing the Internet still costs close to $1,000 or more, although prices are coming down all the time.) And although an enormous amount of information is available on the Internet, the entire contents of the Internet amount to only a tiny fraction of human knowledge, and the information that is there is haphazardly organized, difficult to sift through, and sometimes unreliable.

Still, a tiny fraction of all human knowledge is worth having, even if it is poorly organized. And that's why the Internet has become so popular. People love to surf the Web (I explain what the Web is later in this chapter), hoping to glean some useful bit of information that may make their investment of online time and money worthwhile.

Plus, the Internet is just downright fun.

The Internet: A Network of Networks

The Internet is actually a network of networks. The world is filled with computer networks. Large and small businesses have networks that connect the computers in their offices. Universities have networks that the students and faculty can access. Government organizations have networks. And many people belong to online services, such as CompuServe, America Online, or The Microsoft Network; these online services are themselves large computer networks.

The Internet's job is to connect all these networks together to form one gigantic mega-network. In fact, the very name *Internet* comes from the fact that the Internet allows connections among distinct computer networks.

The Internet consists of several hundreds of thousands of separate computer networks. These networks, in turn, connect millions of computers to one another.

Who Invented the Internet?

Some people are fascinated by history. They subscribe to cable TV just to get the History Channel. If you're one of those history buffs, you may be interested in the following chronicle of the Internet's humble origins. (For maximum effect, play some melancholy violin music in the background as you read the rest of this section.)

In the summer of 1969, the four mop-topped singers from Liverpool were breaking up. The war in Vietnam was escalating. Astronauts Neil Armstrong and Buzz Aldrin walked on the moon. And the Department of Defense built a computer network called ARPANET to link its defense installations with several major universities throughout the United States.

In the early 1970s, ARPANET was getting difficult to manage, so it was split into two networks: one for military use, called MILNET, and the other for nonmilitary use. The nonmilitary network retained the name ARPANET. To link MILNET with ARPANET, a new method of connecting networks, called *Internet Protocol* or just *IP* for short, was invented.

The whole purpose of IP was to enable these two networks to communicate with one another. Fortunately, the designers of IP realized that it wouldn't be too long before other networks wanted to join in the fun, so they designed IP to allow for more than two networks. In fact, their ingenious design allowed for tens of thousands of networks to communicate via IP.

The decision was a fortuitous one, as the Internet quickly began to grow. By the mid-1980s, the original ARPANET reached its limits. Just in time, the National Science Foundation (NSF) decided to get into the game. NSF had built a network called NSFNET to link its huge supercomputers. (*Supercomputers* are those behemoth computers — the kind of computers that, even today, fill entire rooms and are used to calculate the orbits of distant galaxies, discover new prime numbers, and outwit chess masters like Kasparov.)

NSFNET replaced ARPANET as the new background for the Internet. Around that time, such magazines as *Time* and *Newsweek* began writing articles about this new phenomenon called the Internet, and the Net (as it became nicknamed) began to grow like wildfire. Soon NSFNET couldn't keep up with the growth, so several private commercial networks took over management of the Internet backbone. The Internet has grown at a dizzying rate ever since, and who knows how long this frenetic growth rate will continue.

If the story of the Internet has a moral, it is that the Internet has probably been so successful precisely because it's not strictly a commercial or government venture. No one is really in charge of the Internet. Instead, the Internet sprang up pretty much on its own. No rules dictate who can and who cannot join the Internet. Kinda warms your cockles, doesn't it?

The Many Faces of the Internet

The Internet is not a single, monolithic entity that has a consistent look and feel for all its services. Quite the contrary — over the years, many different services have sprung up on the Internet, each with its own style and appearance. Microsoft Internet Explorer has features that enable you to access most, but not all, of these services.

The World Wide Web

The most popular Internet venue is the *World Wide Web*, usually called *the Web* for short. The Web is to the Internet what Windows is to DOS: a graphical interface to what would otherwise be a bland and boring place. The Web enables you to view the information that is available on the Internet using neatly formatted text, stunning pictures, and gee-whiz special effects, such as sounds, animations, and videos.

Information on the World Wide Web is organized into documents called *pages*. A single Web page can be as short as one word, or it can contain hundreds of lines of text. Most pages contain no more information than you can comfortably squeeze onto an 8½-x-11-inch printed page.

Each page on the Web can contain text, graphics, sounds, videos, and — most important — links to other Web pages with related information. For example, a page that contains information about frogs may contain links to other pages with information about princes, Muppets, or hallucinogenic substances.

A *Web site* is a collection of pages related to a particular subject and kept on a single computer, known as a *Web server*. Every Web site has a *home page,* which is the starting point for accessing the pages that are available at the Web site. The home page has *links* that let you access the Web site's other pages in an organized fashion.

Besides links to other pages at the same Web site, a Web page can also have links to pages that live on different Web sites. Thus, clicking a link may take you to an entirely different Web site that's located halfway around the world from the one you were accessing, without jet lag, airsickness, or even a noticeable hesitation!

That's the neat thing about surfing the Web: You can travel the world without leaving your home — and without long-distance charges! Your Internet service provider charges you a flat monthly or hourly rate, whether you're retrieving data from a Web site four miles or four *thousand* miles from your computer.

To access the Web, you need a special program called a Web browser. A *Web browser* knows how to display the special formats and codes used to send information over the World Wide Web. The Web browser reads these special codes over the Internet and translates them into fancy displays and beautiful pictures for your screen. The browser also enables you to follow links from one Web page to another simply by clicking the link.

Just as you can choose among many different word processing or spread-sheet programs, you have your choice of many different Web browsers to use. Internet Explorer 5.5 is the latest and greatest Web browser program from Microsoft. Figure 1-1 shows Internet Explorer 5.5 in action, displaying a page from the World Wide Web.

Internet Explorer isn't the only Web browser on the block, of course. Another popular Web browser is Netscape Navigator. Netscape and Microsoft are in a neck-and-neck race to see who can create the best browser software — kind of like the way the Republicans and Democrats are in a race to see who can create the best campaign reform proposals. Obviously, this book is about exploring the Internet using Internet Explorer. If you use Netscape Navigator, you should probably be reading *Netscape Communicator 4.5 For Dummies,* by Paul Hoffman (published by IDG Books Worldwide, Inc.), instead.

Netscape distributes the latest version of Navigator, 4.7, in a suite of Internet programs called Netscape Communicator. In addition to Navigator, Communicator includes an electronic mail program, a newsgroup program, a special program to help you create your Web pages, and more. (At the time I wrote this, Netscape was finalizing a new version, to be known as Navigator 6.)

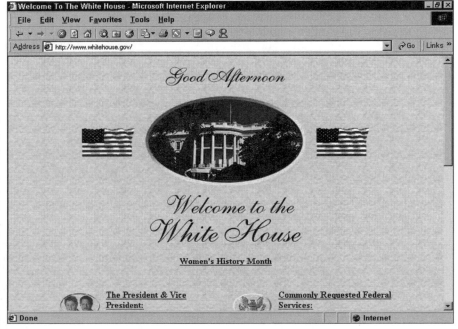

Figure 1-1:
Internet
Explorer
displays
pages from
the World
Wide Web,
such as this
one, the
White
House's
own home
page.

Web browsers, such as Internet Explorer, aren't limited to accessing just the World Wide Web. In fact, you can access most of the other parts of the Internet directly from Internet Explorer or from programs that come with Internet Explorer.

Electronic mail

Electronic mail (usually called *e-mail*) enables you to exchange private messages with any other e-mail user on the Internet, no matter where in the country or world that user lives. Unlike the postal service, Internet e-mail is delivered almost instantly. And unlike Federal Express, you don't have to pay $13 for fast delivery. In fact, Internet e-mail is probably the least expensive, yet most efficient, form of communication available.

E-mail is not just for sending short notes to your friends, either. You can use e-mail to send entire files of information to co-workers. For example, I used Internet e-mail to send the document files for this book to my editor at IDG Books Worldwide, Inc., and she, in turn, used e-mail to send me back corrections and technical questions.

Many programs are available for reading Internet e-mail. Internet Explorer 5.5 comes with a handy e-mail program called Outlook Express. Outlook Express is actually a scaled-down version of a more complete e-mail program called Microsoft Outlook, which is included as a part of Microsoft Office 2000. Although Microsoft Outlook has more features than Outlook Express, Outlook Express is more than adequate for most e-mail users. Figure 1-2 shows Outlook Express in action. Outlook Express is so useful that I've devoted three chapters of this book — 8, 9, and 10 — to showing you how to use it to access your e-mail.

Newsgroups

Newsgroups are online discussion groups — places where users with common interests gather to share ideas. Thousands of newsgroups exist, covering just about every topic imaginable. You can find newsgroups that discuss obscure computer topics, fan clubs for various celebrities, online support groups, and who knows what else.

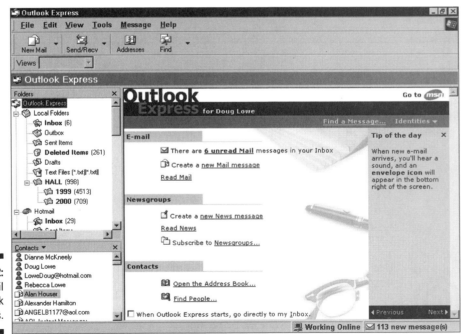

Figure 1-2: Using e-mail with Outlook Express.

Be warned: The Internet is not censored

No censorship exists on the Internet. If you look hard enough, you can find just about anything on the Internet — not all of it wholesome. In addition to information about fly fishing, knitting, and the solar system, you can find photographs of men and women in various states of dress and undress, often engaged in unmentionable acts that would make Hugh Hefner blush.

Unfortunately, you can't do much about the content on the Internet. A few years back, Congress tried to pass a law that would ban indecent content from the Internet, but the Supreme Court ruled such legislation unconstitutional. After all, indecency is a pretty ambiguous concept, and the First Amendment pretty much prohibits Congress from banning any but the most obscene materials from publication on any medium.

However, just because Congress can't prevent people from publishing offensive material on the Internet doesn't mean that you have to view it. Microsoft, along with other Internet companies, has sponsored a voluntary system of ratings that lets you know whether an Internet site contains offensive material. Internet Explorer enables you to control whether you (or anyone in your household) can view such material. The solution's not perfect, but it does go a long way toward controlling the amount of offensive material kids are exposed to. In Chapter 14, I describe Internet Explorer controls for blocking such material.

Most Internet newsgroups are distributed over *Usenet,* a network of special server computers that contain the special software needed to handle newsgroups. As a result, you sometimes see the terms *Usenet* and *newsgroups* used together. However, you can access some newsgroups that aren't a part of Usenet.

As luck would have it, Outlook Express, the handy e-mail program that comes with Internet Explorer, is also adept at handling Internet newsgroups. Figure 1-3 shows Outlook Express accessing a newsgroup — in this case, the newsgroup happens to be devoted to the subject of everyone's favorite comic strip, *Peanuts.* I give you the ins and outs of using Outlook Express to participate in newsgroup discussions in Chapter 12.

Don't be confused by the term *news* in newsgroups. Newsgroups are *not* a news service designed to give you accurate, up-to-date, and unbiased information about current events. Newsgroups are places where people with common interests can share opinions. In this sense, newsgroups are more like talk radio than a news program.

File Transfer Protocol

File Transfer Protocol — or FTP, as it is usually called — is the Internet equivalent of a network file server. FTP is the Internet's primary method of moving files around. Thousands of FTP sites make their files available for downloading. All you have to do is sign in to the FTP site, find the file you want to download, and click.

Internet Explorer has built-in support for FTP, so you can easily log in to an FTP site and download files to your computer. In fact, you don't have to do anything special to access FTP from Internet Explorer; you may not even be aware that you're using FTP.

Instant messages

Instant messaging is an online feature that lets you chat online — that is, you can exchange messages directly with other Internet users, kind of like a phone call with your computer. The most popular instant message service is America Online's AIM (which stands for *AOL Instant Messenger*).

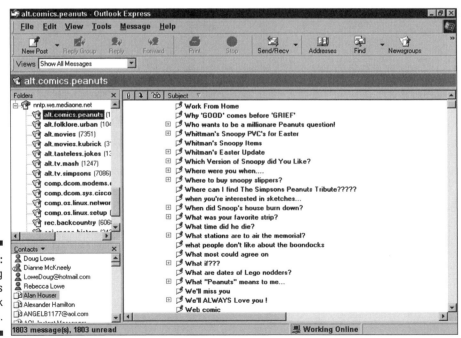

Figure 1-3: Accessing newsgroups with Outlook Express.

Not to be outdone by America Online, Microsoft has its own instant message service, known as *MSN Messenger.* MSN Messenger enables you to create a list of online friends with whom you can chat, either one-on-one or in small groups. Plus, MSN Messenger is integrated with a more sophisticated online chatting program called Microsoft NetMeeting, which sports advanced features, such as audio and video conferencing, a whiteboard on which you and your online friends can doodle, and more. I show you how to use MSN Messenger and Microsoft NetMeeting in Chapter 11.

Another form of online chatting is *Internet Relay Chat,* or *IRC.* Unlike instant message services, such as AIM or MSN Messenger, IRC does not let you set up lists of friends to chat with. Instead, IRC hosts thousands of chat rooms, where anyone can join in on the discussion.

Chapter 2

Getting Connected with Internet Explorer

· ·

In This Chapter

▶ Finding out whether you're already connected to the Internet

▶ Getting connected, if you aren't so lucky

▶ Comparing various Internet pricing plans to get the best deal

▶ Setting up your Internet connection with the Internet Connection Wizard

· ·

The hardest part about using the Internet is figuring out how to get connected to it the first time. After you figure that out, the rest is easy. (Well, relatively easy. Nothing about computers is completely easy!)

This chapter explores the various options for connecting your computer to the Internet using Internet Explorer 5.5. With luck, you may discover that you're already connected to the Internet and Internet Explorer is set up on your computer, so you can skip this chapter and get on with the fun. If you're not so fortunate, read on to find out how to get the job done.

You May Already Be on the Internet. . . .

It's true. You may have been on the Internet for years now and not realized it. And you may have already won $10 million from Publisher's Clearing House, and maybe tomorrow you'll get struck by lightning and your IQ will double.

Actually, the possibility that you already have access to the Internet isn't that outlandish. Here are some reasonable scenarios:

> ✔ If you subscribe to one of the major online services, such as America Online, CompuServe, or The Microsoft Network, you already have access to the Internet. Each of these online services provides a link to the Internet. In the past, online services provided only limited access to

the Internet and were among the more expensive methods of connecting to the Net. But nowadays, the major online services offer full Internet access at competitive prices.

✔ If you use a computer at work, and that computer is a part of a local area network (LAN), and the LAN is connected to the Internet, you may be able to access the Internet via the LAN. Talk to your resident network guru to find out.

✔ The computers at many schools are connected to the Internet. If you're a student, you may be able to bribe your teachers into letting you access the Internet. You may even get extra credit for using the Internet — especially if you use it to do your homework.

✔ Some public libraries have computers that are connected to the Net. With access at a public library, you may still be able to access free e-mail services, such as Hotmail for your electronic mail.

✔ Cybercafés — once found only in trendy cities such as Seattle and San Francisco — have sprouted up around the country. At a cybercafé, you can surf the Web free while sipping a decaf latte and enjoying classical music.

But If You're Not Already on the Internet . . .

If you don't have access to the Internet through one of the sources listed in the preceding section, you have no alternative but to set up your own Internet access at home. Unfortunately, you can't do so without having to contend with at least some of the boring technical details.

Here are a few general tips I want to offer before I get into the details of setting up your Internet access:

✔ Upgrade to one of the latest and greatest versions of Windows: Windows Millennium Edition (I refuse to call it *Windows Me*) or Windows 2000. One favorable feature about these new versions of Windows is that they both have built-in support for the Internet and they come with Internet Explorer built in.

✔ If you plan on connecting to the Internet over the phone (as the overwhelming majority of people do), make sure that your computer is located near a telephone outlet.

✔ If you have a friend who already has access to the Internet, treat him to lunch and pick his brain (well, not literally). Find out what kind of modem he has, who his Internet service provider (ISP) is, how much he is paying for it, what he likes best about it, what he hates about it, what he would do differently, and if he thinks John Travolta should go back to playing nice guys.

✔ If you have a friend who happens to be a computer expert, see if you can bribe her into helping you set up your Internet access. Don't offer cash; bartering is better. Offer to mow her lawn or wash her car.

First, You Need a Modem

The first thing you need to connect your computer to the Internet is a *modem.* If your computer is brand new, you're lucky: It probably already has a modem in it. In that case, all you have to do is plug the modem into the telephone jack by using a phone cord, and you're ready to go.

If your computer doesn't have a modem, you need to purchase and install one yourself. The basic rule of modem-buying is this:

Buy the fastest modem you can afford.

Modems come in a variety of speeds, but the most common speed being hawked at computer stores these days is 56000 bps. Bps stands for *bits per second* and is simply a measure of how fast the modem can pump data through the phone lines. (The term *baud* is sometimes used as a substitute for bps. Both have pretty much the same meaning.) You can purchase a decent 56K modem in the United States for under $50, and if you shop around hard enough, you may find one for as little as $20.

If your computer has an older modem in it, watch out. Older modems may not be fast enough to access the World Wide Web efficiently. If you're working with an older 14400 bps modem or — heaven forbid — a 2400 bps modem, you should definitely replace it with a faster model. If you have a newer 28.8K or 33.6K modem, you can continue to use it. However, your Internet access will be noticeably faster if you upgrade to a 56K modem.

Most modems also enable you to send and receive faxes. Because this feature is handy and doesn't increase the cost of the modem, make sure that the modem you buy includes fax support.

Your modem must be connected to a phone line so that your computer can access the outside world. Unfortunately, whenever you use the Internet, the modem ties up your phone line. Anyone calling your number gets a busy signal, and you can't use the phone to call out for pizza. If being deprived of telephone privileges while you're online proves to be a problem, you can always have the phone company install a separate phone line for your modem. (Or you can use your cell phone to order pizza.)

If the thought of installing a modem nauseates you, pack up your computer and take it to your friendly local computer shop. The folks there can sell you a modem and install it for you for a small charge.

Or . . . You Can Take the Cable or DSL Plunge

If you plan on using the Internet frequently and don't mind spending a few extra dollars for Internet access, you may want to consider one of two relatively new methods of connecting to the Internet: cable and DSL. Cable Internet access works over the same cable that brings 40 billion TV channels into your home, whereas DSL is a digital phone service that works over standard phone lines. Both offer three major advantages over normal dial-up connections:

- Cable and DSL are much faster than dial-up connections. A cable connection can be anywhere from 10 to 200 times faster than a dial-up connection, depending on the service you get. And the speed of a DSL line is comparable to cable.

- With cable and DSL, you are always connected to the Internet. You don't have to connect and disconnect each time you want to go online. No more waiting for the modem to dial your service provider and listening to the annoying modem shriek as it attempts to establish a connection.

What about ISDN?

ISDN, which stands for *Integrated Services Digital Network,* is a digital phone service that was popular a few years ago as an alternative to dial-up connections. ISDN allows data to be sent about twice as fast as a conventional phone line — up to 128 Kbps (kilobits per second) rather than 56 Kbps. As an added plus, a single ISDN line can be logically split into two separate channels, so you can carry on a voice conversation while your computer is connected to the Internet.

Sounds great — the only catch is that it's expensive. An ISDN connection doesn't require a modem. Instead, you use a special ISDN adapter, which will set you back at least $250. In addition, you have to pay the phone company anywhere from $50 to $200 to install the ISDN line, and you pay a monthly fee ranging from $25 to $50 (depending on your area). On top of that, you may be billed by the minute for usage. For example, in my area, an ISDN line costs $24.95 per month, plus usage fees of about a penny a minute.

With the spread of low-cost cable modem access in many areas and the cost of DSL access coming down, ISDN is fast becoming a thing of the past. It was a good idea for its time, but its time has passed.

   ✔ Cable and DSL do not tie up your phone line while you are online. With
     cable, your Internet connection works over your TV cables rather than
     your phone cables. And with DSL, the phone company installs a sepa-
     rate phone line for the DSL service, so your regular phone line is not
     affected.

Unfortunately, there's no such thing as a free lunch, and the high-speed,
always-on connections offered by cable and DSL do not come without a price.
For starters, you can expect to pay a higher monthly access fee for cable or
DSL. In most areas, cable runs about $50/month. The cost for DSL service
depends on the access speed you choose. In some areas, you can get a relatively slow (but still faster than a 56K modem) DSL connection for as little as
$30/month. For higher access speeds, DSL can cost as much as $200/month
or more. (Of course, prices may come down by the time you read this, so be
sure to check.) When you consider cost, remember that the ISP is included
with both DSL and cable (and is covered by their fees).

In addition, both cable and DSL connections require extra equipment.
Both require that your computer have a special type of connection called an
Ethernet port. If your computer doesn't have one, you need to add an Ethernet
interface card. (Fortunately, you can get a relatively inexpensive Ethernet
card for about $25.) Besides the Ethernet port, cable and DSL require their
own modems, which can cost several hundreds of dollars. (In many cases, the
cable or DSL company provides you with the modem as a part of its service.)

DSL stands for *Digital Subscriber Line,* but that won't be on the test.

Next, You Need a Service Provider

An *Internet service provider,* or ISP, is a company that charges you, usually on
a monthly basis, for access to the Internet. The ISP has a bunch of modems
connected to phone lines that you can dial in to. These modems are connected to a computer system, which is in turn connected to the Internet via a
high-speed data link. The ISP's computer acts as a liaison between your computer and the Internet.

Typically, an ISP provides you with the following services in exchange for
your hard-earned money:

   ✔ **Access to the World Wide Web:** Most ISPs let you access any Web site
     on the Internet from your computer. Some ISPs provide built-in filtering
     software that automatically blocks access to pornography and other
     objectionable Web sites.

✔ **Electronic mail:** The ISP assigns you an e-mail address that anyone on the Internet can use to send you mail. You can use Microsoft's Outlook Express, which comes with Internet Explorer, to access your e-mail. See Chapter 8 for more information.

✔ **Access to Internet newsgroups:** In newsgroups, you can follow ongoing discussions about your favorite topics. Read all about newsgroups in Chapter 12.

✔ **Software to access the Internet:** In many cases, this software includes Microsoft Internet Explorer. Or it may include a different Web browser, such as Netscape Navigator. (If Internet Explorer isn't provided by your ISP, you can obtain it free from Microsoft after you set up your Internet connection. Find out how later in this chapter in the section "Finally, You Need Internet Explorer.")

✔ **Technical support, the quality of which varies greatly:** If you have trouble with your Internet connection, try calling your ISP's technical support line. If you're lucky, an actual human being who knows something about computers will pick up the phone and help you solve your problem. Next best: You're put on hold, but someone will eventually answer and help you. Not so good: The technical support line is always busy. Worse: You get a recording that says, "All our support engineers are busy. Please leave a message, and we'll get back to you." Yeah, right.

Basically, two types of companies provide access to the Internet: commercial online services, such as America Online, CompuServe, and The Microsoft Network, and independent Internet service providers. The following sections describe the pros and cons of both types of providers and the Internet access they provide.

Online services

All the major online services enable you to connect to the Internet. On the plus side, you gain access to unique content that's available only to members of the online service. On the minus side, you pay for this extra service. The following are the pricing plans of the three major online services:

✔ **America Online (AOL):** The most popular online service, America Online boasts something like 23 million users. AOL has several pricing plans. The Standard Monthly plan gives you unlimited access to AOL and the Internet for $21.95 per month; if you prepay 12 months, the rate drops to $19.95 per month. The Light Usage plan gives you three hours per month for $4.95, with each additional hour costing $2.50. And the Limited Usage plan gives you five hours for $9.95 per month, with each additional hour costing $2.95.

✔ **CompuServe:** Running second in online service popularity is CompuServe, which claims more than 2.7 million users. CompuServe has two pricing plans. The Best Value Plan gives you 20 hours per month for $9.95, with each additional hour costing $2.95. The Unlimited Plan gives you unlimited access for $19.95 per month. You can lower this to $17 per month if you pay an entire year in advance.

America Online bought out CompuServe, but at least for the time being, AOL and CompuServe continue to operate as separate online services.

✔ **The Microsoft Network (MSN):** MSN is Microsoft's attempt to challenge America Online and CompuServe. MSN offers unlimited access for $21.95 per month.

If you opt to use an online service as your Internet service provider, you need to carefully select the correct pricing plan for the number of hours you intend to use the service. To make this point, Table 2-1 shows the monthly cost for each of the preceding plans for monthly usages of 10, 20, 40, and 60 hours. As you can see, the actual monthly cost varies tremendously depending on which plan you select.

Table 2-1	Pricing Plans Compared			
Price Plan	*10 Hours*	*20 Hours*	*40 Hours*	*60 Hours*
America Online, Standard	$21.95	$21.95	$21.95	$21.95
America Online, Light Usage	$22.45	$47.45	$97.45	$147.45
America Online, Limited Usage	$24.70	$54.20	$113.20	$172.20
CompuServe, Unlimited	$19.95	$19.95	$19.95	$19.95
CompuServe, Best Value	$9.95	$9.95	$68.98	$127.95
The Microsoft Network, Unlimited Access	$21.95	$21.95	$21.95	$21.95

I hear too many horror stories about families who have signed up for America Online or CompuServe, expecting the monthly bill to be only $9.95, only to discover a $200 bill the first month. The problem is that the kids discover the Internet one evening and end up spending four or five hours online every night for two weeks before the parents catch on.

My advice: If you sign up for an online service, always start off with an unlimited access plan. Such a plan may cost you $10 or $15 more if you end up not using it as much as you expect, but that's better than paying $50 to $100 more for exceeding the limited usage plan. And make sure all family members, including the kids, understand how the pricing works.

Basic Internet service providers

The alternative to using a commercial online service is to sign up with a basic Internet service provider, or ISP. ISPs provide the same Internet access that online services do, but they don't provide their own additional content. ISPs are invariably less expensive than commercial online services because they don't have the added expense that results from providing their own proprietary services.

Technically, any company that provides you with Internet access is an ISP, including commercial online services. However, I prefer to use the term *ISP* to refer to a company that specializes in providing only Internet access without providing a separate online service of its own.

You can choose from nationally known service providers, such as NETCOM or AT&T WorldNet Service, or you can select a local ISP. To find the ISPs in your area, check the *Yellow Pages* under Computers — Online Services and Internet (or a similar heading).

Are the online services worth it?

Because you can access the Internet in less-expensive ways, this question naturally comes up: "Are the extra features you get with an online service worth the extra cost?" This may sound like a cop-out, but there's no right or wrong answer to that question. The answer depends on whether you use and benefit from the additional features provided by online services.

One major advantage of online services is their organization. The Internet is a sprawling mess, and sometimes it's hard to find what you want. In contrast, online services are well organized. Information in online services is neatly arranged according to topic. Not so on the Internet.

Another benefit you can probably expect from your online service is customer service support. CompuServe and America Online both have large support staffs that can help to make sure that you get on and stay on the Internet without a lot of technical headaches. The quality of technical support that comes with an ISP varies greatly from one ISP to the next.

Still, if you subscribe to an online service and then discover that you use it only to access the Internet, you may be better off canceling your online service subscription and signing up with a simple Internet service provider instead.

The changing role of online services

The sudden growth of the Internet has had a profound impact on established online services like CompuServe and America Online, and it has even affected newer online services, such as MSN. In the past, online services required you to use software provided by the online service to access the information available at the service. For example, to access America Online, you must use special software provided by America Online. CompuServe and MSN work the same way.

All that is changing, however. Online services are discovering that users prefer to choose access software — so the providers are slowly but surely moving their services to a format that provides users with online access by means of standard Internet Web browsers, such as Netscape Navigator and Internet Explorer.

Now, these developments don't mean that online services are becoming part of the World Wide Web or that you can look forward to free CompuServe or America Online access. The

online services will continue to offer distinctive subscriber-only features, such as discussion forums, file libraries, stock quote services, and reference databases.

The gradual change means a move toward using the same software to access an online service and the World Wide Web and picking which browser program you prefer to use to access your online service.

These changes are evolving slowly. You can't change the software used by millions of subscribers all at once. But the change is certain, and within a few years, all the major online services will let you use Internet Explorer or any other Web browser to access their content.

In fact, MSN is already at that point. The latest version of MSN is Web-based so that you can move seamlessly between Internet Web sites and The Microsoft Network without changing browsers.

Most ISPs offer unlimited access for $15 to $20 per month. Some offer a limited-hours plan for slightly less (for example, 40 hours for $10). Either way, the cost of using an ISP is likely to be less than the cost of using a commercial online service unless you end up using the Internet for only a few hours each month.

Both America Online and MSN let you access their services for a low monthly fee ($9.95 for AOL, $6.95 for MSN), provided that you use your own Internet service provider. In other words, you can access America Online or The Microsoft Network by dialing into your own ISP rather than by dialing one of AOL's or MSN's access numbers.

Finally, You Need Internet Explorer

Naturally, before you can begin to use Internet Explorer, you must install it on your computer. This section explains how.

As you may know, Internet Explorer is free. You can download it from any of several sites on the Internet, and you can use it without charge. There are no restrictions on how you can use it: At home or at the office, Internet Explorer is completely free.

How can the good people at Microsoft afford to distribute Internet Explorer for free? Because they're hoping that the browser will catch on like wildfire. Internet Explorers 3, 4, and 5 were huge successes. Microsoft hopes to build on that success by offering Internet Explorer 5.5 at the same irresistible rate.

For sure, Microsoft plans to make plenty of money from Internet Explorer — not by selling Internet Explorer itself, but by establishing Internet Explorer as the standard Internet browser used by more people than any other browser. Microsoft then plans to make its money by selling the development tools that Web authors and software developers need to create interesting content that is viewable only with Internet Explorer.

Here are some of the ways you can obtain Internet Explorer 5.5:

- ✔ If you already have Internet access and are using another program (such as Netscape Navigator or an earlier version of Internet Explorer), you can download Internet Explorer 5.5 from Microsoft's Web site at www.microsoft.com. Note that the download for Internet Explorer can take several hours if you don't have a cable or DSL connection. Better go to the local video store and rent a movie before proceeding. Or start the download just before you go to bed. The download should be finished by morning.

- ✔ If you recently purchased a new computer, Internet Explorer 5.5 is probably already installed. To find out what version you have, start Internet Explorer by clicking the Internet Explorer icon on your desktop or in the Windows taskbar. Then, choose Help⇨About Internet Explorer. This summons a dialog box that tells you which version of Internet Explorer is installed on your computer.

- ✔ You can subscribe to an Internet service provider that uses Internet Explorer as its default browser. But make sure that the service uses the latest version of Internet Explorer; some ISPs offer only older versions of Internet Explorer.

Internet Explorer has been through several major revisions. The current version, Internet Explorer 5.5, is among the more powerful Web browsers available. If you have an earlier version (5, 4, 3, 2, or 1), be sure to upgrade to Version 5.5 as soon as possible. You can find Internet Explorer 5.5 available for download at www.microsoft.com.

After you download the Internet Explorer file, exit from your Web browser, open the folder into which you downloaded the file, and double-click the file's icon. The Internet Explorer setup program then installs Internet Explorer for you. (Depending on the browser you use, Internet Explorer may automatically install itself after the download finishes. If so, just sit back and enjoy the ride.)

If you don't want to contend with an hours-long download, you can get Internet Explorer 5.5 on CD-ROM from most computer stores for about $5, or you can order it from Microsoft in the USA by calling 800-458-2048.

To actually install the downloaded Internet Explorer 5.5 on your computer, just follow the instructions that appear when you go to the Internet Explorer download page. If you get Internet Explorer 5.5 on a CD-ROM, insert the CD-ROM in your CD-ROM drive and follow the instructions that appear on-screen.

The Internet Explorer 5.5 Setup program asks you several questions before it installs Internet Explorer on your computer. For starters, the Setup program asks if you want to install all of Internet Explorer or just part of it. You have two choices:

✔ **Typical Set of Components:** Installs just those parts of Internet Explorer that you'll probably use, in Microsoft's opinion. This is the easiest and fastest way to install Internet Explorer.

✔ **Customize Your Installation:** Lets you pick exactly which parts of Internet Explorer you want to install. Use this option if you're choosey.

If you have plenty of disk space on your computer and don't mind a long download (as in several hours long unless you have a DSL or cable connection), I suggest that you opt for the Customize Your Installation option, and then select any of the Internet Explorer components you think that you may need. If you select the Typical Installation, you can always return to the download page later and pick up the components you didn't install the first time.

Setup also asks if you want to install an optional feature called the Active Desktop. This feature changes the way the Windows desktop and My Computer windows work. If you choose not to install the Active Desktop now, you can always install it later if you want to.

If you have Windows 98 or Windows 2000 and an Internet connection, you can upgrade to Internet Explorer 5.5 by clicking the Start button and then choosing Settings⇨Windows Update. Performing these steps takes you to the Windows Update site, which automatically offers to install new Windows features, including Internet Explorer 5.5.

Now You Can Set Up Your Internet Connection

In the old days, setting up a connection to the Internet was a complicated affair best handled by computer experts with pocket protectors and tape on their glasses. Now, with Windows 98 or Windows Millenium Edition and Internet Explorer 5.5, configuring your computer to connect to the Internet is a simple, straightforward process. All you have to do is run a special program called the *Internet Connection Wizard*. The wizard handles all the configuration details for you.

To run the Internet Connection Wizard, follow these steps:

1. **Gather the information you need to configure your Internet connection.**

   You need the following information, which your Internet service provider should be able to supply:

   - The name of your Internet service provider
   - The telephone number you dial to connect to the Internet
   - The name and password you must use to access the system
   - Your IP address, unless an IP address is assigned automatically each time you log on
   - The DNS server address, which looks like a bunch of numbers with periods where they don't belong, as in 123.4.56.789
   - Your e-mail address and the address of your e-mail server
   - The address of your Internet news server

2. **Fetch your Windows installation disks or CD-ROM.**

   You may not need these, but the Internet Connection Wizard sometimes asks for them. Better keep your disks handy just in case.

3. **Start the Internet Connection Wizard.**

   Click the Start button on the taskbar and choose Programs⇨ Internet Explorer⇨Connection Wizard. (If you can't find it under Programs⇨Internet Explorer, look under Programs⇨Accessories⇨

Communications.) When you start the Internet Connection Wizard, the dialog box shown in Figure 2-1 greets you and offers you three choices for configuring your computer for the Internet.

Figure 2-1:
The Internet
Connection
Wizard
starts up
and offers
you three
choices.

- The first option enables you to set up a new Internet connection. Choose this option if you don't already have any type of Internet connection or an account with an Internet service provider. The Internet Connection Wizard uses your modem to dial in to a Microsoft computer that maintains a list of Internet service providers. A list of ISPs in your area appears, and you are granted the privilege of signing up with one of these providers and having your connection configured automatically.

- The second option assumes that you have an account with an Internet service provider and you want to transfer it to this computer.

- The third option lets you manually configure your Internet account.

4. **Choose the third option (assuming that you already have an Internet account) and then click Next.**

   The Internet Connection Wizard displays the dialog box shown in Figure 2-2, asking whether you plan to connect to the Internet via an ISP with a modem and phone line or a local area network.

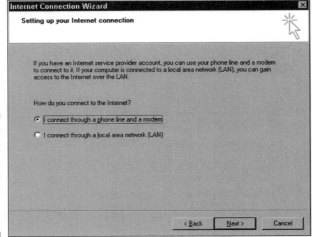

Figure 2-2:
The Internet
Connection
Wizard asks
how you will
connect to
the Internet.

5. Check the appropriate connection option and then click Next.

Assuming you are connecting via an ISP, the Wizard displays a dialog box similar to the one shown in Figure 2-3.

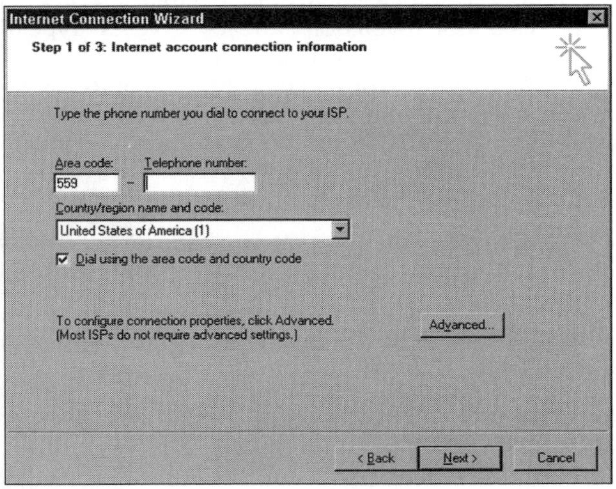

Figure 2-3:
The Internet
Connection
Wizard asks
for your
ISP's phone
number.

6. Type the phone number for your service provider and then click Next.

The dialog box shown in Figure 2-4 appears next.

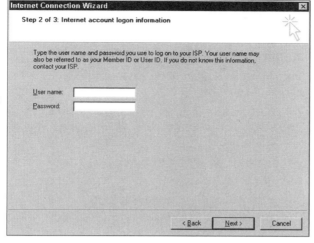

Figure 2-4:
The Internet
Connection
Wizard
wants to
know your
name and
password.

7. **Type your name and password and then click Next.**

Your password is not displayed when you type it, so you don't need to
worry about anyone watching over your shoulder. If you click Next, the
Internet Connection Wizard displays the dialog box shown in Figure 2-5.

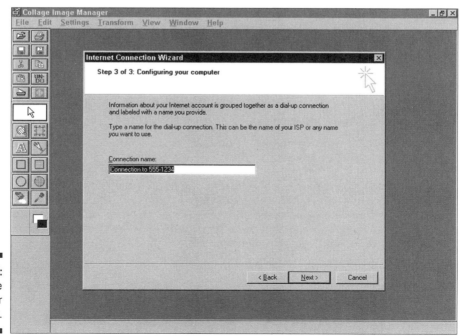

Figure 2-5:
Type a name
for your
connection.

8. **Type a name for your connection and then click Next.**

   You see a series of dialog boxes that enables you to configure the Outlook Express program, which comes with Internet Explorer 5.5, so that it can handle your e-mail and Internet newsgroups.

9. **Type the information requested on each of the Outlook Express configuration screens, clicking Next to move from one screen to the next.**

   You need to type in your e-mail address and the name of your e-mail and Internet news servers. Your Internet service provider should supply you with this information.

   Eventually, the dialog box shown in Figure 2-6 appears.

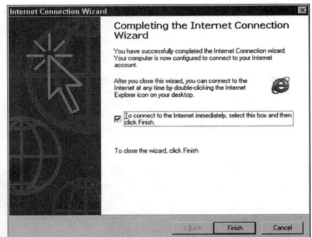

Figure 2-6:
It's about
time.

10. **Click Finish.**

    Your computer grinds and whirls for a moment, and then the Internet Connection Wizard disappears — finally!

Now, you can access the Internet by double-clicking the Internet Explorer icon that appears on your desktop. (If you opted to install the Active Desktop option when you installed Internet Explorer, you don't have to double-click the icon; a single click does the trick.) When the Connection Manager dialog box appears, click Connect and start exploring!

If you need to change any of the advanced settings for your Internet connection, click the Advanced button in Step 6 (refer to Figure 2-3) and then enter the information for the advanced settings you need. Do this only if your ISP uses a SLIP connection rather than a PPP connection or if your ISP tells you to set your browser to use a specific IP or DNS server address. The good news is that you don't have to know anything about what SLIP connections, IP addresses, or DNS server addresses mean. Just type the information your Internet service provider gives you and get on with it.

Part II
Embarking on a World Wide Web Adventure

The 5th Wave   By Rich Tennant

In this part . . .

This is the part of the book where you discover the basics of using Internet Explorer: how to start it, how to use Internet Explorer to browse the World Wide Web, how to look for and find the information you're interested in, how to keep track of your favorite places, and how to get help when you don't know what you're doing.

This is just the beginning of your Internet explorations. After you have these basics under your belt, you'll be ready to take on the most advanced topics covered in the rest of this book. But, as a great king once advised, it is best to begin at the beginning, and go on until you come to the end, and then stop. So grab your pith helmet and prepare for Web Wonderland!

Chapter 3

Pushing Off

- -

In This Chapter

▶ Starting Internet Explorer

▶ Understanding World Wide Web addresses

▶ Displaying pages on the World Wide Web

▶ Printing and saving Web pages

▶ Downloading files from the Internet

▶ Finding information on a page

▶ Exiting Internet Explorer and disconnecting from the Internet

- -

*A*fter you have your Internet connection in place and you've installed Internet Explorer, you're ready to begin your Internet explorations. This chapter shows you how to use the basic features of Internet Explorer to surf the Web. You won't gather intimate knowledge about all the nuances of using Internet Explorer — I save some of the more exotic features for later chapters. In this chapter, I focus on the foundation: how to start Internet Explorer, how to explore the Web, and so on.

Starting Internet Explorer

The first step to surfing the Web using Internet Explorer is starting the program. There are at least three ways to start Internet Explorer.

✔ Double-click the Internet Explorer icon that appears on your desktop. (If you don't have this icon on your desktop, you probably need to install Internet Explorer — read Chapter 2.)

   If you or someone else has configured your Windows desktop to work in single-click mode, a single click of the Internet Explorer desktop icon is sufficient to start Internet Explorer.

✔ Click the Start button on the taskbar and then choose Programs➪Internet Explorer➪Internet Explorer.

✔ Click the small Launch Internet Explorer Browser icon that appears in the taskbar.

Whichever method you opt for, Internet Explorer grinds and churns for a moment. If you use a modem to connect to the Internet and you are not already online, you will be greeted by the Dial-up Connection dialog box shown in Figure 3-1. Type your user ID and password into the appropriate text boxes; then click Connect to proceed.

Figure 3-1:
The Dial-up
Connection
dialog box.

After you click Connect, your computer automatically dials the phone number of your Internet service provider (ISP). If the modem volume is turned up, you will hear a dial tone, two or three rings, and then a few moments of rather obnoxious squealing as the modems establish their connection.

After a connection is established, the Internet Explorer window appears, and you are taken directly to your start page, as shown in Figure 3-2.

If you connect to the Internet via a cable modem, a DSL connection, or a high-speed network connection, you won't see the Dial-up Connection dialog box. Instead, Internet Explorer simply comes to life, as shown in Figure 3-2.

You can resize the Internet Explorer window just as you would any other window. I usually like to work with Internet Explorer maximized so that it fills the entire screen and displays as much of each Web page as possible. To maximize a window, click the Maximize button in the upper-right corner of the Internet Explorer window.

After Internet Explorer dials into your ISP, you may be faced with a window in which you must type login information (see Figure 3-3). For example, my ISP requires me to type in my user ID and password even though the Connection Manager knows my user ID and password. If your ISP tells you to type similar information, you have to follow its instructions.

Figure 3-3:
In some
cases, you
may have to
type in your
user ID and
password to
log in to
your ISP.

Typing login information every time you access the Internet is a big-time hassle. Fortunately, Windows 98 lets you create a special file called a *dial-up script* that supplies the information automatically whenever you dial up your ISP. Creating a dial-up script isn't rocket science, but it's a little more advanced than this chapter can handle. When you grow weary of typing this login information every time you call your ISP, skip to Chapter 16, which explains in detail how to create a dial-up script.

Making Sense of the Internet Explorer Screen

Before I show you how to actually explore the Internet, I want to pause for a moment to examine all the bells and whistles that Microsoft has loaded in the Internet Explorer window. Figure 3-4 shows the Internet Explorer window, maximized for your viewing pleasure, with some of the more important parts labeled for easy identification.

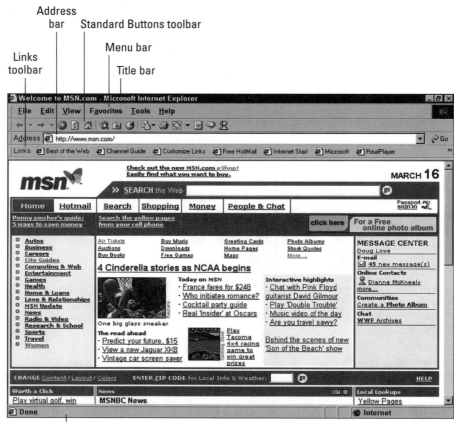

Figure 3-4:
The different parts of the Internet Explorer 5.5 screen.

The following items on the Internet Explorer screen are worthy of note:

✔ **Title bar:** At the very top of the window, the title bar always displays the name of the Internet page you are currently viewing. For example, in Figure 3-4, the title is "Welcome to MSN.com — Microsoft Internet Explorer."

✔ **Menu bar:** Just as in any Windows program, the menu bar lives below the title bar. Internet Explorer's deepest secrets are hidden within the menus located on the menu bar.

✔ **Standard Buttons toolbar:** Beneath the menu bar is the Standard Buttons toolbar, which contains buttons you can click to perform common tasks. The purpose of each of these buttons is summarized in Table 3-1, but don't feel as though you need to understand these buttons at first. As you gain experience with Internet Explorer, the function of each of these buttons becomes apparent.

✔ **Address bar:** Beneath the Standard toolbar is the Address bar, which displays the Internet address (called a URL) of the page currently being displayed in the Address box. You can click the down-arrow button on the right end of the Address box to see addresses of pages you recently visited, and you can type an Internet address in the Address box if you want to go to a specific Web page. (If you don't understand Internet addresses, don't worry. I explain them later in this chapter, under the heading "Understanding Web addresses.")

To the right of the Address box is the Go button, which you can click to cause Internet Explorer to go to the Web page indicated by the address you type in the Address box. Or, if you prefer, you can simply press the Enter key after typing an address.

✔ **Links toolbar:** Below the Address bar is the Links toolbar, which houses a collection of frequently visited Web sites you can access with a single mouse click.

To save space, the Links toolbar may be hidden next to the Address bar. If you can't see the Links toolbar, but the word *Links* appears next to the Address bar, simply double-click the word *Links*. The Links toolbar expands, and the Address toolbar shrinks so that both toolbars are visible. Double-click *Links* again to expand the Links toolbar to the full width of the horizontal bar, shrinking the Address toolbar so that only the word *Address* is visible. Double-click *Links* a third time to shrink the Links toolbar again so that the entire Address toolbar is visible. (You can also resize the Links toolbar by dragging the word *Links* across the horizontal bar. Or you can drag the word *Links* down so that the Links toolbar appears on a separate line beneath the Address toolbar.)

If a toolbar doesn't fit completely on the screen, Internet Explorer displays a double arrow at the upper-right corner of the toolbar. You can click the double arrow to display a menu that lists any toolbar buttons that don't fit in the Internet Explorer window.

   ✔ **Status bar:** The status bar, located at the bottom of the window, periodically displays useful information, such as what Internet Explorer is
   trying to do or how much progress it has made downloading a large file.

   ✔ **Scroll bars:** Located at the right and bottom of the window, the scroll
   bars appear and disappear as needed. Whenever Internet Explorer can't
   display all the information on an Internet page on a single screen, a
   scroll bar appears so that you can scroll to the hidden information.

One other feature of the Internet Explorer screen that's important to know
about but that isn't visible in Figure 3-4 is the Explorer bar. The Explorer bar
is an area on the left side of the main Internet Explorer window area that
comes and goes as needed. There are actually three different incarnations of
the Explorer bar, known as the Search bar, Favorites bar, and History bar,
which appear when you click the Search, Favorites, or History button in the
Standard toolbar. You can see the Explorer bar in action in several places
throughout this book.

Table 3-1	Buttons on the Internet Explorer Standard Buttons Toolbar
Button	*What It Does*
⬅	Moves back to the most recently displayed page
➡	Moves forward to the page you most recently moved back from
⊗	Cancels a time-consuming download
↻	Forces Internet Explorer to obtain a fresh copy of the current page
🏠	Takes you to your start page
🔍	Enables you to search the Internet quickly for topics of interest
📁	Displays a list of your favorite Internet locations
🕐	Displays a list of sites you have recently visited
✉	Switches to the Outlook Express program so you can send and receive e-mail

Button	What It Does
	Prints the current page
	Lets you edit the current Web page
	Lets you access a Microsoft Office 2000 discussion server
	Opens a separate pane at the bottom of the Internet Explorer window to access the Real.com home page, where you can search for and play music and video files
	Starts MSN Messenger for instant communications with your online friends

Oh, the Places You'll Go!

As its name implies, the chief function of Internet Explorer is to enable you to explore the Internet. To do so, you need to know how to get around — that is, how to navigate from one Internet location to another. The following sections explain Internet Explorer's navigation features.

Understanding Web addresses

Just as every house in a neighborhood has a street address, every page on the World Wide Web has an Internet address. The Internet address of a Web page is also called a *Uniform Resource Locator* (URL).

URLs are becoming commonplace in our society. Just think about how many times you've seen addresses such as www.whatever.com appear at the end of a television advertisement. These days, every company that advertises seems to have a Web page.

To use Internet Explorer effectively, you need to know the various parts that make up a typical URL Web address. Typing URLs isn't hard, but it takes some practice.

A URL consists of three parts, written as follows:

```
protocol://host_address/resource_name
```

✔ For World Wide Web pages, the *protocol* portion of the URL is always http (http stands for *Hypertext Transfer Protocol,* but you don't need to know that to use URLs).

✔ The *host address* is the Internet address of the computer on which the Web page resides (for example, www.dummies.com).

✔ The final part, the *resource name,* is a name assigned by the host computer to a specific Web page or other file. In many cases, the resource name contains additional slashes that represent directories on the host system. Most of the time, you can omit the resource name completely if you simply want to display the home page for a company's Web site.

Here are some examples of complete URLs:

```
http://www.yahoo.com
http://www.cbs.com/network/tvshows/mini/lateshow
http://vol.com/~infidel/halloween/halloween.html
```

Notice that all Web page addresses must be prefixed by http://. However, Internet Explorer cleverly adds the http:// automatically, so you don't have to type it yourself. Throughout this book, I leave off the http:// from any World Wide Web address.

Because Internet Explorer always lets you omit the protocol part (http://), and because you can often omit the resource name, the only URL component you usually need to worry about is the host address. Host addresses themselves consist of three components separated from one another by periods, usually called *dots*.

✔ The first part of the Internet address is almost always www, to indicate that the address is for a page on the World Wide Web.

✔ The second part of the Internet address is usually a company or organization name, which is sometimes abbreviated if the full name is too long. Sometimes this second part actually consists of two or more parts in itself separated by periods. For example, in the address www.polis.iupui.edu, the second part is polis.iupui.

✔ The third and final part of an Internet address is a category that indicates the type of organization the name belongs to. The most common categories are

  • **gov:** Government agencies

  • **com:** Private companies

  • **edu:** Universities

  • **org:** Organizations

  • **net:** Networks

Putting these three address parts together, you get addresses, such as www.microsoft.com, www.nasa.gov, and www.ucla.edu.

Going to a specific page

What if a friend gives you the address of a Web page you want to check out? No problem. To visit a specific Web page for which you know the address, all you have to do is follow these simple steps:

1. **Click the mouse in the Address box, which you can find in the Address toolbar.**

   Refer to Figure 3-4.

2. **Type the address of the Web page you want to retrieve.**

3. **Press Enter.**

Internet Explorer has a timesaving feature called AutoComplete that is designed to make typing Web addresses even easier. AutoComplete keeps track of Web addresses that you've recently typed. Then, AutoComplete watches as you type Web addresses and tries to anticipate which address you are typing. As soon as it thinks that it knows, it automatically fills in the rest of the address.

For example, if you recently visited www.microsoft.com and you type www.mi, AutoComplete automatically fills in www.microsoft.com as the complete address. If you visited www.yahoo.com and then type www.ya, AutoComplete fills in www.yahoo.com. If the address AutoComplete suggests is indeed the address you want to type, just press Enter. Otherwise, keep typing — the address AutoComplete suggested disappears the instant you type another letter.

As an added bonus, you don't have to type the www. that comes before most Web addresses and the .com that comes after most addresses. Instead, you can just type the middle portion of the Web address and then press Ctrl+Enter instead of just the Enter key. When you press Ctrl+Enter, Internet Explorer automatically adds http://www. and .com to your Web addresses.

For example, suppose that you want to go to the Microsoft Web site. You could do that by typing **www.microsoft.com** in the Address box and pressing the Enter key. Or, to save time, you could just type **microsoft** and press Ctrl+Enter. Internet Explorer changes microsoft to http:/www.microsoft.com and then retrieves the page.

Note that this trick won't work for government or educational Web pages because their addresses end in .gov or .edu rather than .com.

Many Web addresses are complicated — complicated enough that typing them without making a mistake is difficult. Fortunately, if you already have the Web address in another document, such as a word processing document or e-mail message, you can always copy and paste it into Internet Explorer's Address box. Assuming that Internet Explorer is already running and that you have opened the document that contains the address you want to copy in another window, you can paste the address into Internet Explorer by following these steps:

1. **From Internet Explorer, press Alt+Tab and then open the document or e-mail message that contains the address you want to copy.**

2. **Highlight the entire address and then press Ctrl+C to copy the address to the Windows Clipboard.**

   If you're a mouse fan, you can choose Edit➪Copy.

3. **Press Alt+Tab again to return to Internet Explorer.**

   You may have to press Alt+Tab several times to bring up Internet Explorer, depending on what other programs are currently running.

4. **Click in the Address box in the Address toolbar.**

5. **Press Ctrl+V to paste the address.**

   Or you can use the Edit➪Paste command.

6. **Press Enter.**

Following the links

The most popular method of navigating through the Internet is by following links. A *link* is a bit of text or a graphic on one Web page that leads you to another Web page. A link may lead to another page at the same Web site, or it may lead to a page at a different Web site altogether.

You can easily identify the text links on a Web page because they're underlined and displayed in colors different from the rest of the text. For example, Figure 3-4 is filled with links: <u>Air Tickets</u>, <u>Buy Books</u>, <u>Buy Music</u>, and so on.

In addition to textlinks, many Web pages contain *graphical links* — graphics that you can click to jump to another Web page. Unlike text links, graphical links are not identified with a special color or underlining. But you can spot them by watching the mouse pointer as you glide it over the graphic. If the mouse pointer changes from an arrow to a pointing finger, you know that you've found a link.

In some graphical links, the page you are taken to depends on where in the graphic you click. For technical reasons you don't want to know, this type of graphical link is called an *image map*.

In most cases, Web page designers try to make their graphical links obvious by including text next to them. For example, Figure 3-5 shows the Web page for the National Park Service, which sports the following graphical links:

- ✔ Symbols in Battle
- ✔ Visit Your Parks
- ✔ Links to the Past
- ✔ Nature Net
- ✔ Park Smart
- ✔ Info Zone

You can tell where a link leads by moving the mouse pointer over it. This action displays a message in the status bar indicating the address of the page that will be displayed if you click the link. For example, if you point the mouse at the Links to the Past link on the National Park Service page, the status bar displays the following message:

```
http://www.cr.nps.gov
```

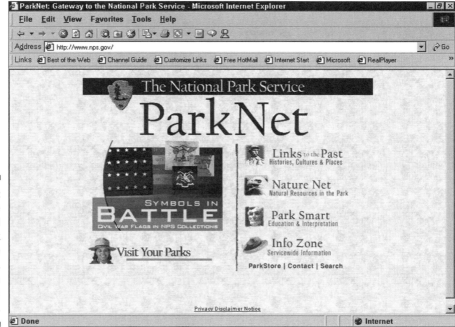

Figure 3-5:
The National Park Service page, loaded with graphic links.

Yes, you can go back

Exploring links on the Web can be like exploring paths in the woods. You see a link that looks promising, so you take it. The page the link leads to has other links that seem interesting, so you pick one and take it. And so it goes until pretty soon you're lost. You should have marked your path with bread crumbs.

Fortunately, Internet Explorer lets you retrace your steps easily. Two buttons on the Standard Buttons toolbar exist for just this purpose:

 ✔ The Back button moves backward along the path you've taken. Clicking this button retraces the links that you followed, only backward. You can click the Back button several times in a row if necessary to retrace your steps through several links.

 ✔ The Forward button moves you forward along your path. As long as you keep plowing ahead, this button is grayed out — meaning you can't use it. However, after you begin to retrace your steps with the Back button, the Forward button becomes active. Clicking the Forward button takes you to the page where you were when you last clicked the Back button.

Both the Back and Forward buttons sport a down arrow, which you can click to reveal a list of Web pages that you've recently visited in the order in which you visited them. This feature enables you to return directly to any page you've visited without having to retrace your steps one page at a time.

It's all history now

 Internet Explorer automatically keeps track of the pages that you've visited not only during your current Internet session, but also in past sessions. To quickly return to one of these pages, click the History button on the Standard Buttons toolbar. The History bar appears on the left side of the Internet Explorer window, as shown in Figure 3-6.

As you can see, the History bar lists the Web pages you've visited today and in past weeks. To return to a page, first click Today or one of the previous week's history folders. A list of Web sites appears, showing all previous stops on your Web page tour. You can then click the site you want to revisit.

To make the History bar disappear, click the History button again or click the Close button in the upper-right corner of the History bar.

 Don't forget that every place you visit is recorded in the history folder. Thus, the history folder provides a record of where you've been and what you've seen . . . and that can be incriminating!

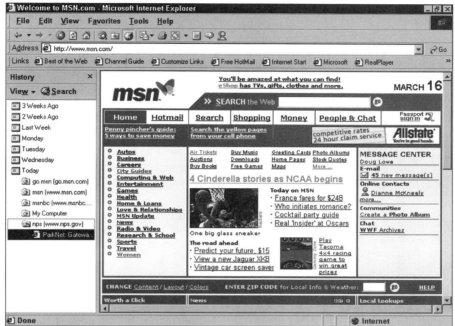

Figure 3-6:
The History
bar.

If your kid denies that he's been sneaking peaks at www.playboy.com, pop up the history folder and find out. Pretty tricky, eh? (Of course, if the kids read this book, they'll know about this trick. Better tear out this page before anyone else sees it.)

Exploring the Web can be fun, but sometimes the exploration turns out to be a wild goose chase. Fortunately, Internet Explorer can bail you out if you find yourself hopelessly lost. Just click the Home button, and you're instantly transported to your start page. You can start over with a clean slate.

If you want to change your start page, may I recommend Chapter 13?

The History bar is actually one manifestation of what Internet Explorer refers to as the Explorer bar. The Explorer bar appears as a separate pane on the left edge of the Internet Explorer window and enables you to navigate through a series of links while the Web page is displayed in the right side of the Window.

Besides the History bar, there are also two other incarnations of the Explorer bar: Search and Favorites. For more information about searching the Web, refer to Chapter 4. For more information about using Favorites, see Chapter 5.

Here are a few tricks you can do with the Explorer bar:

- ✔ You can change the size of the Explorer bar by dragging the vertical divider that divides the Explorer bar from the Web page.

- ✔ You can hide the Explorer bar by clicking the Close button (the X that appears at the top right corner of the Explorer bar) or by clicking the button you clicked to summon the Explorer bar. (For example, if you click the History button to summon the Explorer bar, click the History button again to hide it.)

- ✔ You can switch from one Explorer bar option to another by clicking the appropriate toolbar button. For example, if the History bar is visible, you can switch directly to Favorites or Search by clicking the Favorites or Search buttons.

- ✔ Another way to summon the Explorer bar is to choose View⭢Explorer Bar. This command displays a menu that lists four Explorer bar options: Search, Favorites, History, and None.

Refreshing a Page

The first time that you access a Web page, Internet Explorer copies the entire page over the network from the Web site to your computer. Depending on the size and complexity of the page and the speed of your connection, this process can take a few seconds or a few minutes.

To avoid repeating this download, Internet Explorer saves the information for the page in a special area of your hard disk known as the *cache* (pronounced *cash*). The next time you retrieve the same page from the Web, your computer gets the page directly from your hard disk instead of downloading it again from the Web site. Thus, you get to see the page much faster.

What happens if the page has changed since the last time you downloaded it? Most Web pages don't change very often, but some do. In fact, some pages change daily or even more often. For such pages, you can force Internet Explorer to refresh its view of the page.

 To refresh a page, all you have to do is click the Refresh button and then twiddle your thumbs while Internet Explorer downloads the page. Refreshing a page takes longer than grabbing it from your hard disk, but at least you know that the information is current.

Internet Explorer has an Offline feature that you can use to download new versions of a Web page automatically on a regular basis. You can find everything you need to know about this feature in Chapter 6.

Stop! Enough Already!

Every once in a while, you wander into a Web page that you could do without. The link that led you to the page may have looked interesting, but after you get there, the page isn't what you expected. According to Murphy's Law, that page also will be the page with a 200KB graphic that takes forever to download.

 Fortunately, you're not forced to sit and wait while a large graphic you don't want downloads. All you have to do is click the Stop button, and Internet Explorer cancels the download of the current page. The portion of the page that has already made it to your computer continues to be displayed, but anything that hasn't yet arrived won't. You can then click the Back button to go back to the previous page.

 Sometimes you go to a page that appears to remain blank while a large graphic is downloading. In many cases, simply scrolling the page a bit reveals text that has already been downloaded to your computer, which (for some reason) Internet Explorer has yet to display. If you find yourself staring at a blank page that appears to be in the midst of downloading a large graphic, try clicking one of the scroll bars just to see whether any text is hiding.

Working in Full-Screen View

The Internet Explorer menus and toolbars are nice, but sometimes they get in the way — especially when you're viewing a Web page that is chock full of information. To see more of the Web and less of Internet Explorer's menus and toolbars, switch to full-screen view by choosing View⇨Full Screen or by pressing F11.

Figure 3-7 shows how the National Park Service Web page appears when displayed in full-screen view. As you can see, the Menu bar, Address bar, and Status bar have completely disappeared, and the Standard Buttons toolbar has been reduced to a smaller toolbar at the very top of the screen. To return Internet Explorer to its normal view, press F11 again or click the Restore button that appears at the upper-right corner of the screen.

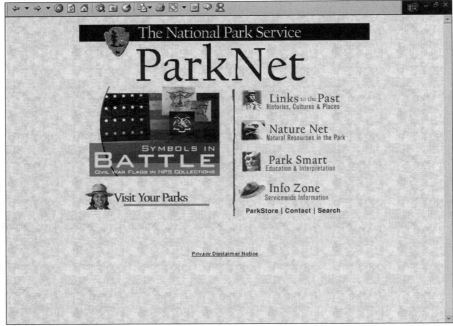

Printing a Web Page

If you find a page with really interesting information that you want to have a hard copy of, all you have to do is print the page. Make sure that your printer's turned on and ready to go and then follow these steps:

1. **Choose File➪Print.**

   The Print dialog box appears, as shown in Figure 3-8.

2. **Stare at the Print dialog box for a moment.**

   If you have more than one printer at your disposal, make sure that the correct printer is selected in the Name drop-down list. If you want to print more than one copy of the page, change the Number of Copies setting.

3. **Click OK.**

4. **Wait a moment while your printer grinds and whirls.**

A faster way to print a Web page — assuming that you want only one copy and you know that the correct printer has already been selected as your default printer — is to simply click the Print button on the toolbar.

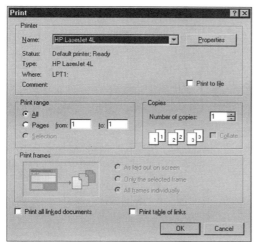

Figure 3-8:
The Print
dialog box.

 Some Web pages are laid out in two or more *frames,* which display content independently of one another. If you attempt to print a page that uses frames, the Print Frames portion of the Print dialog box will be enabled so that you can tell Internet Explorer how you want it to deal with frames when it prints the page. You have three choices:

✔ **As laid out on screen:** Prints all the frames together, as they appear on the screen.

✔ **Only the selected frame:** Prints only the frame that you've selected. This option is available only if you select a frame before calling up the Print dialog box.

✔ **All frames individually:** Prints all of the frames that make up the page separately.

 Internet Explorer 5.5 includes a new Print Preview feature that lets you see how a page will appear when it's printed before you actually send the page to your printer. To use this feature, choose the File⇨Print Preview command. A Print Preview screen appears, as shown in Figure 3-9. To print the page, click Print. To return to Internet Explorer without printing the page, click Close.

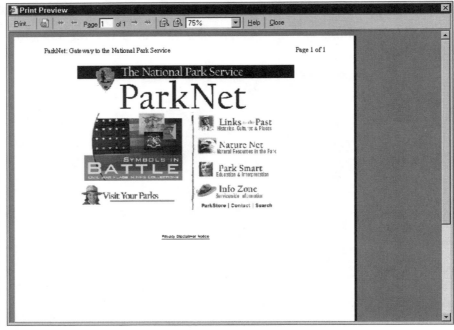

Figure 3-9:
Print
Preview lets
you see how
a page will
appear
before you
actually
print it.

Changing the Font Size

If you consistently find that the text displayed on the Internet is too small, you may want to visit your ophthalmologist. On the other hand, if every once in a while you come across a page that you have to squint at to see, the problem may not be with your eyes; it may be that the text is simply displayed too small.

Fortunately, Internet Explorer provides a simple solution for too-small text. To change the font size, choose View⇨Text Size. This command leads to another menu that lists five font sizes: Largest, Larger, Medium, Smaller, and Smallest. Click the size you want.

 You can also use the Size button to change the font size. When you click the Size button, all the text on a page jumps to a larger size. Each time you click the Size button, the text size increases — until you get to the largest possible size. Clicking the Size button once more returns you to the smallest size.

Unfortunately, the Size button is not normally displayed in the Internet Explorer Standard toolbar. To display the Size button, choose View⇨ Toolbars⇨Customize. This command summons a dialog box that has two side-by-side list boxes. The one on the right lists the buttons that appear on your toolbar; the one on the left lists buttons that you can add to the toolbar. Click the Size button in the left list box and click Add to add the Size button to the toolbar. Finally, click Close. The Size button now appears on your toolbar.

Saving a Web Page

You can save the contents of any Web page to a file on your computer by following these steps:

1. **Choose File⇨Save As.**

   A dialog box like the one shown in Figure 3-10 appears.

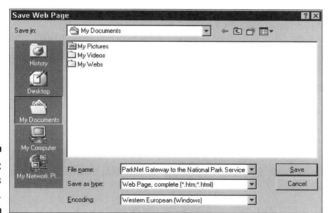

Figure 3-10: The Save As dialog box.

2. **Select a suitable location for the file.**

   By default, Internet Explorer saves the file in your My Documents folder. If this is not an appropriate location, you can browse your way to a better locale.

3. **Type a name for the file you want to save in the File Name field.**

4. **Choose the file type in the Save as Type field.**

   You have four choices:

   - **Web Page, complete:** Saves all the files required to display the page, graphics and all

   - **Web Archive, single file:** Saves the Web page along with all its graphic and other elements as a single file, suitable for e-mailing to your friends

- **Web Page, HTML only:** Saves the page complete with formatting but doesn't save auxiliary files, such as graphic or sound files

- **Text File:** Saves the text without the formatting information

5. **Click the Save button.**

If you don't want to save the entire page as a text file, you can select the text that you do want to save and then press Ctrl+C to copy it. Next, switch to a word processing program, such as Microsoft Word, open an existing document or create a new document, and then press Ctrl+V to paste the copied text into the document.

Saving a Picture

You can save any picture you see in a Web site as a graphic file on your hard disk. To save a picture, all you have to do is follow these steps:

1. **Right-click the picture you want to save.**

   A pop-up menu appears.

2. **Choose the Save Picture As command.**

   A standard Save As dialog box appears.

3. **Navigate to the folder in which you want to save the file.**

4. **Type a new filename for the file if you don't like the one that is supplied.**

5. **Click the Save button.**

Note that you can also choose to use the picture as your desktop wallpaper. Simply right-click the image and then select Set As Wallpaper. Unfortunately, when you do that, Internet Explorer saves the picture as a file named simply Internet Explorer Wallpaper. If you'd rather choose your own name for the file, use the Save Picture As command as described in the preceding steps and save the picture in the C:\Windows folder. (For Windows 95, you have to save the picture as a BMP file, but for Windows 98 or higher, you can leave it as a JPEG.) Then, right-click your desktop, choose the Properties command, and choose the file you saved from the list of image files to use for your wallpaper.

Beware of copyright protections when you save a graphic. Many images, especially artwork, photographs, and company logos, are copyrighted. If you save a graphic that may be protected by copyright law, be sure to get the owner's permission before you use the graphic.

Downloading a File

One of the main reasons that many people use the Internet is to *download* files — that is, to copy files from other computer systems and place them on their own computers. The Internet offers many types of files for downloading: documents, pictures, sounds, movies, animation, and programs.

Internet Explorer makes downloading files easy. In fact, the only hard part is finding the file you want to download. The best way to find a file to download is to use one of the search services described in Chapter 4. For example, if you want to download the popular computer game Doom, use any of the search services to search for the word Doom. You're sure to find several sites from which you can download the file.

To actually download a file, just follow these steps:

1. **Find a Web site that contains a file that you want to download.**

   You may have to use one of the search services described in Chapter 4. Usually, a search leads you to a page that includes a link that you can click to download the file. This link usually, but not always, gives you some indication of how large the file is.

2. **Click the link to download the file.**

   Internet Explorer grinds and churns for a moment. Eventually, the dialog box shown in Figure 3-11 appears.

Figure 3-11:
The File Download dialog box.

3. **Make sure that the Save This Program to Disk option is selected and then click OK.**

   If you want to run the program immediately after you download it, click the Run This Program from Its Current Location option instead.

Assuming you chose the Save This Program to Disk option, a Save As dialog box appears. (If you chose Run This Program from Its Current Location instead, you can skip ahead to Step 5.)

4. **In the Save As dialog box, select the folder in which you want the file to be saved. Then click $\underline{S}$ave.**

A dialog box displays a progress bar that enables you to monitor the download progress, as shown in Figure 3-12.

Figure 3-12:
Downloading
a file.

5. **Wait until the download is finished.**

When the download finishes, a dialog box appears and informs you that the download is complete.

6. **Click OK.**

If you chose the Save This Program to Disk option in Step 3, you're done. If you chose the Run This Program from the Internet option instead, the program you downloaded runs immediately.

Here are some pertinent points to ponder when performing a download:

✔ You should always make sure that you have enough disk space on your hard drive before downloading a large file. Nothing is more frustrating than discovering that you have only 3MB of free disk space an hour after you begin a 4MB download.

✔ To check your free disk space, you can double-click the My Computer icon on your desktop and then click the icon for your C drive. The My Computer window displays the amount of free space on the C drive in the status bar at the bottom of the window.

✔ You don't have to twiddle your thumbs while the file is downloading. In fact, as I write this, I'm downloading a 4MB file from the Internet. To continue with other work, simply click anywhere outside the File Download dialog box. The dialog box kindly steps out of the way so that you can work with other programs while the download continues. You can even use Internet Explorer to browse other Web sites while the download takes its sweet time.

Finding Text

Sometimes you stumble across a large page of text that you know contains some useful tidbit of information, but you can't seem to locate what you want among all those words. When this happens, you can use the Find command to locate text on the page. Simply follow these steps:

1. **Choose Edit⇨Find (or press Ctrl+F).**

   The Find dialog box appears, as shown in Figure 3-13.

Figure 3-13:
The Find
dialog box.

2. **In the Find What text box, type the text that you want to find.**

3. **Click Find Next.**

   Internet Explorer finds the first occurrence of the text on the current page. The Find dialog box remains active so that you can quickly find additional occurrences of the text.

4. **Keep clicking Find Next until you find the text you want.**

5. **Click Cancel to close the Find dialog box.**

Keep in mind that the Find command searches for text only on the current page; it does not search the Internet for other text references to what you're trying to find. To do that type of search, you must use one of the search services that I describe in Chapter 4.

Exiting Internet Explorer

After you finish browsing the Web, you can exit Internet Explorer by using any of the following techniques:

✔ Choose File⇨Close.

✔ Click the Close button, which is located at the top right corner of the Internet Explorer window. (It's the one with an X in it.)

✔ Press Alt+F4.

After closing Internet Explorer, you should disconnect from your Internet service provider. To do so, double-click the modem connection icon that is displayed in the right corner of the Windows taskbar to bring up the Connected dialog box that you see in Figure 3-14. Then click the Disconnect button.

Figure 3-14:
The
Connected
To dialog
box.

Some Internet service providers still insist on charging you for Internet access on an hourly basis. If your ISP charges you by the hour, be aware that connect time charges continue to accumulate if you close Internet Explorer but forget to disconnect from your ISP. The extra time won't hurt if you pay a flat monthly rate with unlimited access, but if you're paying $2.50 or $2.95 per hour, you don't want to remain accidentally connected overnight!

Chapter 4

Searching the Web

● ●

In This Chapter

▶ Searching for information on the Web with the Internet Explorer Search bar

▶ Searching in the Address box

▶ Using search services, such as AltaVista, Lycos, and Yahoo!

● ●

*M*any people think of the Internet as a vast library of online information, but the Internet hardly resembles a library. Libraries are run by compulsive neat freaks known as *librarians,* whose mission in life is to make sure that, at least within their libraries, there is a place for everything and everything is in its place. Unlike a library, the Internet has no librarian. No one person or organization is officially in charge of what goes onto the Internet. Anyone can put anything on the Internet, and no one is responsible for making sure that new entries are cataloged in any way, shape, or form.

Fortunately, all is not lost. Several excellent search services are available to help you locate information on the Internet. Although none of these services is truly comprehensive, several of them come pretty close. No matter what you're looking for, these services are likely to turn up a few Internet sites that pertain to your topic.

Internet Explorer has a built-in search feature called the Search bar that makes searching the Internet simpler than ever before. This chapter shows you how to use the Search bar to find the pages you're looking for.

Finding Stuff Fast

The easiest way to locate information on the Internet is to use the *Search bar*. The Search bar is a pane that appears on the left side of the Internet Explorer window when you click the Search button on the Standard toolbar. The Search bar is designed to enable you to snoop around for information via a search service while simultaneously viewing a Web page.

The Internet Explorer 5.5 Search bar is a great time-saver. You can use it to look for Web pages, addresses, company or organization home pages, online encyclopedia articles, or newsgroup postings. Plus, the Search bar can search more than one search service for the information you are looking for. If the information doesn't turn up in one search service, odds are you'll find it in another.

To use the Search bar, follow these directions:

1. **Click the Search button on the Standard toolbar.**

   The Search bar appears, as shown in Figure 4-1.

2. **Select the type of information you want to search for by clicking one of the options listed under Choose a Category for Your Search.**

   You can use the Search bar to search for Web pages, personal home or e-mail addresses, company home pages, or maps.

   You can click <u>More . . .</u> to reveal three additional categories of searches: Look Up a Word, Find a Picture, and Find in Newsgroups.

3. **Type the word or phrase you're looking for in the text box next to the Search button.**

   For example, type the word **arachnid** in the text box.

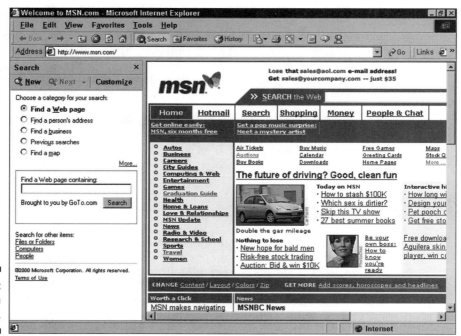

Figure 4-1:
The Search
bar.

4. **Click the Search button.**

   Your search request is submitted to the first search service — for Web page searches, the GoTo.com search service is accessed first.

   When the search service completes its search, the results of the search appear in the Search bar, as shown in Figure 4-2.

5. **If you find something that looks promising, click it.**

   Internet Explorer displays the page you selected on the right side of the Internet Explorer window. Meanwhile, the Search bar remains visible in the left side of the window so that you can choose a different link.

6. **If nothing looks promising, click the link for the next set of entries.**

   Each search service displays only a certain number of *hits* (found Web pages) at a time, typically 10 or 15. If none of the hits at the top part of the Search bar look promising, scroll to the bottom of the Search bar and locate a link that says something along the lines of Next 10 Entries. Clicking this link displays additional results for the search.

7. **If you still can't find what you're looking for, click the Next button at the top of the Search bar.**

   Doing this switches you to another search service, which will probably produce different results from the previous search.

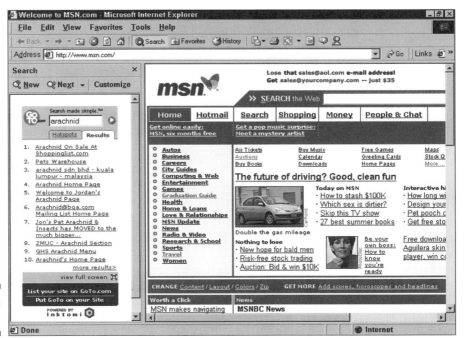

Figure 4-2:
Eureka!

Here are some thoughts to keep in mind when searching:

- If the search comes up empty, try again using a different search word or phrase. For example, try *spider* instead of *arachnid*.

- When picking search words, try to think of words that are specific enough that you don't end up with thousands of hits but general enough to encompass the topic you're trying to find.

- Most of the search services list results in sorted order, with the pages that most closely match your search criteria presented first. In particular, if you search with two words, the pages that contain both words are listed before pages in which just one of the words appears.

- Each of the search services available from the Search bar has its own set of options for customizing your search. For example, you may be able to indicate whether the search should be case-sensitive (so that *RAM* is not the same as *ram*) or whether to search for pages that contain all the words you type or pages that contain any of the words you type.

Customizing the Search Bar

You can customize the search services used by the Search bar — and change the order in which search services are accessed — by clicking Customize in the Search bar's toolbar. This brings up the Customize Search Settings page in a separate window, as shown in Figure 4-3.

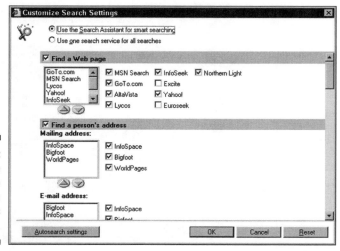

Figure 4-3: The Customize Search Settings page.

The Customize Search Settings page has a separate section for each category of information you can search for from the Search bar. Within each category, you'll find one or more search services with check boxes, and a list box that indicates the order in which the search services will be used by the Search bar.

As you can see, some of the services listed are checked, and others are not. To add or remove a service from the Search bar, just click the service's check box.

To change the order in which the search services will be accessed, first select the service whose order you want to change by clicking its entry in the list box. Then, click the up or down arrows that appear beneath the list box to move the service you selected.

At the very bottom of the Customize Search Settings page, you find a list box that lists all the search categories. You can use this list box to change the order in which the search categories appear in the Search bar.

After you have finished playing with the search settings, click the Update button that appears at the bottom of the Customize Search Settings page to apply any changes that you made to your Search bar.

Searching from the Address Bar

One of the nifty features of Internet Explorer 5.5 is called *Autosearch.* Autosearch is a way to search the Internet quickly for specific information without even going to a search service. Simply type the word Find, Go, or a question mark in the Address box, followed by the word or words you want to look up. For example, to search for *arachnid,* type **find arachnid**, **go arachnid**, or **? arachnid** in the Address box. Internet Explorer picks a search service to look up the word or phrase you typed and displays the results in the Search Bar, as shown in Figure 4-4.

Figure 4-4:
Type **find
arachnid** to
search for
spidery stuff
automati-
cally.

Using Popular Search Services

The Internet Explorer Search bar lets you quickly access nine popular search services. If you find the narrow confines of the Internet Explorer Search bar limiting, you can also access the search services directly. To work with a search service in the entire Internet Explorer window, type the service's Internet address in the Address box and press Enter.

Each of these services has its own peculiar approach to categorizing informa- tion and searching its database in response to your queries. As a result, you should experiment with the various services to determine which one best suits your needs.

AltaVista

www.altavista.com

AltaVista is a large and fast catalog of individual Web pages and Usenet discussion groups found throughout the Internet. The search network uses a special program called a *spider,* which automatically reads and catalogs three million Web pages every day. The AltaVista catalog lists tens of millions of Web pages. Figure 4-5 gives you a glimpse of the AltaVista home page.

One of the drawbacks of AltaVista is its huge size. Many searches return thousands (or even millions) of Web pages. For example, when I searched AltaVista for the word *arachnid,* it found 26,997 pages. As a result, you have to plow through pages and pages of results looking for Web sites that might contain the information you're looking for.

However, AltaVista does offer very powerful advanced search capabilities. If you're a bit of a computer guru and want a powerful search tool, AltaVista is worth checking out.

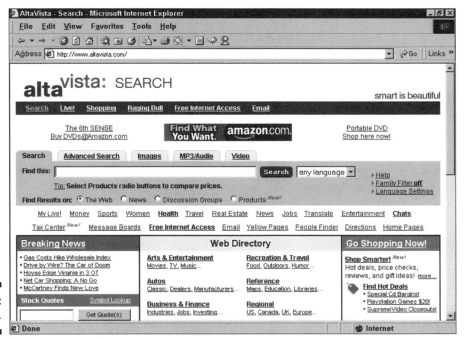

Figure 4-5:
AltaVista.

EuroSeek

`www.euroseek.com`

As its name implies, EuroSeek is a search services that focuses on Web sites in Europe. One of the unique strengths of EuroSeek is its ability to operate in any of nearly 30 languages. So, if you are more comfortable searching in Bulgarian or Lithuanian, EuroSeek is the place to go. Figure 4-6 shows the EuroSeek home page.

Excite

`www.excite.com`

Excite is a search service that catalogs more than 50 million Web pages. In addition to this huge index of Web pages, Excite also features thousands of reviews prepared by the Excite services editorial staff; it also indexes Usenet newsgroup postings and classified ads. The Excite opening page appears in Figure 4-7.

Figure 4-6: EuroSeek.

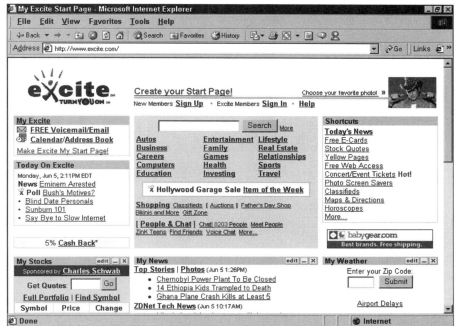

GoTo.com

```
www.goto.com
```

As Figure 4-8 shows, the GoTo.com home page is not cluttered by advertisements like most search services' home pages. That's because GoTo.com doesn't make its money by selling space for banner ads. Instead, advertisers pay GoTo.com for priority placement in its search results.

Infoseek (GO.com)

```
www.infoseek.go.com
```

Infoseek is owned by GO.com, an online megacompany that split off from Disney's Buena Vista Internet Group. Besides Infoseek, GO.com oversees some of the most popular sites on the Internet, including ABC.com, Disney.com, and ESPN.com.

Figure 4-8:
GoTo.com.

Infoseek is a large database that indexes millions of Web pages. It also enables you to browse through category listings or search by keywords. In addition to its Web index and directory, Infoseek enables you to search for e-mail addresses and search Usenet newsgroups and news stories from Reuters News. The Infoseek main page appears in Figure 4-9.

Lycos

www.lycos.com

Lycos is a huge Web index compiled by the computer nerds at Carnegie Mellon University. Lycos is primarily a keyword search tool, but it also includes categories you can browse. It's my personal favorite when I'm looking for obscure information. Figure 4-10 shows the Lycos opening page.

Lycos includes such features as a travel guide that lets you reserve flights and a hotel room, view city maps or driving directions, and more; an online shopping center with links to several thousand online stores; music downloads; and many more features.

Figure 4-9:
Infoseek.

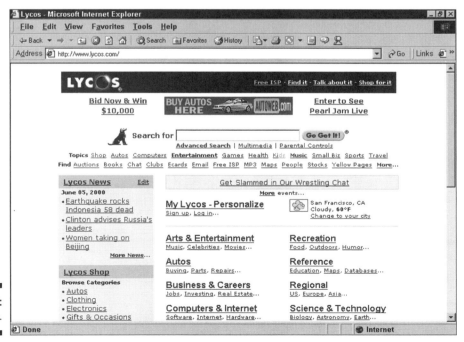

Figure 4-10:
Lycos.

MSN Search

search.msn.com

MSN Search is the Microsoft Network search site, which includes not only a searchable database of Web sites, but also a categorized Web directory, *White Pages* where you can look up personal addresses, and *Yellow Pages* where you can look up business addresses. Figure 4-11 shows the MSN Search home page.

Northern Light

www.northernlight.com

Northern Light is possibly the largest Web index available, with more than 220 million entries in its database. In addition to a huge index of Web pages, Northern Light also features indexes of popular publications such as *The Wall Street Journal, Business Week,* and *Fortune.* Figure 4-12 shows the Northern Light home page.

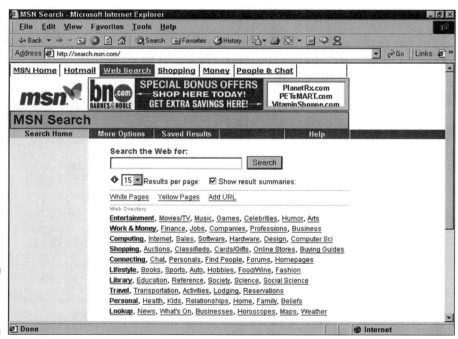

Figure 4-11:
MSN
Search.

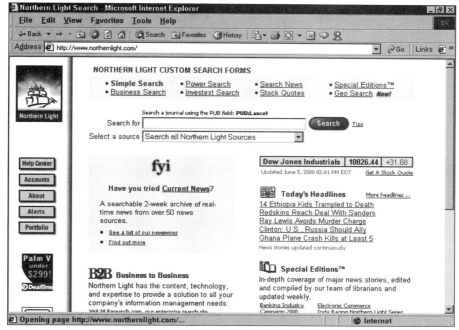

Figure 4-12:
Northern-
Light.com.

Yahoo!

www.yahoo.com

Yahoo! is one of the most popular Web directories around. Unlike search engines such as AltaVista and MSN Search, Yahoo! is a listing of tens of thousands of Web sites organized into categories, such as Arts & Humanities, Business & Economy, Computers & Internet, Education, and so on. You can browse through the Yahoo! categories or search for specific pages by keyword. The Yahoo! opening page appears in Figure 4-13.

Yahoo! is excellent for searching categorized information, but its keyword search abilities aren't as strong as other services such as Lycos or AltaVista.

Yahoo! was founded by two college students at Stanford University. Rumor has it that Yahoo! stands for Yet Another Hierarchical Officious Oracle, but the two student founders deny the allegation.

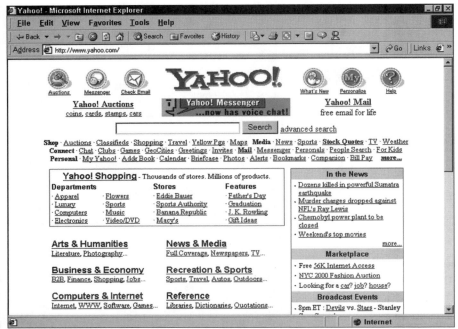

Figure 4-13:
Yahoo!.

Chapter 5

Getting around the Web Quickly

· ·

In This Chapter

▶ Creating a list of your favorite Web pages

▶ Using the Favorites bar

▶ Using the Links toolbar

▶ Adding and removing links from the Links toolbar

· ·

*T*he World Wide Web offers millions of interesting destinations. Exploring them all just to see what's available would be fun, assuming you could live long enough. But after you see a few hundred or a few thousand Web pages, you'll probably come to realize that not all Web pages are created equal. You soon settle on a few Web sites that are your personal favorites. This chapter shows you how to use two features of Internet Explorer 5.5 that are designed to make it easier to access frequently visited pages: Favorites and the Links toolbar.

Playing Favorites

The Internet Explorer Favorites feature is designed to expedite travel to your favorite Web sites without you having to remember a bunch of Web addresses or navigate your way through link after link. The Favorites feature is basically a menu on the Internet Explorer menu bar that lists links to your favorite Web sites. You can add links to and remove links from the Favorites menu whenever you want. The following sections describe how to use Internet Explorer's Favorites feature.

Another popular term for Favorites is *bookmarks*.

Adding a Web page to the Favorites menu

To designate a Web page as one of your Favorites so that you can find it fast later, follow these steps:

1. **Browse your way to the page you want to add to your list of favorite pages.**

2. **Choose the Favorites⇨Add to Favorites command.**

   The Add Favorite dialog box appears, as shown in Figure 5-1. The Name text box displays the name of the Web site that you want to add to your Favorites menu.

3. **Change the Web site's Name if you wish.**

   In many cases, the name proposed by Internet Explorer is acceptable. But if you want to change the name, you can do so by typing a new name in the Name field.

4. **Click OK.**

   Internet Explorer adds the Web page to your Favorites menu.

The Make Available Offline check box in the Add Favorite dialog box enables you to *synchronize* to a Web page so that you are automatically notified whenever the Web page changes. For now, leave this option unchecked. I show you how to use the Make Available Offline option in Chapter 6.

If you're on a Web page that contains a link to another Web page that you want to add to your Favorites menu, you can right-click the link you want to add. and then Choose Add Favorite from the pop-up menu. This trick adds the link to your Favorites menu without actually taking you to that Web site.

Going to one of your favorite places

After you add your favorite Web pages to your Favorites menu, you can open the menu to jet away to any of the pages it contains. Here's how:

1. **Choose F̲avorites from the menu bar.**

   The Favorites menu reveals your list of favorite places, as shown in Figure 5-2. Your Favorites menu undoubtedly contains a different collection of links than mine, so don't panic if your Favorites menu doesn't resemble the one shown in Figure 5-2.

2. **Select the Web page you want to view, and off you go.**

   Notice that the Favorites menu in Figure 5-2 includes several submenus that contain my favorite Web pages organized into categories. You can find instructions for setting up submenus like these in the next section, "Using Favorites folders."

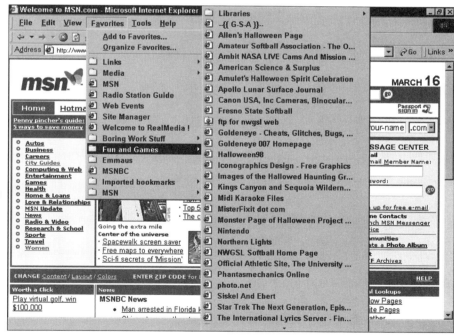

Figure 5-2:
The
Favorites
menu
contains
your list of
favorite
places.

Using Favorites folders

If you keep adding pages to it, pretty soon the Favorites menu becomes so full of links to your favorite sites that you can't find anything. To ease crowding on the Favorites menu and to help you organize your favorite links, Internet Explorer enables you to create separate folders in which you can categorize your favorite sites.

To create a Favorites folder in which to place a link to the Web page you're viewing, follow these steps:

1. **Choose Favorites⇨Add to Favorites.**

   The Add Favorite dialog box appears.

2. **Click Create In.**

   The Add Favorite dialog box expands, as shown in Figure 5-3.

Figure 5-3: Adding a page to a Favorites folder.

3. **Click the New Folder button.**

4. **Type a name for the new folder.**

5. **Click OK.**

The folders within the Favorites menu appear as menu items with arrows next to them. If you point the mouse to one of these menu items, a second menu appears, listing the contents of the folder.

If you want to place a link to a Web page in an existing folder, follow these steps:

1. **Choose F̲avorites⇨A̲dd to Favorites.**

   The Add Favorite dialog box appears.

2. **Click C̲reate In.**

   The Add Favorite dialog box expands.

3. **In the Create I̲n list, select the folder in which you want to store the new link.**

4. **Click OK.**

Organizing your Favorites

Eventually, your Favorites menu becomes filled with Web links that no longer hold your interest, are out of date, or just need to be reorganized. When you reach this point, it's time to roll up your sleeves and reorganize your Favorites. Fortunately, Internet Explorer provides a command just for this purpose.

To organize your Favorites, choose the F̲avorites⇨O̲rganize Favorites command. The Organize Favorites dialog box appears, as shown in Figure 5-4.

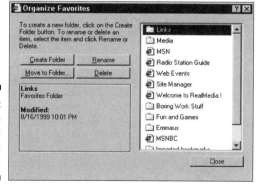

Figure 5-4:
The Organize Favorites dialog box.

The buttons in the Organize Favorites dialog box enable you to create, rename, move, or delete items around in your Favorites folders.

✔ To create a new folder, click the Create Folder button. Doing this creates a new folder named, naturally, New Folder. Type a new name for the folder and then press Enter.

✔ To rename a page or a folder, select the page or folder and click the Rename button. Type a new name for the page or folder and then click OK.

✔ To move a page or a folder to another folder, select the page or folder. Click the Move to Folder button and then click the folder you want to move the page or folder to. (To simply change the position of a folder or page in the Favorites list, you can click just the page or folder and then drag it to a new location.)

✔ To delete a page or a folder, select the page or folder and then click the Delete button. A dialog box appears asking if you are sure that you want to delete the folder or page; click Yes.

You can also right-click items on the Organize Favorites dialog box to summon a shortcut menu that contains options for deleting or renaming pages or folders.

If you are a Netscape user, you can quickly transfer bookmarks from Netscape into Internet Explorer Favorites (or vice versa) by choosing the File⇨Import and Export command. Choosing this summons the Import/Export Wizard, which walks you step-by-step through the process of exchanging favorites between Internet Explorer and Netscape Navigator.

Using the Favorites button on the Standard toolbar

The Favorites button on the Standard toolbar works a little differently from the Favorites menu. When you click the Favorites button, a separate Favorites bar appears on the left side of the Internet Explorer window, as shown in Figure 5-5. This bar enables you to view the list of your favorite Web pages while viewing a Web page at the same time in the right-hand portion of the Internet Explorer window.

To display any of the Web pages in your Favorites, just click the link for the page. To remove the Favorites bar so that the Web page once again occupies the entire window, just click the Favorites button on the Standard toolbar again, or click the Close button at the upper-right corner of the Favorites bar.

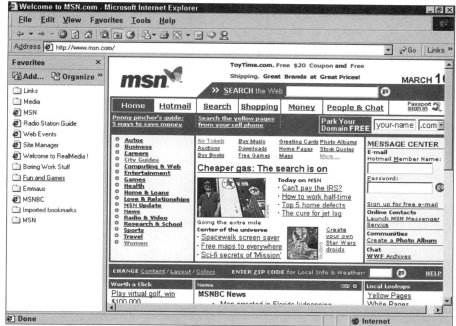

Figure 5-5:
The
Favorites
bar in
action.

Using the Links Toolbar

Internet Explorer Favorites are a great way to keep track of all the Web pages
you visit periodically. However, Internet Explorer provides an even more convenient method of quickly visiting up to five of your absolute favorite Web
sites: the Links toolbar. The Links toolbar enables you to place links to a
select group of your very favorite Web pages on a toolbar that's always available at the click of a mouse.

When you first install Internet Explorer, the Links toolbar is configured with
the following default links:

✓ **Best of the Web:** A listing of links to various pages throughout the
   Internet that Microsoft deems to be "tops."

✓ **Channel Guide:** A listing of Internet channels you can subscribe to. For
   more information about channels, see Chapter 6.

✓ **Customize Links:** Takes you to a help page that displays information
   about how you can customize the Links toolbar.

✓ **Free Hotmail:** Takes you to a page that offers a free e-mail service.

✓ **Internet Start:** Takes you to Microsoft's Internet Start page (which is also the default home page displayed when you click the Home button).

✓ **Microsoft:** Microsoft's home page.

✓ **RealPlayer:** Home page for Real.com, which allows you to listen to live audio and video broadcasts over the Internet.

✓ **Windows Update:** Informs you of updates to your Windows software.

✓ **Windows:** The main Windows page at the Microsoft Web site.

Accessing the Links toolbar

Ordinarily, the Links toolbar is covered up by the Address toolbar. To reveal the Links toolbar, double-click the word *Links* near the top right of the Internet Explorer window. The Links toolbar appears, as shown in Figure 5-6.

To display one of the pages on the Links toolbar, just click its button. To show the Address toolbar again, double-click the word *Address* to the left of the Links toolbar.

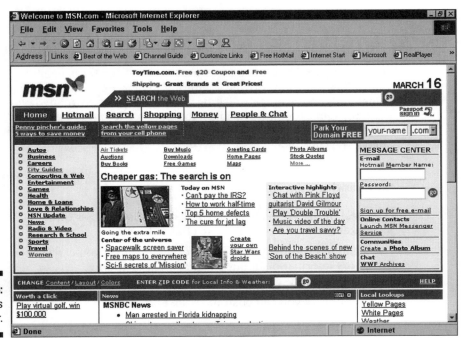

Figure 5-6:
The Links toolbar.

Depending on the number of links that you create for the Links toolbar and the size of the Internet Explorer window, Internet Explorer may not be able to squeeze all of your links onto the visible portion of the Links toolbar. If not, you can click the right arrow that appears at the upper right corner of the Links toolbar to display a menu of the additional links.

Here are two other ways you can position the Links toolbar:

✔ You can position the Links toolbar beneath the Address toolbar so that both toolbars are visible at the same time. To do so, click the word Links and hold down the mouse button. Then, drag the toolbar down until the Links toolbar pops into place beneath the Address toolbar; then release the mouse button.

✔ You can position and adjust the size of the Links and Address toolbars so that both are visible and share the same line, as shown in Figure 5-7. Just drag the Links toolbar left instead of down. As you drag the Links toolbar to the left, the Address toolbar is resized automatically to make room for the Links toolbar.

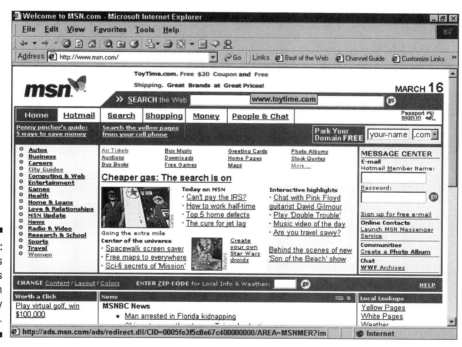

Figure 5-7:
The Address and Links toolbars can live side by side.

Adding a link

Internet Explorer enables you to customize the Links toolbar by removing any or all of the default links and by adding additional links of your own. To add a link of your own to the Links toolbar, follow these steps:

1. **Browse your way to the Web page that you want to add to the Links toolbar.**

2. **Choose the Favorites⇨Add to Favorites command.**

   The Add Favorite dialog box appears (refer to Figure 5-1).

3. **Click the Create In button.**

   The Add Favorite dialog box expands to show your Favorites folders (refer to Figure 5-3).

4. **Click the Links folder.**

5. **Click OK.**

The page that you displayed in Step 1 is added to the Links toolbar. If the page doesn't appear on the Links toolbar, you can click the small right-pointing arrow that appears at the right edge of the toolbar. This displays a menu that lists those links that don't fit in the visible portion of the Links toolbar.

You can quickly add the currently displayed page to the Links toolbar by dragging the page icon from the Address bar to the Links toolbar.

Removing a link

To remove a link from the Links toolbar, follow these steps:

1. **Call up the Favorites⇨Organize Favorites command.**

   The Organize Favorites dialog box appears. (It was shown back in Figure 5-4.)

2. **Double-click the Links folder.**

   The Links folder appears, showing all the links that are on your Links toolbar.

3. **Select the link you want to remove.**

4. **Click the Delete button.**

   A dialog box appears, asking if you really want to delete the link.

5. **Click Yes.**

You're done! The link that you deleted is removed from the Links toolbar.

 Another way to delete a link is by right-clicking the link in the Links toolbar and then choosing the Delete command from the pop-up menu that appears. A dialog box appears asking if you are sure that you want to delete the link. Click Yes, and the link is deleted.

Chapter 6

Working Offline

- -

In This Chapter

▶ Viewing Web pages offline

▶ Changing your offline viewing options

- -

*O*ne of the major annoyances of the Internet is that you always have to be connected online to access the Web. That requirement can be a major hassle for folks who have to share the computer phone line with a teenager, or for those who want to tote a laptop computer to the park and access the Web while watching kids play on a swing.

The Internet Explorer offline browsing feature comes in handy in those circumstances. The *offline browsing feature* lets you designate certain pages for offline browsing, which means that you can access those pages even if your computer isn't connected to the Internet.

Offline browsing works by keeping a copy of your offline pages on your computer's own hard disk. That way, if you want to visit a page without connecting to the Internet, Internet Explorer can retrieve a copy of the page from your hard disk without connecting to the Internet.

Obviously, if the online version of a Web page changes, the offline copy of the Web page becomes outdated. Fortunately, the offline browsing feature lets you *synchronize* the offline copy of a Web page with the online copy by downloading an updated version of the page to your hard drive. You can synchronize your offline pages manually, or you can tell Internet Explorer to auto-matically synchronize your pages on a regular basis — for example, every night at 2 a.m., when your teenager isn't using the phone (well, maybe).

Back in Internet Explorer 4, the offline browsing feature was known as *subscriptions*. Microsoft, in its infinite wisdom, decided that too many users were confused by the term *subscription,* so it decided to eliminate the term *subscription* and repackage the same feature in Internet Explorer 5 and 5.5 under the name *offline browsing*.

Making a Page Available Offline

Suppose you discover a Web site that you want to visit often, but you don't want to connect to the Internet every time you visit the page. Here is the procedure for setting up a page for offline browsing:

1. **Browse your way to the site you want to view offline.**

   For example, I like to follow the exploits of the Fresno State softball team, whose home page is at `www.fansonly.com/schools/fres/sports/w-softbl/fres-w-softbl-body.html`.

2. **Choose the Favorites⇨Add to Favorites command.**

   This command summons the Add Favorite dialog box, shown in Figure 6-1.

Figure 6-1:
The Add
Favorite
dialog box.

3. **If you don't like the name provided in the Name field, change it.**

   Most of the time, the name is acceptable, so you can usually skip this step.

4. **Choose the Make Available Offline option in the Add Favorite dialog box.**

   This option configures the Web page properly so that you can view it offline.

5. **Click OK.**

   The Add Favorite dialog box vanishes. Internet Explorer immediately synchronizes your offline copy of the Web page. This action may take a few moments, so be patient. While the Web page is synchronizing, a dialog box appears to let you know that the page is being synchronized. The dialog box vanishes after the page is synchronized.

6. You're done.

You have now successfully set up the page for offline viewing.

If you want to remove a page from your collection of offline pages, choose Favorites⇨Organize Favorites. Then, in the Organize Favorites dialog box, click the page you no longer want to access offline and uncheck the Make Available Offline option.

Viewing Web Pages Offline

To view Web pages offline, disconnect your computer from the Internet if it's connected. Then, start up Internet Explorer. Doing so summons the Dial-up Connection dialog box shown in Figure 6-2.

Figure 6-2:
The Dial-up
Connection
dialog box.

Normally, you type your user ID and password in the Dial-up Connection dialog box and then click the Connect button to connect your computer to the Internet. To work offline, click the Work Offline button instead. This action starts Internet Explorer in Offline mode, as shown in Figure 6-3. When in Offline mode, the title bar reads [Working Offline].

To access an offline page, just select the page from your Favorites menu.

Internet Explorer continues in Offline mode until you disable Offline mode by choosing the File⇨Work Offline command.

Figure 6-3:
Internet
Explorer in
Offline
mode.

If you close Internet Explorer while working in Offline mode, you will be returned to Offline mode the next time you start Internet Explorer. After you set Internet Explorer to work in Offline mode, Internet Explorer will always start up in Offline mode until you choose File⇨Work Offline again to disable Offline mode.

Synchronizing Your Offline Pages

To bring your offline Web pages up-to-date, start up Internet Explorer and connect to the Internet. Next, follow these steps:

1. **Choose Tools⇨Synchronize.**

   Doing so summons the Items to Synchronize dialog box, shown in Figure 6-4.

2. **Select the pages you want to synchronize.**

   Initially, all of your offline pages are selected. Click the check box next to any Web page that you do not want to synchronize to deselect that item.

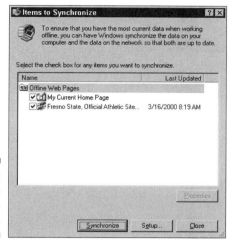

Figure 6-4:
The Items to
Synchronize
dialog box.

3. Click Synchronize.

Internet Explorer proceeds to download fresh copies of each of the
pages you selected. This process takes awhile, so now is a good time to
fetch a cup of coffee. A dialog box appears to keep you informed of
Internet Explorer progress. When all the pages are synchronized,
Internet Explorer briefly displays a `Synchronization complete` message. Then, the progress dialog box disappears.

If you want to set up Internet Explorer so that it automatically synchronizes
your pages on a regular basis, choose the Favorites⇨Synchronize command
to summon the Items to Synchronize dialog box; then click Setup. The
Synchronization Settings dialog box appears, as shown in Figure 6-5.

The Synchronization Settings dialog box lets you set up three types of automatic updates for your offline Web pages.

 ✔ **Logon:** Lets you select pages that automatically update whenever you
    log on to the Internet.

 ✔ **On Idle:** Lets you select pages that automatically update whenever your
    computer is idle. For example, you can tell Internet Explorer to begin
    synchronizing your offline pages anytime your computer has been idle
    for more than 15 minutes.

 ✔ **Scheduled:** Lets you set up a schedule for regularly synchronizing your
    offline pages. For example, you can have your computer automatically
    start up the Internet and synchronize your offline pages every morning
    at 2 a.m.

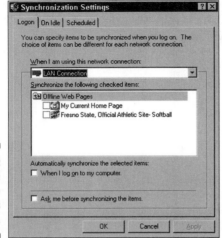

Figure 6-5:
The
Synchroniza-
tion Settings
dialog box.

Chapter 7

Getting Help While You Explore

. . . .

In This Chapter

▶ Getting assistance with the Internet Explorer Help features

▶ Using Windows Millennium troubleshooters

▶ Finding help on the Internet

. . . .

*I*magine that you have a pet Internet guru who sits at your side while you surf the Web, ready and willing to answer your questions with straightforward responses spoken in plain English, gently but firmly correcting you when you make silly mistakes, never giggling at you behind your back? All you have to do is supply a steady stream of pizza and Diet Coke, let him or her out twice a day, and absorb the wisdom of the master.

The next best thing to having your own personal Internet guide is using the built-in Help features of Internet Explorer. No matter how lost you become while exploring the Internet, help is but a few keystrokes or mouse clicks away.

Summoning Help

Internet Explorer comes with an excellent built-in Help system that can probably answer your most burning questions about the Web and Internet Explorer. You can summon this help in any of the following ways:

▸ **Press F1.** This action catapults you into the Internet Explorer Help system.

▸ **Choose Help⇨Help Topics.** This menu command is the mouse lover's equivalent to pressing F1.

▸ **Click the Question Mark icon.** Dialog boxes often have a question mark icon near the upper-right corner. Click this icon to transform the mouse pointer into a big question mark. You can then click any field in the dialog box to call up specific help for that field.

Getting to Know the Help Window

When you call up the Internet Explorer Help system, a separate window, like the one shown in Figure 7-1, appears. The Help window is divided into three main areas: a toolbar at the top, a contents area at the left, and the actual Help text on the right. As you can see, the contents portion of the Help window has four tabs across the top labeled Contents, Index, Search, and Favorites. All four tabs access the same Help information, but in a different fashion. The Contents tab groups Help topics by category, whereas the Index tab lists all Help topics in alphabetical order. The Search tab lets you look up Help information based on the word that you type. And the Favorites tab lets you create your own customized list of the Help topics you access most often.

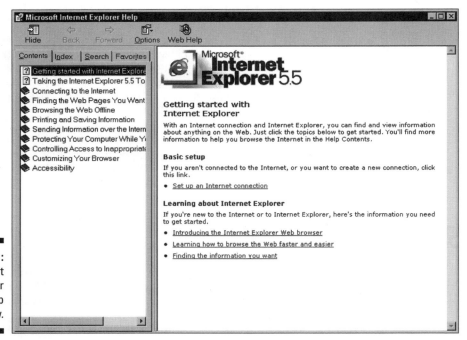

Figure 7-1:
The Internet
Explorer
Help
window.

Scanning the Contents

Clicking the Contents tab of the Help window displays a window that lists Internet Explorer Help topics by category. As Figure 7-1 shows, each category has a closed-book icon next to it. To expand a category, double-click the book icon. The Help topics associated with that category appear, and the closed-book icon changes to an open book. In addition, a category may include subcategories, which may themselves have additional subcategories.

Notice that individual Help topics (as compared with categories that contain several topics) are represented by an icon that resembles a page with a big question mark. To display an individual Help topic, click the icon for the topic you want to display. The Help information for the topic appears on the right side of the Help window, and the Contents remain visible on the left. For example, Figure 7-2 shows the Help Contents after you open the Finding the Web Pages You Want category and click the topic Listing Your Favorite Pages for Quick Viewing.

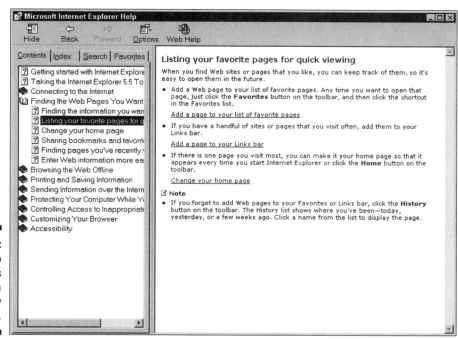

Figure 7-2:
Help
Contents
with a
category
expanded.

Many Help topics include links to other Help topics. For example, the Help topic shown in Figure 7-2 includes three links to other related topics: Add a page to your list of favorite pages, Add a page to your Links bar, and Change your home page. These links work just like the links in a Web document: Click once to follow the link.

When you have followed a link to another Help topic, you can click the Back button in the Help toolbar to return to the previous page.

Scanning the Index

The Help Index, shown in Figure 7-3, lists all the Internet Explorer Help topics in alphabetical order. To get help on a particular Help topic, scroll through the list of Help topics. When you find a topic that interests you, click the topic to display the appropriate Help page.

To find a Help topic quickly, type the first few letters of the topic in the text box that appears at the top of the Index tab. Doing this automatically scrolls the index to the topic you are interested in.

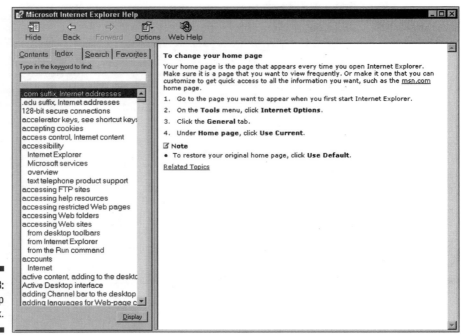

Figure 7-3:
The Help
Index.

Searching for Help Topics

You can also search for Help topics by clicking the Search tab in the Help dialog box, typing a word or phrase, and then clicking the List Topics button. Doing so displays a list of all the Help topics containing the word or phrase you typed. For example, Figure 7-4 shows the results of a search for the word *favorites*. Double-click any of the topics listed to display the Help topic.

Listing Your Favorite Help Topics

If you find yourself returning to a particular Help topic over and over again, you can add that Help topic to the Favorites tab so that you can call it up quickly when you need it. Figure 7-5 shows the Favorites tab with a few of my favorite Help topics added.

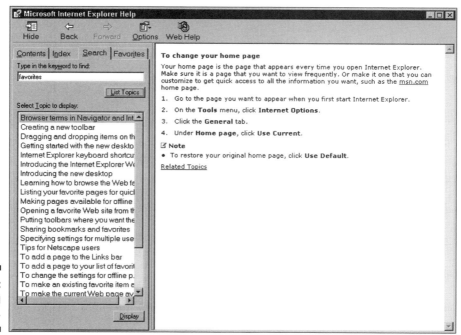

Figure 7-4:
Searching
for help.

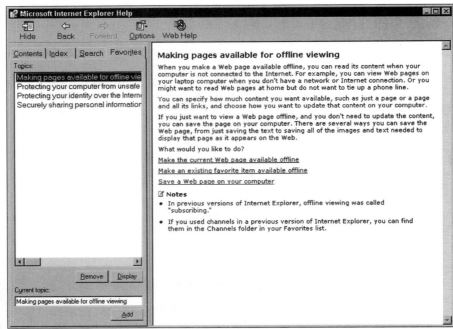

Figure 7-5:
These are a
few of my
favorite
Help topics.

To add a Help topic to the Help Favorites, just follow these steps:

1. **Use the Contents, Index, or Search tabs to call up the Help topic you want to add to Favorites.**

2. **Click the Favorites tab.**

3. **Click the Add button.**

That's all there is to it.

To display a topic you've added to Help Favorites, click the Favorites tab and then double-click the topic you want to display. (If double-clicking gives you cramps, you can just click the topic once to select it and then click the Display button.)

To remove a Help topic from Favorites, click the Favorites tab, click the topic you want to remove, and click the Remove button.

Troubleshooting at Your Fingertips

If you don't find the clue you're looking for in the Internet Explorer Help feature, you may find the answer buried within the Help files that come with Windows Millennium itself. In fact, the Windows Millennium Help system includes several special troubleshooting features that can walk you through typical causes of common problems. (Previous versions of Windows include similar troubleshooters.)

To conjure up one of the Windows Millennium troubleshooters, follow these steps:

1. **Click the Start button located on the taskbar and then choose <u>H</u>elp.**

   The Windows Millennium Help page appears, as shown in Figure 7-6.

2. **Click the Troubleshooting link (under "What would you like help with?") and then click Troubleshooting.**

   A list of several Internet and Web troubleshooting topics appears.

3. **Choose the troubleshooting topic that interests you.**

   For example, if you are having trouble with your modem, click <u>Modem Troubleshooter</u>. Figure 7-7 shows the Modem Troubleshooter.

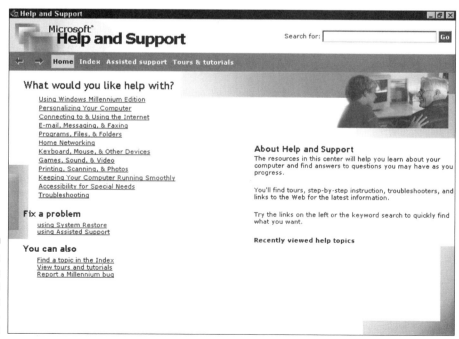

Figure 7-6: The Windows Millennium Help screen.

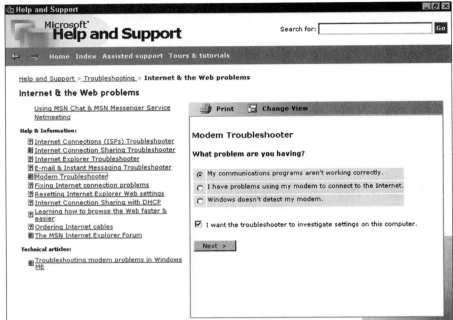

Figure 7-7:
The Modem
Trouble-
shooter.

4. **To use the troubleshooter, answer each of the troubleshooter's questions by clicking the appropriate button.**

   With luck, the troubleshooter leads you to the solution you seek.

Getting Help Online

If you can't find help for a specific problem in the Internet Explorer Help files, you can always turn to your online comrades on the Internet. The first place to check for online help is Microsoft's own Web page that's devoted to Internet Explorer technical support. You can call up this Web page by starting Internet Explorer and then choosing Help➪Online Support. Or, you can manually navigate to the Internet Explorer technical support Web site at support.microsoft.com.

The Internet Explorer Support Home page, shown in Figure 7-8, provides up-to-date information about the latest releases of Internet Explorer. This Web page also includes links to pages that list frequently asked questions (FAQs), known problems with Internet Explorer, and other helpful information.

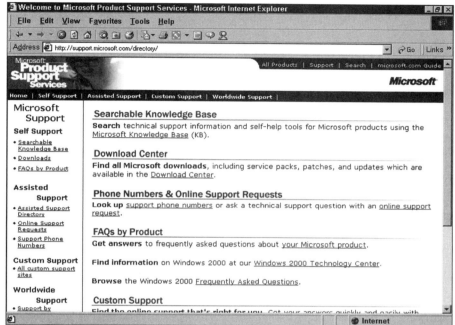

Figure 7-8:
Microsoft's
online
support
page.

Part III

Getting Connected with Outlook Express

The 5th Wave   By Rich Tennant

It's an e-mail from my mother. She wants me to know how happy she is for us.

In this part . . .

*I*nternet Explorer comes with a companion program known as Outlook Express, a handy e-mail program that lets you send and receive electronic messages to and from your friends on the Internet. The chapters in this part show you how to use the basic features of Outlook Express, such as creating new mail messages, reading mail you have received, dealing with attachments, and setting up an address book that contains the e-mail addresses of the people you frequently exchange mail with. In addition, you'll learn how to use some of Outlook Express's more advanced features, such as adding an automatic signature to the end of your messages, setting up mail filters to screen out junk mail, accessing newsgroups, and working with more than one e-mail account.

You'll also learn how to use Outlook Express to access Microsoft's free e-mail service (Hotmail), as well as how to use MSN Messenger and NetMeeting to chat with your online buddies.

Chapter 8

E-mailing with Outlook Express

In This Chapter

▶ Reading your e-mail

▶ Sending e-mail messages

▶ Dealing with attachments

▶ Formatting your e-mail messages with HTML

▶ Using the Address Book

*O*ne of the most common reasons people dare to venture forth onto the Internet is to use electronic mail — *e-mail,* as it's called. E-mail lets you exchange messages with your Internet-connected friends and colleagues. E-mail is much faster than regular mail, even mail delivered by Mr. McFeeley, the bespectacled mailman on *Mr. Rogers' Neighborhood* ("Speedy Delivery!").

Sending an e-mail message is much like sending a letter through regular mail. In both cases, you write your message, put an address on it, and send it off through an established mail system. Eventually, the recipient of the message receives your note, opens it, reads it, and (if you're lucky) answers by sending a message back.

But e-mail offers certain advantages over regular mail. For example, e-mail arrives at its destination in a matter of minutes, not days. E-mail can be delivered any day of the week, including Sundays. And, as a special bonus, no way yet exists for your great-aunt to send you a fruitcake through e-mail.

About the only reason that the post office exists anymore, other than transporting fruitcake, is that e-mail only works when both the sender and the receiver have computers that are connected to the Internet. In other words, you can't send e-mail to someone who isn't on the Internet.

Internet Explorer 5.5 comes with a handy e-mail program called Outlook Express, which is actually a scaled-down version of the more powerful Outlook program that comes with Microsoft Office. Outlook Express handles not only Internet e-mail, but also newsgroups. (You can find out about newsgroups in Chapter 12.) In this chapter, I focus on using Outlook Express for reading and sending e-mail.

Outlook Express and its older sibling Microsoft Outlook are not the only e-mail programs available. Internet Explorer's chief competitor — the Netscape Communicator Suite — comes with a powerful e-mail program called *Netscape Messenger*. Fortunately, all e-mail programs can get along with one another, so you can use Outlook Express to exchange e-mail with your friends, whether they are using Outlook Express or Outlook, Netscape Messenger, or any other e-mail program.

Starting Outlook Express

As with all Windows programs, you can start Outlook Express a few different ways. Here are some of the more popular methods:

✔ On the Windows 98 or higher taskbar, click the Launch Outlook Express button.

✔ Click the Start button and choose Programs⇨Internet Explorer⇨Outlook Express.

✔ In Internet Explorer, choose Tools⇨Mail and News⇨Read Mail.

✔ In Internet Explorer, click the Mail button and then choose Read Mail from the pop-up menu that appears.

However you open it, Outlook Express springs to life, displaying the window shown in Figure 8-1.

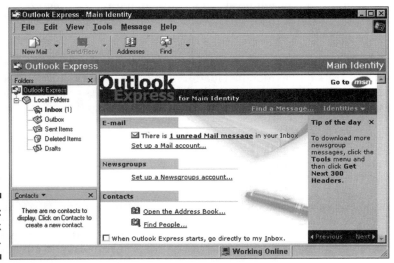

Figure 8-1:
Outlook
Express.

Hotmail: The poor man's e-mail

Hotmail is a free e-mail service offered by the Microsoft Network (also known as *MSN*). Hotmail is a Web-based e-mail service, which means that you can access it from any Web browser (including Internet Explorer) by going to www.Hotmail.com. The Hotmail Web site includes Web pages that allow you to see e-mail messages that have been sent to you and send e-mail to other Internet users.

To make Hotmail even easier to use, Microsoft enables you to set up and use a Hotmail account directly from Outlook Express. Then you can use Outlook Express to send and receive e-mail messages to and from your Hotmail account.

You can find complete information for using Hotmail with Outlook Express in Chapter 10.

Each time you start Outlook Express, the program automatically checks to see whether you have any new mail. Provided that you leave Outlook Express open (you can minimize it if you want), Outlook Express periodically checks to see whether new mail has arrived. Any new messages that you haven't yet read appear in boldface in the Inbox pane.

Sending E-mail

To send e-mail, all you have to do is follow these steps:

1. **Click the New Mail button on the left side of the toolbar.**

   Or choose Message⇨New Message, or use the keyboard shortcut Ctrl+N. Whichever option you choose, a new, blank message appears, as shown in Figure 8-2.

2. **Type the Internet address of the person to whom you want to send the message.**

   The To: field is automatically selected when the New Message dialog box appears, so you can just type in the recipient's address.

   Note that you can send mail to more than one recipient by typing more than one name or address in the To: field. Type a comma or semicolon between each name.

   For examples of different kinds of Internet addresses, check out the "Addressing your e-mail" sidebar later in this chapter.

   If you frequently send e-mail to a particular person, you can add that person's e-mail address to your Address Book. Then you can easily retrieve that person's e-mail address from your Address Book whenever you send him or her a message without having to retype the entire address each time. For more information about using the Address Book, see the section "Using the Address Book."

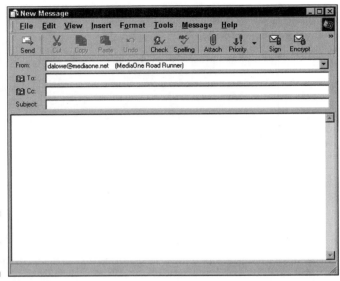

Figure 8-2:
A new
message.

3. **If you want to send a copy of the message to another user, type that person's address in the Cc: field.**

   Click in the Cc: field and then type the address or addresses of anyone to whom you want to send a copy of the message.

   If you want to send a copy of a message to someone else but you don't want the other recipients to know about it, use the Bcc: field instead of the Cc: field. A copy of the message is sent to each person listed in the Bcc: field, but the people listed in the To: and Cc: fields aren't notified of the Bcc: recipients. (If the Bcc: field doesn't appear in the New Message window, choose the View⇨Bcc command to enable this optional field.)

4. **Type a succinct but clear title for the message in the Subject field.**

   Click in the Subject field, and then type the subject of your message. For example, type **Let's Do Lunch** or **Jetson, You're Fired!**

5. **Type your message in the message area of the New Message dialog box.**

   Figure 8-3 shows what a message looks like with all this information typed in and ready to go.

6. **When you finish typing your message, click the Send button.**

   Outlook Express dismisses the New Message dialog box and sends the message to the intended recipients.

   If you're working in Internet Explorer and you want to send some quick e-mail without starting up Outlook Express, just click the Mail button in the toolbar and choose New Message from the pop-up menu that appears. The New Message command takes you straight to a New Document window, where you can compose and deliver your message without starting Outlook Express.

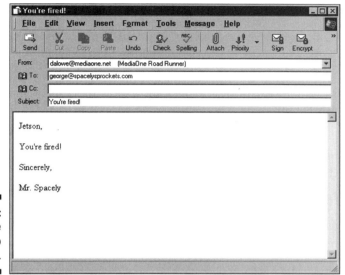

Figure 8-3:
A message
all ready to
be sent.

Instead of typing a full Internet address, you can simply type the person's name if you already created an entry for that person in your Address Book. For more information, see the section "Using the Address Book."

Addressing your e-mail

Before you send e-mail, you need to know the address of the person to whom the message is intended (just like that pesky post office expects with paper mail). The easiest way to find out someone's e-mail address is to ask for it.

To send e-mail to a user of one of the major online services, compose the user's e-mail address as follows:

✔ For America Online users, type the username followed by @aol.com. For example, Lurch@aol.com.

✔ For CompuServe users, type the screen name followed by @cs.com. For example, Gomez@cs.com. (Older CompuServe accounts, known as *CompuServe Classic accounts,* have numeric account numbers such as 12345.6789. To send mail to a CompuServe Classic account, use the numeric user ID followed by @compuserve.com, but use a period rather than a comma to separate the two parts of the numeric user ID. For example: 12345.6789@compuserve.com.

✔ For users of The Microsoft Network, type the username followed by @msn.com. For example, BillG@msn.com. (No, that's not really Bill Gates's e-mail address. So please don't flood The Microsoft Network with hate mail — or love mail — for Bill!)

If you're not sure whether you typed the names and addresses correctly, click the Check Names button. This feature checks the names you typed against the Address Book to reveal any errors. (Outlook Express assumes that any name typed in the form of an Internet address — rather than bounced off the Address Book — is correct.) The Check Names feature checks to make sure that the address is in the correct format but does not check to make sure that the address actually exists. (For more information about using the Address Book, see the section "Using the Address Book" later in this chapter.)

Checking Your Message for Spelling Errors

If you have Microsoft Office or any of its programs (Word, Excel, or PowerPoint), Outlook Express includes a bonus feature: a spell checker that is capable of catching those embarrassing spelling errors before they go out to the Internet. The spell checker checks the spelling of every word in your message, looking up the words in its massive dictionary. Any misspelling is brought to your attention, and the spell checker is under strict orders from Bill Gates himself not to giggle or snicker at any of your misspellings, even if you insist on putting an *e* at the end of *potato*. The spell checker even gives you the opportunity to tell it that you are right and it is wrong — and that it should learn how to spell the way you do.

To spell check your messages, follow these steps:

1. **In the New Message window, choose Tools⇨Spelling after you have finished composing your message.**

   The spell checker comes to life, looking up your words in hopes of finding a mistake.

2. **Try not to be annoyed if the spell checker finds a spelling error.**

   Hey, you're the one who told it to look for spelling mistakes; don't get mad if it finds some. If the spell checker finds an error, it highlights the offending word and displays the misspelled word along with a suggested correction, as shown in Figure 8-4.

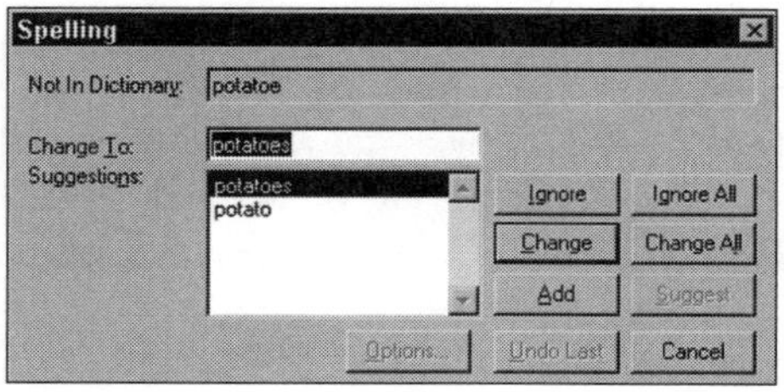

Figure 8-4: The spell checker can be very annoying.

Spelling	
Not In Dictionary:	potatoe
Change To:	potatoes
Suggestions:	potatoes
	potato

Ignore   Ignore All
Change   Change All
Add   Suggest
Options...   Undo Last   Cancel

3. **Choose the correct spelling, and then click Change or click Ignore to skip to the next word the spell checker doesn't recognize.**

   • If you agree that the word is misspelled, scan the list of suggested corrections and click the one that you like. Then click Change.

   • If, on the other hand, you prefer your own spelling, click Ignore. To prevent the spell checker from asking you over and over again about a particular word that it doesn't recognize (such as someone's name), click Ignore All.

   If the correct spelling doesn't appear in the list, type the correct spelling for the word in the Change To box. Then click Change.

4. **Repeat Steps 2 and 3 until the spell checker gives up.**

   When you see the message The spelling check is complete, your work is done.

Sending Attachments

An *attachment* is a file that you send along with your message. Sending an attachment is kind of like paper-clipping a separate document to a letter. In fact, Outlook Express uses a paper clip icon to indicate that a message has an attachment, and the button you click to add an attachment sports a paper clip design as well.

Here is the procedure for adding an attachment to an outgoing message:

1. **Click the Attach File button.**

   The Insert Attachment dialog box, shown in Figure 8-5, appears.

2. **Rummage through the folders on your hard drive until you find the file you want to insert.**

   When you find the file that you want to attach, click the filename to select it.

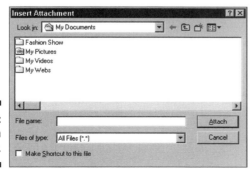

Figure 8-5:
Inserting an
attachment.

3. **Click Attach.**

   The file is inserted into the message as an attachment. An icon for the attachment appears in a special Attach line that is inserted beneath the Subject field in the message header, as shown in Figure 8-6.

4. **Finish the message, and then click the Send button.**

   Finish typing the message you want to send, and then click Send to send the message on its way.

Here are some things to consider when you send attachments:

✔ Be aware that sending large attachments can sometimes cause e-mail troubles, especially for attachments that approach a megabyte or more in size. If possible, you should mail several smaller attachments instead of one large one.

✔ If the attachment is large, consider shrinking it with a file compression program, such as WinZip, before you attach it. (You can download WinZip from www.winzip.com.)

✔ If you attach a file and then change your mind before you have sent the message, you can remove the attachment by right-clicking the attachment's name in the Attach: line and then choosing Remove from the pop-up menu that appears.

Figure 8-6: E-mail attachments are shown in a separate Attach: line in the heading portion of the message.

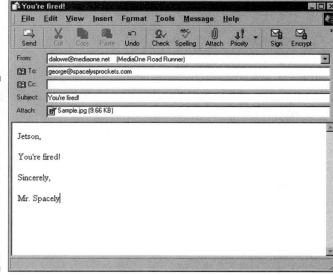

Using HTML Formatting

Outlook Express has a nifty feature that enables you to add formatting to your e-mail messages. For example, you can change the font, size, or color of your message text, and you can insert pictures to liven things up. Figure 8-7 shows how you can make even the rudest of messages seem friendly by using Outlook Express formatting.

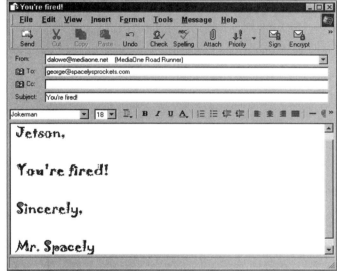

Figure 8-7:
A message
that uses
HTML
formatting.

To accomplish its formatting virtuosity, Outlook Express employs the same HTML formatting codes used to create pages on the World Wide Web. Of course, when you send an HTML-formatted message to another Internet user, that user must have a mail program that's capable of reading messages formatted with HTML. Otherwise, your beautiful formats will be for naught.

To apply HTML formatting, you use the special HTML formatting toolbar that appears in the New Message window. If your New Message window doesn't have this toolbar, summon the Format⇨Rich Text (HTML) command.

Table 8-1 shows how you can use the various buttons and controls on the HTML formatting toolbar to enhance the text in your e-mail messages.

Table 8-1	Controls on the HTML Formatting Toolbar
Control	**Format**
Arial	Changes the font
10	Sets the size of the text font
	Selects a heading style or other style for the text
B	Makes the text bold
I	Makes the text italic
<u>U</u>	Underlines the text
	Changes the text color
	Creates a numbered list
	Creates a bulleted list
	Decreases the indentation
	Increases the indentation
	Left-aligns the text
	Centers the text
	Right-aligns the text
	Aligns the text on left and right
	Inserts a horizontal line
	Creates a hyperlink
	Inserts a picture

Receiving E-mail

E-mail wouldn't be much good if it worked like a send-only set, sending out messages but not receiving them. (I once had an aunt who worked that way.) Fortunately, you can receive e-mail as well as send it — assuming, of course, that you have friends who write.

To read e-mail that other users have sent you, follow these steps:

1. **Start Outlook Express.**

   Refer back to the section "Starting Outlook Express" at the beginning of this chapter if you're not sure how.

2. **Go to the Inbox by clicking the Inbox icon.**

   The Inbox icon appears in the list of folders on the left side of the Outlook Express window. When you go to the Inbox, Outlook Express displays a list of all the messages that you've received, as shown in Figure 8-8. Any new messages you have not read are displayed in bold-face type.

3. **Double-click a new message to read it.**

   The message is displayed in its own window.

   If the message is small, you can skip this step. Instead, just read the message in the preview pane that appears in the main Outlook Express window.

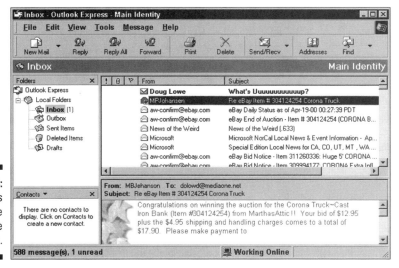

Figure 8-8:
Messages wait to be read in the Inbox.

4. **Read the message.**

5. **After you read the message, dispense with it in one of the following ways:**

- If the message is worthy of reply, click the Reply button. A new message window appears, allowing you to compose a reply. The To: field is automatically set to the user who sent you the message, the subject is automatically set to RE: (whatever the original subject was), and the complete text of the original message is inserted at the bottom of the new message. Compose your reply and then click the Send button.

- If the message was originally sent to several people, you can click the Reply to All button to send a reply to all of the original recipients.

- If the message was intended for someone else, or if you think some-one else should see it (maybe it contains a juicy bit of gossip!), click the Forward button. A new message window appears, enabling you to select the user or users to whom you want to forward the mes-sage. The original message is inserted at the bottom of the new mes-sage, with space left at the top for you to type an explanation of why you think the message qualifies for more audience (Hey Mr. Spacely, get a load of this!).

- To print the message, click the Print button.

- If the message is unworthy even of filing, click the Delete button. Poof!

When you first install Outlook Express, you automatically receive two mes-sages in your Inbox: one welcoming you to Outlook Express and the other describing the security features that are available in Outlook Express. Be sure to read both of these messages.

Saving an Attachment as a File

If someone is kind enough to send you a message that includes an attached file, you can save the attachment as a separate file by following these steps:

1. **Open the message that has the attachment.**

   You can tell which messages have attachments by looking for the paper clip icon next to the message in the message list.

2. **Right-click the attachment icon and then choose the Save As command from the pop-up menu.**

   A Save As dialog box appears.

3. **Choose the location where you want to save the file.**

   You can use the controls on the standard Save As dialog box to navigate to a different drive or folder.

4. **Type a filename for the file.**

   Outlook Express, always trying to help out, proposes a filename. You need to type a new filename only if you don't like the filename that Outlook Express suggests.

5. **Click Save.**

   The attachment is saved as a file.

   If the attachment is a graphic image, Outlook Express displays the image directly in the message when you open the message. As a result, you don't have to do anything special to view images your friends send to you via e-mail.

   Beware of attachments from unfamiliar sources: They may contain a virus that could infect your computer. Unfortunately, Outlook Express doesn't have any built-in virus protection. So if you are concerned about viruses (and you should be), purchase and install separate virus protection software.

Using the Address Book

Most Internet users have a relatively small number of people with whom they exchange e-mail on a regular basis. Rather than retype their addresses every time you send e-mail to these people, you can store your most commonly used addresses in the Outlook Express Address Book. As an added benefit, the Address Book enables you to refer to your e-mail friends by name (for example, George Jetson) rather than by address (george@spacelysprockets.com).

Adding a name to the Address Book

Before you can use the Address Book, you must add the names of your e-mail correspondents to it. The best time to add someone to the Address Book is after you receive e-mail from that person. Here's the procedure:

1. **Open an e-mail message from someone whose e-mail address you want to add to the Address Book.**

   Outlook Express displays the message.

2. **Right-click the user's name and then choose Add to Address Book.**

   A dialog box similar to the one in Figure 8-9 appears, describing the person's e-mail address information.

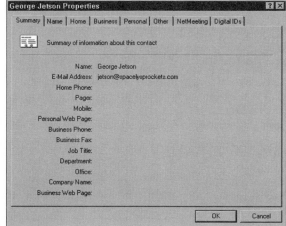

Figure 8-9:
The
Summary
tab lists
contact
information.

3. **If the summary information is incorrect, click the Name tab. Then type the correct address information into the appropriate fields.**

   Figure 8-10 shows the dialog box that appears after you click the Name tab. In some cases, these fields may already correctly contain the person's name. More often, however, the First field contains the person's e-mail address and the Middle and Last fields are blank.

   As you type the first, middle, and last names, Outlook Express automatically fills in the complete name in the Display field. For example, if you type **George** in the First field and **Jetson** in the Last field, the Display field is automatically set to George Jetson.

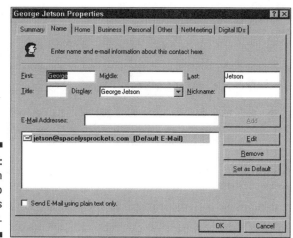

Figure 8-10:
Adding an
address to
the Address
Book.

4. Click OK.

The address shows up in the Address Book.

5. Close the message.

Thereafter, you can access the person's address in the Address Book.

You can configure Outlook Express to automatically add addresses to your Address Book whenever you reply to a message. To accomplish this feat of automation, choose Tools⇨Options, click the Send tab, select the Automatically Put People I Reply to in My Address Book option, and then click OK.

For those times when you want to add someone to your Address Book who hasn't sent you e-mail yet, follow these steps:

1. In Outlook Express, choose Tools⇨Address Book.

Or click the Address Book button or press Ctrl+Shift+B. One way or the other, the Address Book window appears, as shown in Figure 8-11.

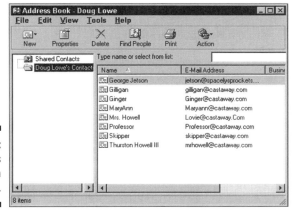

Figure 8-11: The Address Book main window.

2. Click the New button; then choose New Contact from the menu that appears.

If you prefer, you can choose File⇨New Contact or press Ctrl+N. In any event, the Properties dialog box appears. (Refer to Figure 8-10.)

3. Type the information for the new Address Book entry.

At a minimum, type the person's first and last name and e-mail address. If you want, you can include additional information, such as phone numbers and addresses under the Home, Business, Personal, and Other tabs.

4. Click OK.

The Address Book adds your new entry.

Sending a message to someone in the Address Book

To send a message to a user who's already in the Address Book, follow these steps:

 1. **In the New Message window, click the little Address Book icon next to the To: field.**

The Select Recipients dialog box appears, as shown in Figure 8-12.

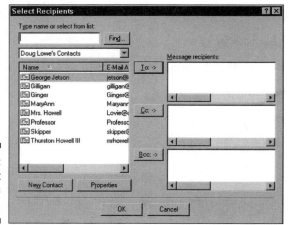

Figure 8-12: The Select Recipients dialog box.

2. **Double-click the name of the person to whom you want to send e-mail.**

The person's name appears in the To: list on the right side of the dialog box. If double-clicking is against your religion, just click once on the person's name and then click the To: button.

You can add more than one name to the To: list. You can also add names to the Cc: or Bcc: lists by clicking the Cc: or Bcc" button. (Bcc stands for Blind carbon copy; names you add to the Bcc: list receive a copy of the message, but other recipients of the message don't know that a copy was sent to the Bcc: recipient.)

3. **After you have selected all the names you want, click OK.**

Poof! You're back at the New Message dialog box, and the names you selected appear in the To:, Cc:, and Bcc: fields.

Changing or deleting Address Book entries

On occasion, one of your e-mail buddies switches Internet service providers and gives you a new Internet address. Or you may lose touch with someone and decide to remove his or her name from your Address Book. Either way, the following steps guide you through the process of keeping your Address Book up to date:

1. **From Outlook Express, click the Address Book button or choose Tools⇨Address Book.**

   The Address Book dialog box appears. (Refer to Figure 8-11.)

2. **Click the address you want to change or delete.**

3. **To delete the address, click the Delete button.**

   Or, if you prefer, you can right-click the name and then choose Delete from the shortcut menu.

4. **To change the address, click the Properties button.**

   After the Properties dialog box appears, make any necessary changes and then click OK.

5. **Click OK when you're finished.**

Working with Address Book folders

With Outlook Express, you can organize your Address Book contacts into folders, much like you can organize your files into folders in Windows Explorer. By default, Outlook Express dumps all your Address Book contacts into a single folder named Contacts. This method is okay if you have just a few dozen contacts. But if you have more contacts than you can easily keep track of in a single folder, you should consider creating additional folders to help you categorize your contacts. For example, you can create folders with names, such as Business or Friends and Relatives or Washed-Out 60s Sitcom Stars.

The following procedure shows you how to create an Address Book folder and move one or more existing contacts from the Contacts folder to the new folder:

1. **In the Address Book window, click the New button; then choose New Folder from the menu that appears.**

   If you prefer, you can choose File⇨New Folder or press Ctrl+R. Outlook Express then asks for a name for the new folder, using the dialog box shown in Figure 8-13.

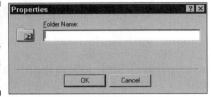

Figure 8-13:
Creating a
new
Address
Book folder.

2. Type a name for the new folder; then click OK.

Outlook Express returns you to the Address Book window. Your newly created folder appears in the list of folders at the left side of the Address Book window, as shown in Figure 8-14.

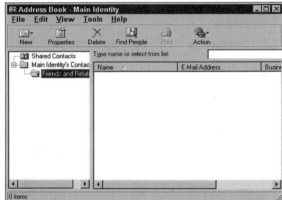

Figure 8-14:
A new
folder is
born.

3. Click the Contacts folder in the folder list at the left side of the Address Book window.

This opens the Contacts folder.

4. Drag each contact that you want to move from the Contacts folder to the folder you created in Step 2.

To *drag* a contact, start by positioning the cursor over the contact name, clicking the left mouse button, and holding the button on the contact name. Next, while holding the mouse button down, move the mouse pointer to the new folder that appears in the folder list at the left side of the Address Book window. When the cursor is over the folder into which you want to move the contact, release the mouse button. Outlook Express moves the Address Book entry to the new folder.

5. That's all!

Here are a few additional details you should know about:

✔ If you can't see the folder list at the left side of the Address Book window, you can display it by choosing View➪Folders and Groups.

✔ If you want to change the name of a folder, right-click the folder and select the Properties command from the shortcut menu. Doing this summons the Folder Properties dialog box, where you can type a new name for the folder. Click OK, and you're done.

✔ To send mail to a recipient that you've placed in a folder, call up the Select Recipients dialog box as usual (by clicking the To button while composing a new message). The Select Recipients dialog box contains a drop-down list that lists your folders. Use this drop-down list to select the folder that contains the address of the person you want to send mail to.

Synchronizing mail accounts

Most e-mail accounts provided by Internet service providers automatically delete your e-mail messages from the mail server when you receive the mail to your Inbox. If you use only one computer to access your e-mail, this arrangement works fine. But what if you want to access your e-mail from two or more computers? For example, suppose you want to access e-mail from your computer at work and your computer at home. If you do, some of your messages may wind up in the Inbox on your office computer, while other messages may be in the Inbox on your home computer. Neither computer contains all the messages that you've received.

If you access mail from two or more computers, you may want to consider setting up a special type of e-mail account called an IMAP account. IMAP mail accounts do not automatically delete messages from the server whenever you download mail to your Inbox. Instead, IMAP accounts keep copies of downloaded messages and enable you to synchronize the Inbox on each computer you use to access your e-mail. To synchronize your e-mail account, choose the Tools➪Synchronize All command.

Unfortunately, not all Internet service providers offer IMAP accounts. You have to ask your ISP if it can set up an IMAP account for you.

Chapter 9

E-mail Shortcuts and Tricks

In This Chapter

▶ Using and creating Outlook Express folders

▶ Filtering your mail with message rules

▶ Using stationery to make your messages more attractive

▶ Adding signatures to the end of your messages

▶ Looking up lost e-mail addresses

▶ Using mailing groups

▶ Assuming a new identity

▶ Using digital signature and encryption

*I*f you send or receive more than a few e-mail messages each week, you'll want to check out the timesaving shortcuts and tricks in this chapter. Here, you can find out how to save time by setting up folders to sort your e-mail messages, filter out messages you don't want to read, set up Outlook Express for more than one user, and more.

You can also find out about Outlook Express features that let you dress up your e-mail. Stationery lets you change text fonts and add colorful backgrounds, and signatures let you automatically add your name, address, phone number, and perhaps a catchy phrase to the end of all your messages.

Have fun!

Using Outlook Express Folders

When you first install Outlook Express, five message folders are set up to store and organize messages you have sent and received. These folders are displayed as icons on the left side of the main Outlook Express window. You will spend most of your time working in the Inbox folder, which contains messages you have received. But you can display the contents of other folders by clicking the icon for the folder you want to view.

The five message folders that are initially set up for Outlook Express are

- **Inbox:** Where Outlook Express stores your incoming messages
- **Outbox:** Where Outlook Express stores your outgoing messages until they're sent to their intended recipients
- **Sent Items:** Where Outlook Express places copies of messages you have sent
- **Deleted Items:** Where Outlook Express stores deleted messages (much like the Windows Recycle Bin, the Deleted items folder enables you to undelete a deleted message if you later decide that you want the message back)
- **Drafts:** Where Outlook Express stores messages that you have not yet finished. For example, suppose your favorite episode of *Gilligan's Island* comes on while you are in the middle of composing a long message. Just click the Close button (the little X in the upper right-hand corner of the New Message window), then choose <u>Y</u>es when Outlook Express asks if you want to save the message. Outlook Express saves your message in the Drafts folder so that you can return to it after Gilligan spoils the rescue attempt.

Outlook Express also enables you to create your own message folders. For example, you may want to create separate folders for different categories of messages, such as work-related, friends and family, and so on. Or you may want to create date-related folders for storing older messages. For example, you can create a 2000 folder to save all the messages you receive in 2000.

This section explains how to work with message folders.

Don't confuse the mail folders that I describe in this section with Address Book folders, which I describe in Chapter 8. Address Book folders let you organize contacts in your Address Book. In contrast, Outlook Express folders let you organize mail messages you have sent or received.

Creating a new folder

Before you start saving important messages, it's wise to create one or more folders in which to save the messages. I use just a single folder, named Saved Items, but you may want to create several folders for saving messages according to their content. For example, you can create a Personal Items folder for personal messages and a Business Items folder for business messages. You can come up with your own scheme for organizing saved messages, but my advice is to keep your method simple. If you create 40 folders for storing saved messages, you run the risk of forgetting which message is in which folder.

To create a new folder, follow these steps:

1. **Click Local Folders in the Outlook Express folders list.**

2. **Choose File⇨Folder⇨New Folder.**

   The Create Folder dialog box appears, as shown in Figure 9-1.

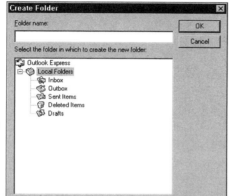

Figure 9-1:
The Create
Folder
dialog box.

3. **Type a name for the new folder.**

   For example, type **Work Items**.

4. **Click OK.**

The new folder is visible in the folder tree on the left side of the Outlook Express window. If you click on the new folder, the message There are no items in this view appears in the folder view area, indicating that the folder you have just created is empty.

Moving messages to another folder

After you create a folder for your messages, moving a message to the folder is easy. Just follow these steps:

1. **In the Inbox, position the mouse pointer over the message you want to move.**

2. **Click and hold the left mouse button. While holding the left button, drag the message to the folder in which you want it stored.**

   The folder is located in the folder tree on the left side of the Outlook Express window.

3. **Release the mouse button when the mouse pointer is over the folder that you want to move the message to.**

   The message moves to the folder you selected and is deleted from the Inbox folder.

If you prefer, you can make a copy of the message rather than move the message. Just hold down the Ctrl key before dragging the message to the new folder.

If dragging isn't your cup of tea, you can move or copy a message by right-clicking the message that you want to move or copy and then choosing the Move to Folder or Copy to Folder command from the pop-up menu that appears. This action brings up a dialog box that enables you to designate the folder you want to move or copy the message to.

Filtering Your Mail

A common complaint of frequent e-mail users is receiving too much unsolicited mail. Outlook Express has several features that let you deal with this problem, as I describe in this section.

Using message rules

One way to deal with the problem of unwanted mail is to create *message rules*. Message rules let you set up Outlook Express so that it automatically takes a specific action whenever a certain type of message arrives. For example, you can set up a message rule to automatically delete any message sent to you from a specific e-mail address. Or you can have Outlook Express automatically move any message that contains specific text in the subject line to a folder that you've created.

A message rule consists of two parts. The first part is a called a *condition*. The condition identifies which specific e-mail messages the rule applies to. Outlook Express lets you use conditions to filter the following types of messages:

 ✔ Messages that contain specific names or words in the From, To, or Cc lines

 ✔ Messages that contain specific words in the Subject line

 ✔ Messages that are larger than a size you specify

 ✔ Messages that are marked as high priority

 ✔ Messages that are encrypted

 ✔ Messages that have attachments

✔ Messages that are sent to a specific mail account you specify (This option is particularly useful when you have subscribed to more than one e-mail service and want to route incoming messages into different folders based on the account the messages were sent to.)

✔ All other messages (This option is useful if you want to perform some special action for messages that aren't handled by other filters you set up.)

You can specify more than one condition for a message rule. For example, you can set up a rule to handle all messages that contain the word *Picture* in the Subject line and are larger than 10K.

The second part of a message rule is the *action,* which indicates what you want Outlook Express to do with messages that meet the criteria for the rule's condition. You can choose any of the following actions for each of your message rules:

✔ Move the message to a specific folder

✔ Copy the message to a specific folder, leaving the original in your Inbox

✔ Delete the message

✔ Forward the message to another person

✔ Reply to the message

✔ Highlight the message with a color of your choosing

✔ Flag the message

✔ Mark the message as having already been read

✔ Do not download the message from the server

✔ Delete the message from the server (Some servers keep a copy of messages that have been sent to you.)

As with conditions, you can specify more than one action for each message rule. For example, you can create a rule that automatically deletes messages you don't want to read and sends a reply message that says something like, "Stop sending me mail!"

To illustrate how to set up a message rule, suppose you want to create a rule that automatically moves all messages that have a specific word in the Subject line to a folder. Here's how to do it:

1. **Choose Tools⇨Message Rules⇨Mail from the main Outlook Express window.**

   This action summons the New Mail Rule dialog box, shown in Figure 9-2.

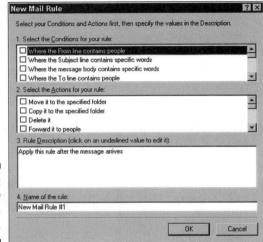

Figure 9-2:
The New
Mail Rule
dialog box.

If you have previously created a message rule, the Message Rules dialog box appears instead of the New Mail Rule dialog box. The Message Rules dialog box is shown later in this section, in Figure 9-4. To summon the New Mail Rule dialog box, click the New button in the Message Rules dialog box.

2. **Choose Where the Subject Line Contains Specific Words for the condition.**

   When you do, the following line is added to the Rule Description text box:

   ```
   Where the Subject line contains specific words
   ```

3. **Click <u>contains specific words</u> in the Rule <u>D</u>escription text box.**

   The Type Specific Words dialog box appears, as shown in Figure 9-3.

Figure 9-3:
The Type
Specific
Words
dialog box.

4. Type a word or phrase in the text box and then click Add.

The word or phrase you typed appears in the bottom of the Type Specific Words dialog box. For example, if you type **SARAH:** in the text box, the following appears at the bottom of the Type Specific Words dialog box:

```
Where the Subject line contains

SARAH:
```

You can type additional words or phrases in the text box. Each time you type a word or phrase, click the Add button to add the words to the Words list at the bottom of the dialog box.

5. Click OK.

You are returned to the New Message Rule dialog box. The condition line in the Rule Description text box now shows the message rule you have created — for example,

```
Where the Subject line contains 'SARAH:'
```

6. Choose Move It to the Specified Folder for the rule action.

When you do, the following line is added to the Description text box:

```
Move it to the specified folder
```

7. Click specified in the Rule Description text box.

A dialog box showing all your Outlook Express folders appears.

8. Click the folder that you want the messages moved to; then click OK.

When you return to the New Mail Rule dialog box, the message rule description is adjusted to indicate the folder you selected. For example, if you select Sarah's Mail for the folder, the Rule Description contains this line:

```
Move it to the Sarah's Mail folder
```

9. Type a meaningful name for the rule in the Name of the Rule text box.

For example, **Sarah's Messages**.

10. Click OK.

The New Message Rule dialog box gives way to the Message Rules dialog box, shown in Figure 9-4. This dialog box lists all of the message rules you have created.

11. Click OK.

From now on, any message you receive with the word you specified in the Subject line (in this case, "SARAH:") is automatically moved to the folder you specified (in this case, "Sarah's Mail").

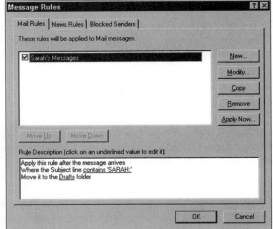

Figure 9-4:
The
Message
Rules dialog
box.

If you create more than one message rule, the rules are applied to your incoming mail in the order in which they are listed in the Message Rules dialog box. For example, suppose you create a rule to move all messages with the word *SARAH:* in the subject line to the Sarah's Mail folder and then create a second rule to delete any message from george@spacelysprockets.com. If george@spacelysprockets.com sends you a message with SARAH: in the subject line, that message is moved to the Sarah's Mail folder because of the first message rule. However, if you reverse the order of the rules so that the Delete-messages-from- george@spacelysprockets.com rule appears first, the message would be deleted.

You can change the order in which rules are listed in the Message Rules dialog box by using the Move Up and Move Down buttons.

To delete a rule, click the rule to select it and then click Remove.

Blocking senders

Another way to deal with unwanted mail is to create a Block Senders list, which is simply a list of e-mail addresses from which Outlook Express refuses to accept mail. Any mail received from a sender on the Blocked Senders list is automatically moved to the Deleted Items folder.

If you receive a piece of obnoxious mail from someone, you can quickly add that person to your Blocked Senders list by clicking the message in your Inbox and then choosing the Message➪Block Sender command. A dialog box appears to inform you that the person has been added to your Blocked Senders list.

To review the list of e-mail senders you have blocked, choose <u>T</u>ools⇨ Message Rules⇨Block <u>S</u>enders List. This command summons the dialog box shown in Figure 9-5, which shows all of the e-mail senders you have blocked. The buttons on this dialog box enable you to add, remove, or modify any of these blocked senders.

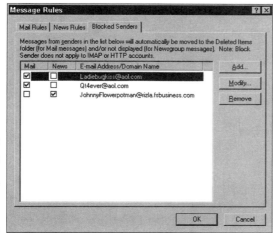

Figure 9-5:
Managing
your
Blocked
Senders list.

Using Stationery

Outlook Express lets you attractively format your e-mail messages using what it calls *stationery.* Stationery lets you create fancy messages with background images, alternative text fonts, and even boilerplate text. This section shows you how to create messages that use stationery and how to set the default stationery that will be used for all new messages.

For stationery to work, you must activate HTML formatting. To do so, choose the F<u>o</u>rmat⇨<u>R</u>ich Text (HTML) command when you create the message.

Creating a message with stationery

Outlook Express comes with 14 different stationery selections for you to choose from. To create an e-mail message using one of these 14 stationery options, follow these steps:

1. In Outlook Express, choose the <u>M</u>essage⇨New Message Using⇨ Select Stationery command.

The Select Stationery dialog box appears, as shown in Figure 9-6.

2. Select the stationery you want to use and then click OK.

A New Message window appears, using the stationery you selected. For example, Figure 9-7 shows a New Message window that uses the Ivy stationery.

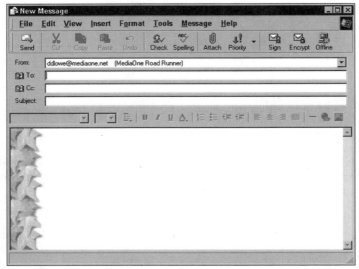

3. Compose and send your message.

Note that some of the stationery selections include sample text for your message. For example, several of the stationery choices have the text Your message here in the stationery. To compose your message, you should delete the Your message here text and then type your own text in its place.

Here are a few other tidbits of useful stationery information:

✔ Outlook Express keeps track of up to ten of your most recent stationery choices. The ten most recently used stationery selections appear as menu choices when you choose the Message➪New Message Using command.

✔ In Outlook Express, you can click the arrow that appears next to the New Message button to reveal a menu that includes the ten most recent stationery selections.

✔ If you want to change the stationery of a message while you are in the New Message window, choose Format➪Apply Stationery and select the stationery you want to use.

✔ To remove stationery, choose Format➪Apply Stationery➪No Stationery.

✔ If the Format➪Apply Stationery command is not available, use the Format➪Rich Text (HTML) command to enable stationery. You can then use the Format➪Apply Stationery command.

Setting the default stationery

If you find some stationery that you want to use for all of your messages, you can set that stationery as the default by following these steps:

1. **From Outlook Express, choose Tools➪Options. When the Options dialog box appears, click the Compose tab.**

   A dialog box showing various options for composing new messages appears, as shown in Figure 9-8.

2. **Click in the Mail check box to activate stationery for new mail messages.**

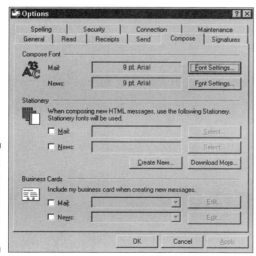

Figure 9-8:
The
Compose
tab of the
Options
dialog box.

3. **Click the Select button.**

   This summons the Select Stationery dialog box (refer to Figure 9-6).

4. **Select the stationery that you want to use and then click OK.**

   You return to the Options dialog box. The stationery you selected is listed next to the Mail check box.

5. **Click OK again.**

   The Options dialog box disappears. From now on, all your e-mail messages will use the stationery you just selected.

Creating new stationery

If you aren't satisfied with any of the stationery selections that come with Outlook Express, you can easily create your own stationery. Outlook Express includes the Stationery Setup Wizard to simplify the process of creating stationery.

To access the Stationery Setup Wizard, follow these steps:

1. **Choose the Tools⇨Options command and then click the Compose tab.**

   This step summons a dialog box that lists the options used for composing new messages, shown in Figure 9-8 (earlier in this section).

2. **Click the Create New button.**

   The Stationery Setup Wizard appears, as shown in Figure 9-9.

Figure 9-9:
The
Stationery
Setup
Wizard
comes to
life.

3. **Click Next.**

   The Stationery Setup Wizard displays options for the message background, as shown in Figure 9-10.

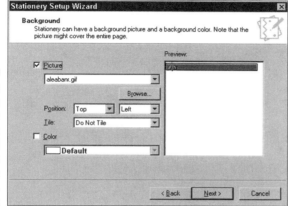

Figure 9-10:
The
Stationery
Setup
Wizard
lets you
choose a
background.

4. **Set the background options and then click Next.**

   You can set the background of your stationery to a picture or to a solid color. To use a picture, click Picture and then select one of the pictures listed in the drop-down box or click the Browse button to select any image file you want to use. You can also set the picture's position, and you can specify how you want the picture to be tiled: horizontally, vertically, filling the entire page, or not tiled.

   To use a solid color for the background, click Color and then choose the color you want to use from the drop-down list.

   After you select the background you want, click Next. The Stationery Setup Wizard displays the font options that will be used for your message, as shown in Figure 9-11.

5. **Choose the font options that you want to use and click Next.**

   The Stationery Setup Wizard lets you choose the font, size, and color from drop-down lists. In addition, you can use the Bold and Italic check boxes to use bold or italic text.

   When you click Next, the Stationery Setup Wizard displays the margin options, as shown in Figure 9-12.

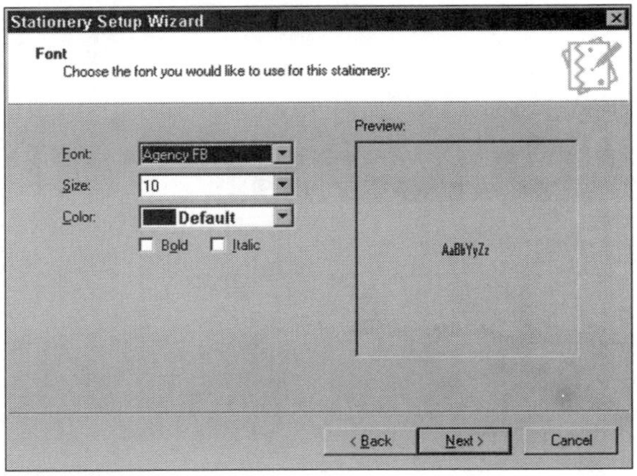

Figure 9-11:
Pick a font,
any font.

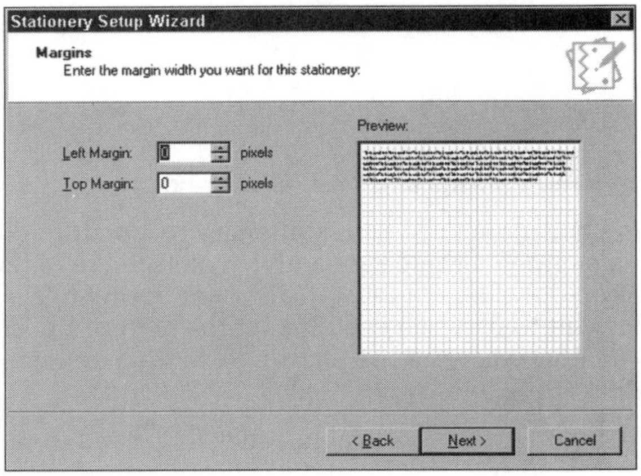

Figure 9-12:
The
Stationery
Wizard
issues a
margin call.

6. **Adjust the margin settings and then click Next.**

   The Stationery Setup Wizard next asks for a name for your new
   stationery, as shown in Figure 9-13.

7. **Type a name for your new stationery and click Finish.**

   After you click Finish, Outlook Express creates the new stationery and
   returns you to the Options dialog box (refer to Figure 9-8).

8. **Click OK to dismiss the Options dialog box.**

   You're done! You can now use your new stationery.

Figure 9-13:
Time to name your stationery.

Another way to get more stationery is to click the Download More button in the Compose tab of the Options dialog box. This fires up Internet Explorer and takes you to a page at Microsoft's Web site. You can download additional stationery files from this page, as shown in Figure 9-14.

Figure 9-14:
You can download additional stationery from Microsoft's Home Publishing Web site.

Signing Off with Signatures

A *signature* is a bit of text you can easily insert at the end of your messages. Signatures usually include information such as your name, the address of your home page (if you have one), and a witty saying. You can configure Outlook Express to automatically insert a signature at the end of every message, or you can insert a signature manually whenever you want to use one.

To create a signature, follow these steps:

1. **In Outlook Express, choose Tools⇨Options.**

   Doing so summons the Options dialog box.

2. **Click the Signatures tab.**

   By doing so, you summon the Signatures options, shown in Figure 9-15.

Figure 9-15:
Creating a
signature.

3. **Click in the text box that appears in the Edit Signature portion of the dialog box and then type the text you want to use for a signature.**

   To create a signature that consists of more than one line, just hit the Enter key when you want to create a new line.

4. **If you want the signature to be automatically attached to every message you send, choose the Add Signatures to All Outgoing Messages option.**

   If you do not select this option, you have to manually insert the signature. I list the steps to do so later in this section.

5. Click OK.

The Options dialog box is dismissed.

You can create more than one signature by clicking the New button. A new signature (named Signature #2) appears in the Signatures list box. You can change the text for any signature by first selecting the signature from the Signatures list box and then editing the signature text in the Edit Signature text box.

If you want to change the name of a signature, select the signature in the Signatures list box, click the Rename button, and then type a new name for the signature.

To manually insert a signature into a new message, choose Insert➪Signature when you create the new message. If you have created more than one signature, the Insert➪Signature command leads you to a menu that lists all your signatures.

Looking Up an E-mail Address

Outlook Express includes a built-in link to several Internet search services that can help you find an e-mail address for an individual or business. To use this feature, choose Edit➪Find➪ People. The Find People dialog box shown in Figure 9-16 appears.

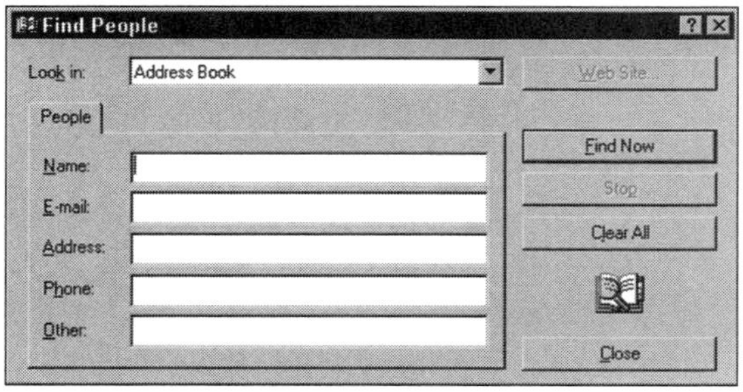

Figure 9-16:
The Find
People
dialog box.

This dialog box enables you to access the following address databases and services:

- ✔ Your very own Address Book
- ✔ Yahoo! People Search
- ✔ Bigfoot

✔ InfoSpace

✔ InfoSpace Business

✔ SwitchBoard

✔ Verisign

✔ WhoWhere?

To search for a person's e-mail address, first select the search service you want to use from the drop-down list. Then type the person's name and click the Find Now button. After a brief delay, the Find People dialog box expands to show a list of all those who match the name you typed, as shown in Figure 9-17.

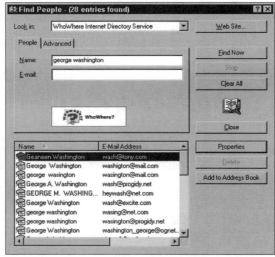

Figure 9-17: Check out all the George Washingtons.

If the name you're looking for doesn't appear in the list, you can try again with a different search service. If the name does appear, select it and then click the Add to Address Book command.

Creating and Using Mailing Groups

If you find that you frequently send mail to a particular group of people, you can create a special type of Address Book entry known as a *mailing group*. A mailing group is simply a list of people selected from your Address Book. When you send a message to the group, Outlook Express automatically sends a copy of the message to each person in the group.

To create a mailing group, follow these steps:

1. **Click the Address Book button in the Outlook Express toolbar.**

   The Address Book appears. (If you forgot what it looks like, refer to Figure 8-11 in Chapter 8.)

2. **Create an Address Book entry for each person you want to include in the group.**

   If all of the people in the group are already in your Address Book, you can skip this step.

3. **Click the New button and then choose New Group from the menu that appears.**

   Or choose File➪New Group. Either way, a Properties dialog box for a new mailing group appears, as shown in Figure 9-18.

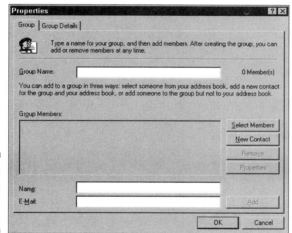

Figure 9-18: Creating a new mailing group.

4. **Type a name for the new group in the Group Name text box.**

   For example, to create a group that consists of your friends who are stranded on a desert isle, type something like castaways.

5. **Click the Select Members button.**

   The Select Group Members dialog box appears, as shown in Figure 9-19.

6. **To add a member to the group, click the member from the list on the left side of the dialog box and then click the Select button.**

   Alternatively, you can simply double-click the name in the left-hand list. Either way, Outlook Express adds the name to the Members list box on the right side of the Select Group Members dialog box.

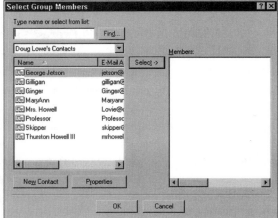

Figure 9-19:
Selecting group members for a mailing group.

7. **Repeat Step 6 for each person you want to add to the group.**

   If you accidentally add the wrong person to the group, you can remove that person by selecting his or her name in the Members list box and pressing the Delete key.

8. **After you finish adding names to the group, click OK.**

   You are returned to the Properties dialog box for the group. The names that you selected for the group appear in the Members list box.

9. **Click OK.**

   The Address Book reappears, as shown in Figure 9-20. The name of the group you created appears in the list at the left side of the Address Book window. If you select the group, the names of the group members appear in the window, as well.

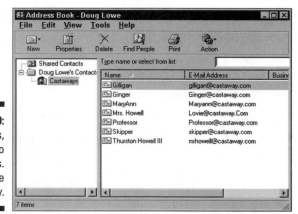

Figure 9-20:
No phones, no lights, no motor cars. Not a single luxury.

10. **Click the Close button (the X in the upper-right corner of the window) to dismiss the Address Book.**

   You're done!

 After you create a group, sending mail to the group is easy. When you are composing a new message, click the To button to summon the Select Recipients dialog box. The groups that you created are highlighted in the Select Recipients dialog box by a special icon (shown in the margin).

Here are a few additional points to keep in mind when you work with groups:

- A person's e-mail address can appear in more than one group. This feature lets you include Thurston Howell III not only in the Castaways group, but also in another group named Eccentric Millionaires (along with Bill Gates and Ross Perot).

- You can easily add names to an existing group by clicking the group name in an Address Book window and then clicking the Properties button. When the Group Properties dialog box appears, click Select Members and add your new member to the group.

- To remove a person from the group, call up the Group Properties dialog box. Then click the member you want to remove and click the Remove button.

Changing Identities

If more than one person uses your computer to access e-mail or Internet newsgroups, you may want to consider creating a separate Outlook Express *identity* for each person. Each identity can have its own Inbox and other Outlook Express folders, separate contacts in the Address Book, and separate newsgroup subscriptions. In other words, identities make it easy for two or more people to share a computer without getting their e-mail and newsgroups mixed up.

For identities to work best, each person who has an identity should have a separate e-mail account with your Internet service provider. Many Internet service providers let you set up additional e-mail names for family members. If not, you can set up a separate Hotmail account for each identity. Either way, everyone with an identity will be able to receive their own e-mail messages when they log on to Outlook Express by using their individual identities. (For more information about using Outlook Express with Hotmail, see Chapter 10.)

Here are the steps to create a new identity:

1 Choose the File➪Identities➪Add New Identity command.

This summons the dialog box shown in Figure 9-21.

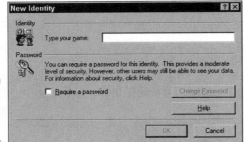

Figure 9-21:
Creating an
identity.

2. **Type a name for the new identity in the text box.**

3. **If you want to create a password for the identity, check the Require a Password check box.**

4. **Click OK to create the identity.**

When Outlook Express offers to switch to the new identity, click Yes. Outlook Express then starts the Internet Connection Wizard, which asks you for important information, such as your full name, e-mail address, and the Internet address for your mail server. Type all of this information dutifully, and Outlook Express creates the new identity for you.

After you have created an identity, you can switch to that identity at any time by choosing the File➪Switch Identity command. This brings up the dialog box shown in Figure 9-22, which lists the identities you have created. Click the identity you want to switch to and then click OK.

Figure 9-22:
Switching
identities.

If you have created more than one identity for Outlook Express, an Exit and Log Off Identity command appears on the File menu. You should use this command whenever you exit Outlook Express. That way, the Switch Identities dialog box (refer to Figure 9-22) appears the next time you start Outlook Express so that you can choose the identity you want to work with.

Reading Mail Offline

Outlook Express includes an offline reading feature that lets you dial in to the Internet, download your mail, and then disconnect from the Internet so that you can read your mail offline. This feature is useful if

- ✔ Your Internet service provider charges by the hour.
- ✔ You want to download your e-mail to a laptop computer and then take your computer to the park and read your mail.
- ✔ You want to free up your phone line so your teenager can use it while you read your e-mail.

To set up Outlook Express to work offline, choose the Tools⇨Options command and click the Connection tab. Select the Hang Up After Sending and Receiving option, and then click OK.

To download your e-mail so that you can read it offline, click the Send and Receive button in the toolbar. Outlook Express uses your modem to connect your computer to your Internet service provider, establish a connection with your e-mail server, download all your e-mail messages to your Inbox, and then disconnect your computer from the Internet. You can then read your mail, compose replies, or create new messages. When you are finished, click the Send and Receive button again to connect to the Internet and send your replies and new messages.

Sending and Receiving Secure Messages

If you're involved in top-secret nuclear arms negotiations, living in Fryburg under the Federal Witness Protection program, or if you're just plain paranoid, you may want to use Outlook Express's security features to send and receive messages. Outlook Express has two methods for securing your e-mail: *encryption,* which scrambles the text of your message so that no one other than the intended recipient can read the message, and *digital signing,* which guarantees the sender's identity.

Before you can use either encryption or digital signing, you must obtain a *digital ID,* which is sort of the online equivalent of a driver's license. You can get digital IDs from several certification authorities on the Internet for a modest fee (about $15 per year).

The first time you attempt to send an encrypted or signed message, Outlook Express displays the dialog box shown in Figure 9-23. Click Get Digital ID to access a special Microsoft Web site that contains links to several digital ID suppliers. Then follow one of the links to one of the certification authorities to obtain a digital ID.

Figure 9-23:
Outlook
Express
offers to
pick up a
digital ID
for you.

After you have obtained your digital ID, sending a secure message is easy:

✔ To encrypt a message, choose the Tools➪Encrypt command when you compose the message.

✔ To sign the message, choose Tools➪Digitally Sign.

When you receive a message that has been encrypted, Outlook Express automatically decodes the message for you. If the message has been signed, Outlook Express verifies the sender's digital ID and displays a warning message if there is a problem with the ID — for example, if the ID has expired.

Chapter 10

Using Outlook Express with Hotmail

In This Chapter

▶ Signing up for a new Hotmail account

▶ Configuring Outlook Express to work with an existing Hotmail account

▶ Accessing your Hotmail account from Outlook Express

▶ Accessing your Hotmail account from a Web browser

*H*otmail is a free e-mail service that does not require you to use a special e-mail program such as Outlook Express. Instead, Hotmail works through the World Wide Web, so you can access your Hotmail e-mail account using Internet Explorer or any other Web browser.

The best part about Hotmail is that it's free. Microsoft makes money from Hotmail by selling advertising for the Hotmail Web site — not by charging membership fees. Unfortunately, this means that you have to put up with sometimes obnoxious advertisements when you check your mail, but at least you don't have to pay for your Hotmail account.

Because Hotmail has become popular, Microsoft decided to add support for Hotmail accounts to Outlook Express. As a result, you can use Outlook Express to access your ISP e-mail account as well as any number of Hotmail accounts. This chapter shows you how to set up and use Hotmail from Outlook Express.

Why Bother with Hotmail?

Since you must have an Internet account to access Hotmail, and most Internet accounts come with an e-mail account, why would you bother setting up a Hotmail account? There are several reasons:

✔ You can access your Hotmail account from any computer that is connected to the Internet, provided the computer has a current version of Internet Explorer or Netscape Navigator. This feature is a great plus if you need to access your e-mail account while you are travelling.

✔ With your ISP e-mail account, your e-mail address changes if you decide to switch to a different ISP. In contrast, Hotmail lets you set up a permanent e-mail address that won't change even if you decide to switch to a different ISP.

✔ If several members of your family use the Internet through a single ISP account, each person can create his or her own Hotmail e-mail account. Although some ISPs let you have more than one e-mail account, many give you only one, requiring that all your family members share a common e-mail account.

✔ If you have an e-mail account at the company where you work, you can use Hotmail to set up a private e-mail account for personal mail. You won't have to worry about your boss snooping through your personal e-mail.

Signing Up for a Hotmail Account

Before you can use Hotmail, you must sign up for a Hotmail account. Fortunately, Hotmail accounts are free, and the procedure for setting up an account is pretty simple. Just follow these steps:

1. **From Outlook Express, choose the Tools⇨New Account Setup⇨ Hotmail command.**

   The Setup Hotmail Account Wizard appears, as shown in Figure 10-1.

Figure 10-1: The Setup Hotmail Account Wizard.

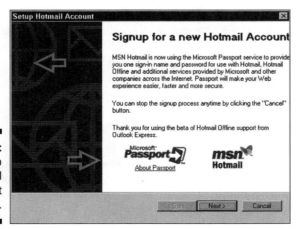

2. **Click Next.**

   Doing this takes you to the Profile Information page, shown in Figure 10-2.

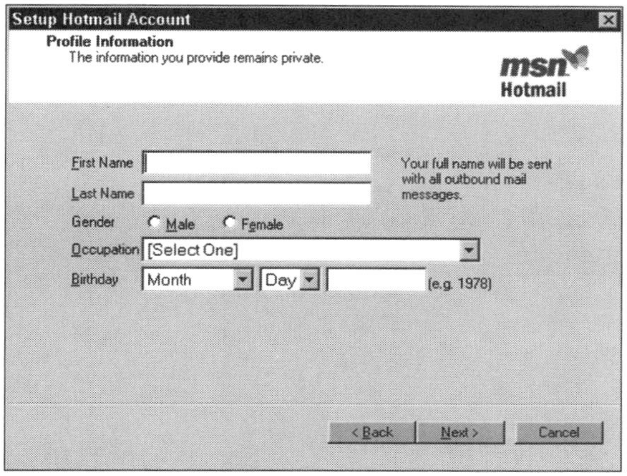

Figure 10-2:
The Profile
Information
page.

3. **Fill in the information requested on the Profile Information page.**

   Hotmail wants to know your first and last names, your gender (one only, please), occupation, and birthday.

4. **Click Next.**

   The Region and Time Zone page appears, as shown in Figure 10-3.

5. **Fill in the information requested on the Region and Time Zone page.**

   Hotmail wants to know what country or region you live in, your state and zip code (these fields may change if you pick a country other than the United States), and your time zone.

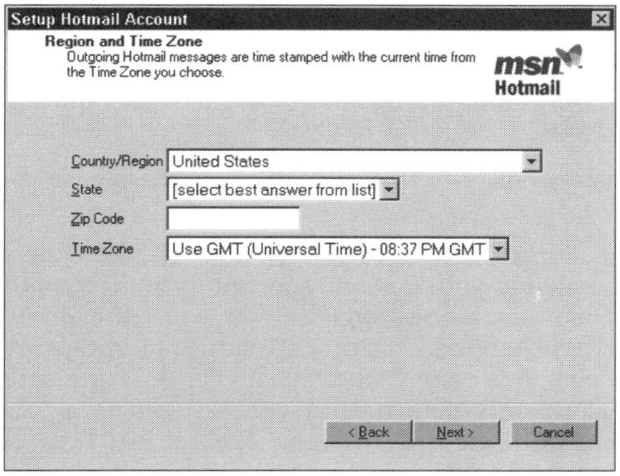

Figure 10-3:
The Region
and Time
Zone page.

6. Click Next.

The Account Information page appears, as shown in Figure 10-4.

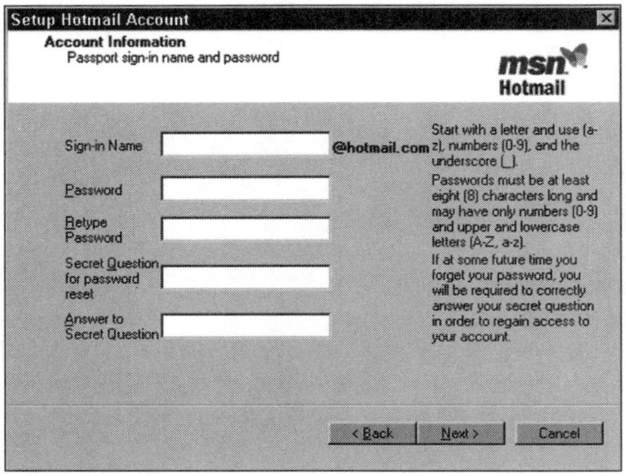

Figure 10-4:
The
Account
Information
page.

7. Type the sign-in name that you want to use.

Your sign-in name is combined with @Hotmail.com to form your complete e-mail address. For example, if your sign-in name is George, your e-mail address is George@Hotmail.com.

Don't fret too much over the sign-in name. Because Hotmail already has a few million users, odds are good that the name you want to use has already been taken. (You can see what to do if that happens a few steps later in this procedure.)

8. Type the password that you want to use for your e-mail account twice — once in the Password field and again in the Retype Password field.

For security reasons, your password is not displayed on the screen as you type it. Hotmail asks you to type the password twice to make sure that you typed it in correctly.

9. Type a secret question and the answer to the secret question in the appropriate fields.

The secret question is used to verify your identity in case you forget your password.

Make sure the answer to your question is truly secret. Otherwise, anyone can break into your Hotmail account by answering the question. For example, don't use a question like "Who wrote the Monroe Doctrine?" or "Who's buried in Grant's Tomb?" Questions such as "What is my mother's maiden name?" and "What year did I graduate from high school?" are also pretty easy to figure out. Try something obscure that only you would know, such as "What are the last five digits of my checking account number?"

10. **Click Next.**

The Internet Directories page appears, as shown in Figure 10-5.

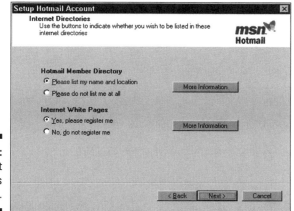

Figure 10-5:
The Internet
Directories
page.

11. **Indicate whether you want to be listed in Hotmail's directories.**

Hotmail maintains two databases of Internet users in which you can be listed — a Hotmail member directory, which contains listings only for Hotmail users and the Internet White Pages directory, which is not limited to Hotmail users.

12. **Click Next.**

Ninety-nine percent of the time, Hotmail next informs you that the sign-in name you chose has already been taken. For example, Figure 10-6 shows the screen I saw when I requested "DummyGuy" as my sign-in name. As you can see, Hotmail suggests a few alternatives to the name you requested. (If by some miracle your sign-in name is accepted the first time around, do a cartwheel and head straight to Step 14.)

13. **Pick one of the alternatives suggested by Hotmail or type a new sign-in name in the text box.**

If you type a new sign-in name, you may again pick a name that is already in use. In other words, you may have to repeat this step several times before you get a name you like.

Most of the good names are already taken. You can keep trying to get a cool name, such as Mulder, DarthMaul, or Mini-Me. But trust me, the good names are already taken. You may as well just pick one of the alternatives suggested by Hotmail. If you want a cool name, you'll probably have to attach a number to the end of it, such as minime38994.

Figure 10-6:
Sorry, that
name is
already
taken.

14. Click Next.

Hotmail congratulates you for successfully setting up an account, as
shown in Figure 10-7.

Figure 10-7:
Your new
e-mail
address.

15. Click Next.

Next comes the Hotmail Terms of Service page (shown in Figure 10-8),
which explains in a mere 2,713 words composed by Microsoft's legal
department the rules that you have to follow if you want to use Hotmail.

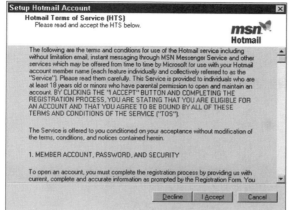

Figure 10-8:
Hotmail's
Terms of
Service
page.

16. **Read the rules.**

   The rules say that you must behave yourself. For example, you can't send junk mail, chain letters, obscene material, or be otherwise obnoxious to other netizens.

17. **Click I Accept.**

   The next page up is the Inbox Protector page (shown in Figure 10-9), on which you can elect to use Hotmail's Inbox Protector feature, designed to screen out junk mail from your inbox. Because Hotmail accounts can quickly get flooded with junk mail, I recommend you use the Inbox Protector.

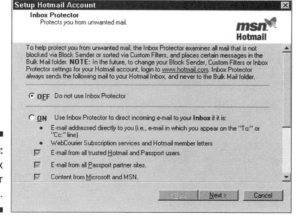

Figure 10-9:
The Inbox
Protector
page.

18. **Click Next.**

The WebCourier page appears, as shown in Figure 10-10. This page lists various mail services you can sign up for.

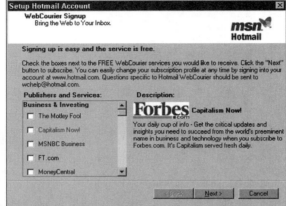

Figure 10-10:
The
WebCourier
page.

19. **Check any of the services you want to sign up for and then click Next.**

Finally, Hotmail displays the congratulatory page shown in Figure 10-11. You are now the proud parent of a Hotmail account.

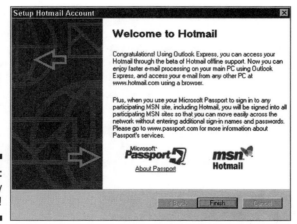

Figure 10-11:
Oh happy
day!

20. **Click Finish.**

The Hotmail Setup Wizard disappears, replaced by the Outlook Express window, shown in Figure 10-12. Don't relax . . . you're not done yet.

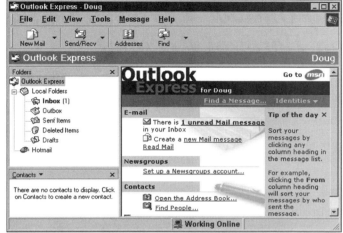

Figure 10-12:
A Hotmail account has been created in Outlook Express.

21. **Click the Hotmail icon in the Outlook Express folder list.**

    A dialog box appears, informing you that you have not set up any folders for the Hotmail account and asking if you want to do so now.

22. **Click Yes.**

    After a brief delay, the folder list is updated to show the folders in your Hotmail account, as shown in Figure 10-13.

    Now you're done!

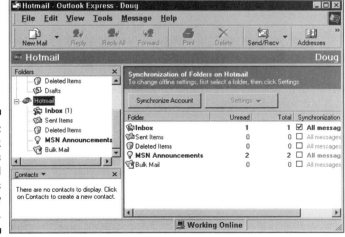

Figure 10-13:
Your Outlook Express Hotmail account is ready to use.

Configuring Outlook Express to Use an Existing Hotmail Account

If you already have a Hotmail account, you can easily configure Outlook Express to use it. Just follow these steps:

1. In Outlook Express, choose the Tools⇨Accounts command.

The dialog box shown in Figure 10-14 appears. This dialog box lists all the Internet accounts Outlook Express is configured to work with.

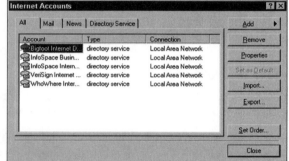

Figure 10-14:
The Internet Accounts dialog box.

2. Click the Add button and then choose Mail from the menu that appears.

The first page of the Internet Connection Wizard appears, as shown in Figure 10-15.

3. Type the name you want to use as your display name and then click Next.

The display name is the name that Outlook Express puts in the From field when you send a message to someone. Usually, you should just type your real name here.

When you click Next, the Internet E-mail Address page appears, as shown in Figure 10-16.

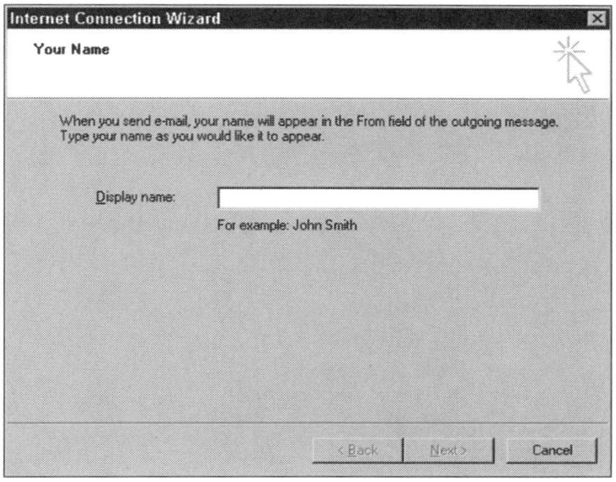

Figure 10-15:
The Internet
Connection
Wizard is
ready to
guide you
through the
task of con-
figuring
Outlook
Express to
use your
Hotmail
account.

Figure 10-15: The Internet Connection Wizard is ready to guide you through the task of configuring Outlook Express to use your Hotmail account.

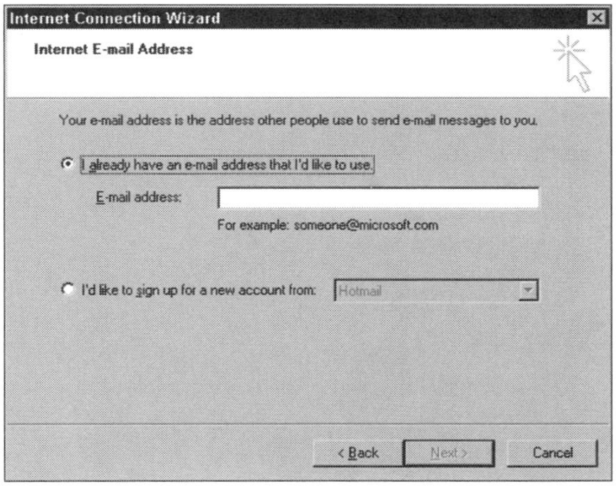

Figure 10-16: The Internet Connection Wizard asks for your Hotmail address.

4. **Type your complete Hotmail e-mail address in the E-mail Address field and then click Next.**

   For example, if your Hotmail account name is Gilligan, type `gilligan@Hotmail.com` in the E-mail Address field. When you click Next, the E-mail Server Names page appears, as shown in Figure 10-17.

5. **Choose HTTP for the incoming mail server type and choose Hotmail for the HTTP mail service provider and then click Next.**

   HTTP is the default choice for the incoming mail server type, and Hotmail is the default for the HTTP mail service provider, so all you have to do here is make sure that the HTTP and Hotmail options are selected. When you click Next, the Internet Mail Logon page appears, as shown in Figure 10-18.

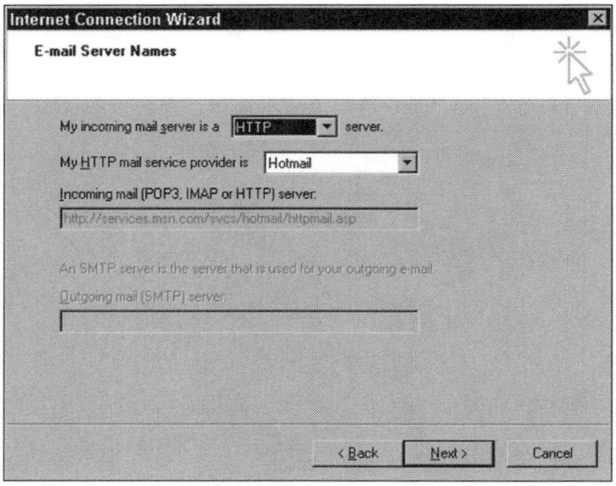

Figure 10-17:
The E-mail
Server
Names
page.

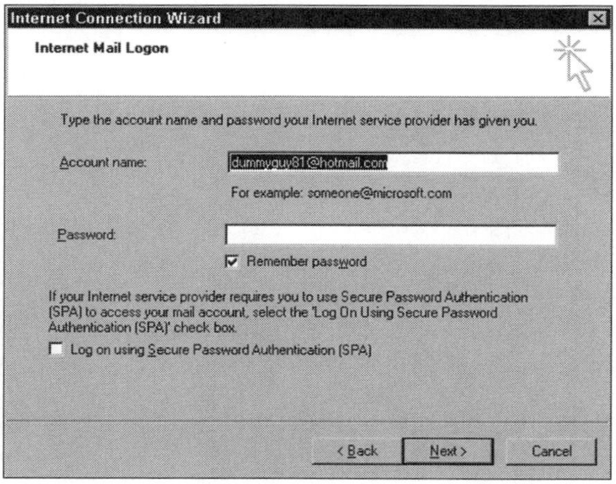

Figure 10-18:
The Internet
Mail Logon
page.

6. Type your Hotmail password in the Password field and then click Next.

The last page of the Internet Connection Wizard appears, congratulating you for successfully setting up Outlook Express for your Hotmail account. Aren't you proud?

7. Click Finish.

You are returned to the Internet Accounts dialog box, which now includes the Hotmail account you just added.

8. Click Close.

A dialog box appears, asking if you want to download the message folders for the Hotmail account.

9. **Click Yes.**

   Outlook Express grinds and whirs for a moment while it downloads the folders for your account. When the Outlook Express window reappears, you're done.

Using Outlook Express to Access Your Hotmail Account

After you have set up your Hotmail account, you can access it from Outlook Express to send and receive mail. Although using a Hotmail account from Outlook Express is similar to using your regular e-mail account, there are a few differences:

✔ To read your incoming mail, scroll down the Folders list to the Hotmail folders and click on the Inbox. You can read messages and send replies the same as you do with your regular e-mail account.

✔ Unlike regular e-mail accounts, Hotmail keeps a copy of all your e-mail messages on its servers. That way, you can access your Hotmail inbox from another computer and still read your mail. However, Hotmail limits the total size of all your e-mail messages to 2MB. When your stored messages exceed the 2MB limit, Hotmail sends you mail to let you know that you should delete some messages. If you don't delete messages within a few days, Hotmail automatically deletes some of your messages. Because of this, you should make a point of regularly deleting old messages.

✔ To send a message via your Hotmail account, you must first tell Outlook Express that you want to send the message using Hotmail rather than your regular e-mail account. You can do that by clicking the Hotmail icon in the folder list before you click the New Mail button. Or you can click the New Mail button and then choose your Hotmail account from the drop-down list that appears in the From: header of the New Message dialog box.

Using Hotmail from the Web

One of the benefits of using Hotmail is that you can access it from any computer that has a connection to the Internet and a Web browser. All you have to do is connect to the Internet, go to the Hotmail home page at `www.Hotmail.com`, and sign in using your Hotmail sign-in name and password. Figure 10-19 shows the page that appears when you access your Hotmail account.

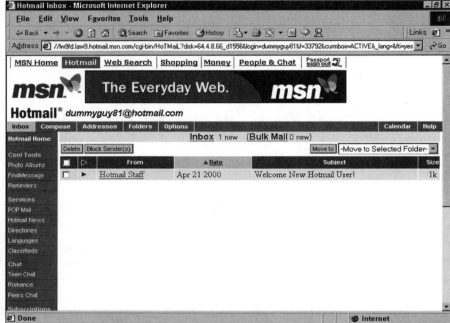

Figure 10-19:
Accessing
your Hotmail
account
from
the Web.

Across the top of the Hotmail page is a horizontal menu that lets you access several basic Hotmail functions:

- **Inbox:** Lets you read mail that has been sent to you. Incoming messages are listed in the middle of the page.

  In Figure 10-19, you can see that I've received one message: a welcome message from the Hotmail staff. You, too, will receive this friendly welcome when you join Hotmail.

  To read a message in your Inbox, just click the underlined name of the message in the From column.

  You can delete one or more messages by clicking the check boxes for the messages you want to delete and then clicking the Delete button near the top of the Inbox message list.

- **Compose:** Lets you create an e-mail message to send to someone else. A separate Compose page appears, with fields you can fill in for the To address, Subject, and message text. You can also spell check your message, attach pictures or other files, and use stationery.

✔ **Addresses:** Lets you keep track of e-mail addresses of the people you frequently send mail to. Note that your Hotmail Address Book is separate from your Outlook Express Address Book. The first time you click Addresses, you're taken to an empty Hotmail address book — even if you have dozens or hundreds of names stored in your Outlook Express Address Book.

✔ **Folders:** Lets you organize your e-mail by storing messages in folders. Hotmail has several built-in folders:

  • **Inbox:** Holds incoming e-mail messages.

  • **Sent Messages:** Holds messages you've already sent.

  • **Drafts:** Holds drafts of messages until you're ready to send them.

  • **Trash Can:** Holds messages you have deleted.

You can also create your own folders to help you organize messages you have received.

✔ **Options:** Lets you set options that affect how Hotmail works. You can use the Options page to change your display name, password, and other account information. You can also set up message filters and a blocked senders list. And you can access a Hotmail feature called the Inbox Protector that's designed to limit the amount of junk mail that reaches your inbox. You can also use the Options page to set up a signature that is automatically attached to messages you send.

✔ **Calendar:** Calls up MSN Calendar, a Web site that lets you keep track of your schedule, create to-do lists, and compose other notes. You can also use MSN Calendar to schedule appointments with other MSN Calendar users.

✔ **Help:** Provides information about using Hotmail.

Chapter 11

The Instant Message Connection

In This Chapter

▶ Installing and running the MSN Messenger Service

▶ Building a contact list of online friends

▶ Sending and receiving instant messages

▶ Using Microsoft's NetMeeting for more sophisticated online chatting

*T*his chapter shows you how to use two Internet Explorer programs that are designed to let you chat online with other Internet users: MSN Messenger Service and NetMeeting.

The MSN Messenger Service — which I'll call MSN Messenger for short — is a basic instant message program that lets you find out if your friends are currently connected to the Internet and exchange instant messages with them. MSN Messenger is similar to the popular America Online program, AOL Instant Messenger (also known as AIM).

NetMeeting is a much more complicated program that enables you to communicate with other Internet users — not just with instant messages, but also with voice and video if your computer is equipped with a microphone or a video camera.

Using MSN Messenger

To use MSN Messenger to chat online with your friends, you must first set up MSN Messenger to identify your friends. In addition, the friends you want to communicate with through MSN Messenger must have the service installed on their computers. After everything is set up, whenever your friends log on to the Internet, you are alerted. When MSN Messenger informs you that one of your friends is online, you can easily send a message, which your friend receives almost immediately. MSN Messenger is a great way to stay in touch with your Internet friends.

Although MSN Messenger is similar to AOL Instant Messenger, MSN Messenger and AIM are competing services. Unfortunately, that means that MSN Messenger users and AIM users cannot talk to one another. To talk to one of your online buddies, you and your friend must both use the same service — either MSN Messenger or AIM.

Setting up MSN Messenger

MSN Messenger is available as a part of Internet Explorer 5.5 and is also included in Windows Millennium Edition. To find out if MSN Messenger has been installed on your computer, look for the MSN Messenger icon on your Windows taskbar. If the icon is there, you can skip this section and begin using MSN Messenger.

If the MSN Messenger icon is not present in your taskbar, you must install MSN Messenger before you can use it. To install MSN Messenger on a Windows Millennium computer, just follow these steps:

1. **Click the Start button on the Windows taskbar, then choose Settings⇨ Control Panel.**

   The Control Panel window appears.

2. **Double-click the Add/Remove Programs icon.**

   The Add/Remove Programs dialog box appears.

3. **Click the Windows Setup tab.**

   The Windows Setup options appear, which list the various components you can add or remove from Windows.

4. **Click Communications in the Components list, and then click Details.**

   A list of Windows communications features appears.

5. **Click the MSN Messenger check box.**

6. **Click OK to return to the Windows setup components, and then click OK again to dismiss the Add/Remove Programs dialog box.**

   Windows chugs and churns for a few moments while it sets up MSN Messenger.

If you don't have Windows Millennium Edition, you can download MSN Messenger from Microsoft's Web site at messenger.msn.com.

Running MSN Messenger

After you have installed MSN Messenger, MSN Messenger runs automatically each time that you start your computer. If you have closed the MSN Messenger window or if you have turned off the option that automatically runs MSN Messenger, you can start MSN Messenger using one of the following methods:

- ✔ Double-click the MSN Messenger icon on the Windows taskbar.
- ✔ Click the Start button on the Windows taskbar, then choose Programs⇨MSN Messenger.
- ✔ From Internet Explorer, choose the Tools⇨MSN Messenger command.
- ✔ From Outlook Express, choose the Tools⇨MSN Messenger command.

Whichever method you use to start MSN Messenger, a window similar to the one shown in Figure 11-1 appears. In the center of the MSN Messenger window is a list of your online contacts, indicating which contacts are currently online and which are not. You can send instant messages to any of your contacts who are currently online. (As you can see, the MSN Messenger contact list is empty. For information about adding contacts, see the section "Adding Contacts" later in this chapter.)

Figure 11-1:
The MSN
Messenger
window.

Below the menu bar at the top of the MSN Messenger window is a toolbar, which contains the following icons:

✔ **Add:** Adds a person to your contact list.

✔ **Send:** Sends an instant message to another MSN Messenger user.

✔ **Status:** Changes your MSN Messenger status. Use this button to let people know that you are away from your computer, out to lunch, or that you just don't want to be bothered.

✔ **Mail:** Starts Internet Explorer and calls up your Hotmail inbox so you can read your e-mail.

At the bottom of the MSN Messenger window is a Search text box, which lets you quickly search the Internet using Microsoft's own msn.com search service. To use this feature, type one or more words you want to search for in the Search text box, and then click the Search button. MSN Messenger submits your search to msn.com's search page and then calls up a separate browser window to display the results.

Adding contacts

Before you can use MSN Messenger to send instant messages to your online friends, you must first create a list of your online contacts. The tricky part is that each of your online contacts must also have the MSN Messenger software and an account with a free Microsoft service known as *Passport*. If you try to add someone to your contact list who does not have the MSN Messenger software or a Passport account, MSN Messenger asks for your permission to send that person an e-mail message telling him how to download and install the MSN Messenger and sign up with Passport.

Note that both Hotmail and Microsoft's MSN Internet Access service are automatically linked to Passport. So if your friend has a Hotmail account or uses MSN Internet Access to connect to the Internet, he or she already has a Passport account.

To add someone to your MSN Messenger contact list, first find out that person's e-mail address. Then, follow these steps:

1. **Click the Add button on the MSN Messenger toolbar.**

   The Add a Contact dialog box appears, as shown in Figure 11-2.

2. **Check the By E-mail Address option and then click the <u>N</u>ext button.**

   This action summons the dialog box where you provide your contact's e-mail address, shown in Figure 11-3.

Figure 11-2:
The Add a
Contact
dialog box.

Figure 11-3:
Type your
friend's
e-mail
address.

3. Type your contact's e-mail address in the text box and click Next.

If MSN Messenger finds a Passport account for the e-mail address you entered, a dialog box similar to that shown in Figure 11-4 is displayed. Otherwise, MSN Messenger informs you that you cannot add this person to your contact list until he or she sets up a Passport account. As a favor, MSN Messenger offers to send your friend an e-mail message explaining how he or she can sign up with Passport and use MSN Messenger.

4. If you want to send e-mail to your friend instructing him how to download and install MSN Messenger, click the Yes option.

If you are sure that the person already has MSN Messenger installed, click the No button so that the e-mail message is not sent.

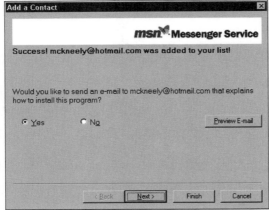

Figure 11-4:
Congratula-
tions! You
have suc-
cessfully
added your
friend to
your contact
list.

If you do choose to send an e-mail message, click the Preview E-mail button to see a preview of the e-mail message that will be sent to your friend.

5. **Click the Next button.**

   Another dialog box appears, congratulating you once again for success-fully adding a contact to your contact list.

6. **To add another contact, click the Next button and repeat Steps 2 through 5.**

7. **When you are through adding contacts, click the Finish button.**

   You are returned to the MSN Messenger window, where the contact list shows the new contacts you added.

Here are a few points to ponder concerning the contact list:

✔ If you don't know the e-mail address of the person you want to add to your contact list, check the Search for a Contact option instead of the By E-mail Address option in Step 2. This summons the dialog box shown in Figure 11-5, which allows you to search Hotmail's database by name, city, state, and country.

✔ The By Passport option in Step 2 (refer to Figure 11-2) lets you locate a contact by entering his or her Passport sign-in name. If your friend does not have a Hotmail or MSN Internet Access account but has created a Passport account, you can use this option to add him or her to your contact list.

✔ To remove a contact, click the contact to select it, and then choose File⇨Delete Contact or just press the Delete key.

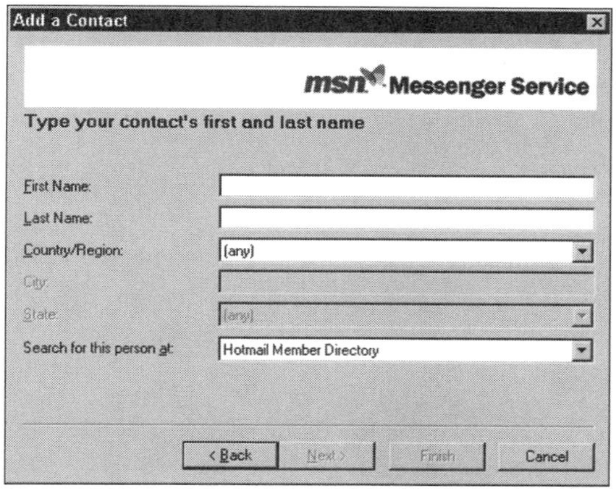

Figure 11-5:
Searching
for contacts
by name,
city, state,
and country.

Add a Contact

msn Messenger Service

Type your contact's first and last name

First Name:

Last Name:

Country/Region: [any]

City:

State: [any]

Search for this person at: Hotmail Member Directory

< Back   Next >   Finish   Cancel

Sending an instant message

Suppose you're busy at work playing Solitaire on your computer one day, and it suddenly occurs to you that one of your friends is probably playing Solitaire too, and wouldn't it be nice to find out. MSN Messenger is designed to enable precisely this kind of important communication. Just follow these steps to send your friend an instant message:

1. **Double-click the contact that you want to send a message to.**

   Or, if you prefer, click the Send button, and then choose the person to whom you want to send the message from the list of online contacts that appears. Either way, an Instant Message dialog box appears, as shown in Figure 11-6.

   You can only send instant messages to contacts that appear in the Contacts Currently Online section of the MSN Messenger contact list. You cannot send messages to the contacts that appear in the Contacts Not Online section.

2. **Type the message you want to send in the text box at the bottom of the Instant Message dialog box.**

   For example, type **Hey, are you playing Solitaire too?**.

3. **Click the Send button.**

   Or, if you prefer, just press the Enter key.

That's all there is to it. Your message is sent over the Internet to your online friend. Your friend will receive the message in a matter of seconds.

Figure 11-6:
Sending an
instant
message.

You can also send a message to someone who is not on your contact list, provided that person has an MSN Messenger account and you know the person's Hotmail address. To send a message to someone who is not on your contact list, click the Send button, then choose Other from the menu that appears. Type the person's MSN Messenger logon name (her Hotmail address, minus the @Hotmail.com), and then click OK.

MSN Messenger conversations are not limited to just two participants. As many as five people can join together in an instant conversation. To invite someone else to join a conversation, click the Invite button, choose To Join This Conversation from the menu that appears, and then choose another one of your online contacts from the list that appears.

Receiving an instant message

When someone sends you an instant message, a sound plays on your computer and a flashing window appears on the Windows taskbar. Click the flashing window on the taskbar to open the Instant Message window, as shown in Figure 11-7.

You can reply to the message by composing a message of your own in the text box at the bottom of the Instant Message window and then clicking the Send button or pressing Enter.

You and your friend can talk back and forth like this for hours if you want. When you're ready to leave the conversation, choose File⇨Close or click the Close button (the X in the upper right-hand corner) of the Instant Message window.

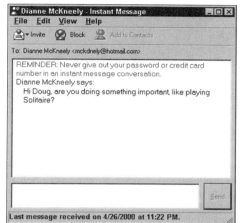

Figure 11-7:
Receiving
an instant
message.

Gone fishing: Letting your friends know that you're offline

If you are going to leave your computer or are unable to participate in instant message conversations for some other reason, you can let MSN Messenger know so that other MSN Messenger users will know that you are not available. Actually, you can choose from several different status settings:

- ✓ **Online:** You are at your computer, able and willing to accept instant messages.

- ✓ **Busy:** You can't talk now because you're busy doing something else.

- ✓ **Be Right Back:** You can't talk now, but you'll be back soon.

- ✓ **Away:** You can't receive messages because you are not at your computer.

- ✓ **On the Phone:** You are engaged in a low-tech conversation.

- ✓ **Out to Lunch:** Either literally or figuratively.

- ✓ **Appear Offline:** You are at your computer, but will appear to be offline to anyone who attempts to contact you via MSN Messenger. You can still send messages of your own, however.

To change your status, click the Status button, and then choose the status option you want to use from the menu that appears.

Keep in mind that other MSN Messenger users who have added you to their contact list can see your status and can still send you messages. The only exception is if you change your status to Appear Offline. If you do, you will appear to be offline to other MSN Messenger users.

If you change your status to Busy, Be Right Back, Away, On the Phone, or Out to Lunch, be sure to change your status back to Online when you return.

Using NetMeeting

Microsoft NetMeeting is an advanced instant messaging program that provides features such as audio and video communications. You can think of NetMeeting as MSN Messenger on steroids.

NetMeeting offers the following instant communication features:

- ✔ **Voice communication:** If you have a microphone plugged into your computer's sound card, you can use NetMeeting like a telephone. You can talk to people all over the world without paying long distance phone charges!

- ✔ **Video:** If your computer is equipped with a video camera, you can send a video picture of yourself to someone else on the Net. Likewise, you can view video images when you connect with someone whose computer has a video camera.

- ✔ **Whiteboard:** This feature is similar to Windows Paint. Whiteboard displays a drawing area in which all the participants in a conference can doodle.

- ✔ **Chat:** This feature works similarly to MSN Messenger. NetMeeting chat enables more than two users to join together in a conference and type messages to one another. (Only two users can use voice or video communications.)

- ✔ **File transfer:** You guessed it — file transfer enables you to send files to other NetMeeting users.

- ✔ **Program sharing:** This feature enables other NetMeeting users to see on their screens an application that you're running on your computer. You can also share applications so that several NetMeeting users can work together on a single document over the Internet.

- ✔ **Remote desktop sharing:** This feature allows a remote computer to access your desktop, which is great for accessing files and programs on another computer or troubleshooting problems.

NetMeeting is included on the Internet Explorer 5.5 CD-ROM and comes with Windows Millennium. However, if you downloaded Internet Explorer 5.5 and you're using an earlier version of Windows, you may not have NetMeeting on your computer. If not, you can download NetMeeting from the NetMeeting home page at www.microsoft.com/windows/netmeeting.

Placing a NetMeeting call

In NetMeeting, you place a *call* to establish a connection between you and another NetMeeting user. To call someone with NetMeeting, you must first connect to the Internet via your Internet Service Provider. Once you are online, follow these steps:

1. **Start NetMeeting by double-clicking the NetMeeting icon on your desktop.**

   Or, if you prefer, you can start NetMeeting by clicking the Start button on the Windows taskbar and then choosing Programs⇨Accessories⇨ Communications⇨NetMeeting. Either way, NetMeeting comes to life and displays the window shown in Figure 11-8.

Figure 11-8:
The main NetMeeting window.

2. **Click the Find Someone in a Directory button.**

   This brings up the Find Someone window, shown in Figure 11-9. As you can see, the Find Someone window lists your MSN Messenger contacts.

   If your MSN Messenger contacts do not appear in the Find Someone window, choose Microsoft Internet Directory in the Select a Directory drop-down list located at the top of the Find Someone window.

3. **Click the name of the person you want to call.**

   NetMeeting attempts to contact the user you selected. This process may take a few moments, so be patient. Messages appear next to the name of the person that you are attempting to call to let you know the status of your call.

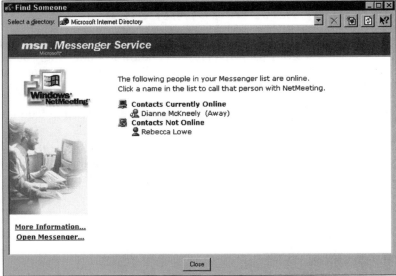

Figure 11-9:
The Find
Someone
window lists
your MSN
Messenger
contacts.

If the person you're trying to call is already in another call, NetMeeting extends the offer to barge in on the conference. However, the members in that conference may decide not to let you in, so don't be surprised if your call goes unanswered. And if they do let you in, you will be able to exchange voice or video with only one of them at a time.

When the connection is finally established, you are returned to the NetMeeting main window, as shown Figure 11-10.

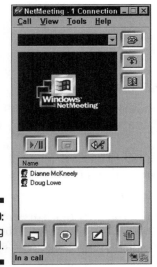

Figure 11-10:
NetMeeting
in a call.

4. **Talk into your microphone.**

   NetMeeting works just like a telephone. You talk into the microphone, and you can hear the person on the other end of the line through your computer's speakers.

5. **Watch the video screen.**

   If you have connected with someone who has a video camera, crude images appear in the video window. Don't expect broadcast quality.

6. **When you're done, say good-bye and click the End Call button.**

   That's all there is to it!

You can also start a NetMeeting call directly from MSN Messenger. In MSN Messenger, choose Tools➪Send an Invitation➪To Start NetMeeting. This brings up a menu of your contacts who are currently online; just choose the person you want to call from this menu. For example, to call Dianne, choose Tools➪Send an Invitation➪To Start NetMeeting➪Dianne.

Using the NetMeeting chat feature

NetMeeting includes a text chat feature that is similar to MSN Messenger. To use NetMeeting Chat, follow these steps:

1. **Call up another NetMeeting user.**

   See the section "Placing a NetMeeting call" earlier in this chapter.

2. **Click the Chat button.**

   Or, if you are allergic to buttons, choose Tools➪Chat or press Ctrl+T. Whichever method you use, up springs the Chat window shown in Figure 11-11.

Figure 11-11:
The
NetMeeting
Chat
window.

3. **Type something in the text box at the bottom of the Chat window.**

4. **Press Enter to send your message.**

Or click the Send button. Messages that other NetMeeting users send are displayed automatically.

5. **When you're finished chatting, choose File⇨Exit.**

You can also close Chat by clicking the Close button in the upper-right corner of the Chat window.

Drawing on the Whiteboard

Another way to communicate in NetMeeting is with Whiteboard, which is sort of like an Internet version of the venerable Paint accessory that comes with Windows. The difference between the two programs is that both you and your friend on the other end of the call can doodle on the Whiteboard, and you can instantly see each other's artistic endeavors.

To use Whiteboard, follow these steps:

1. **Establish a call to another NetMeeting user.**

See the section "Placing a NetMeeting call" earlier in this chapter.

2. **Click the Whiteboard button.**

If buttons are against your religion, you can choose Tools⇨Whiteboard instead. Or just press Ctrl+W. Whichever method you use, the Whiteboard appears, as shown in Figure 11-12.

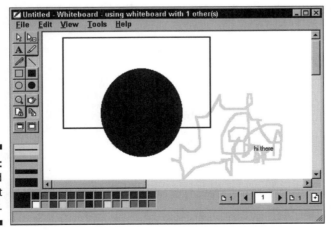

Figure 11-12:
Whiteboard looks a lot like Paint.

3. **Draw something.**

   If you know how to use Microsoft Paint, you already know how to use Whiteboard. Just select one of the drawing tools in the toolbar on the left edge of the Whiteboard window and then doodle something in the drawing area. (You can find an explanation of each of the drawing tools at the end of this section.)

4. **Gasp in amazement when Whiteboard appears to draw stuff all by itself.**

   Actually, Whiteboard isn't drawing that stuff, your counterpart on the other end of the NetMeeting call is. The whole point of Whiteboard is that any of the NetMeeting participants can draw on the Whiteboard at the same time. Anything one person draws on NetMeeting's Whiteboard automatically shows up on every participant's computer.

5. **If the drawing is worth hanging on to, choose File⇨Save to save the drawing or File⇨Print to print it.**

6. **When you're done, close Whiteboard by clicking the Close button (you know, the one with the X on it that's in the upper-right corner of the window).**

   Alternatively, you can choose File⇨Exit.

The following paragraphs describe the various drawing tools that are located in the Whiteboard's toolbar:

✔ **Selector:** Use this tool to move objects around the drawing area or to delete objects. To move an object, click the Selector tool, and then point to the object that you want to move. Press and hold the left mouse button, and drag the object to its new location. To delete an object, click the Selector tool, click the object you want to delete, and then press the Delete key.

✔ **Eraser:** Use this tool to delete an object from the drawing area. First click the Eraser tool, and then click the object you want to delete.

✔ **Text:** Add text to the drawing by clicking the text tool, and then clicking anywhere in the drawing area and typing your text. You can change the font, size, color, and other text formats by clicking the Font Options button at the bottom of the Whiteboard window.

✔ **Highlighter:** Quickly highlight any region of the Whiteboard by clicking this button and then dragging it over the region you want to highlight. You can change the color of the highlighter by clicking one of the colors at the bottom-left corner of the Whiteboard window.

✔ **Pen:** Use this tool to draw on the Whiteboard.

✔ **Line:** Use this tool to draw straight lines on the Whiteboard.

✔ **Unfilled Rectangle:** Use this tool to draw a rectangle or square.

✔ **Filled Rectangle:** Use this tool to draw a rectangle or square filled with a solid color.

✔ **Unfilled Ellipse:** Use this tool to draw an ellipse or circle.

✔ **Filled Ellipse:** Use this tool to draw an ellipse or circle filled with a solid color.

✔ **Zoom:** Click this tool to zoom in for a closer look at the picture.

✔ **Remote Pointer:** Click this button to activate a special pointer that appears on everyone else's Whiteboard. You can move the remote pointer around by dragging it with your mouse.

✔ **Lock Contents:** Click this button to prevent other users from modifying the contents of the Whiteboard. Click it again to unlock it. Note that any user in a conference can lock the Whiteboard.

✔ **Unsynchronize:** Click this button to prevent NetMeeting from showing changes other users make to the Whiteboard. Unsynchronizing allows you to draw on the Whiteboard without being distracted by the doodlings of other users.

✔ **Select Area:** You can copy a selected area from anywhere on your screen into the Whiteboard by clicking this button and then dragging a rectangle over the area you want to copy. When you release the mouse button, the area you selected is automatically pasted into the Whiteboard.

✔ **Select Window:** Copy the contents of another window into the Whiteboard by clicking this button and then clicking anywhere in the window you want to include. As soon as you click the mouse, the contents of the window you clicked are automatically pasted into the Whiteboard.

The Whiteboard can contain more than one drawing page. To display a different page, use the Next Page or Previous Page buttons located at the bottom of the Whiteboard window. To create a new page, click the Insert New Page button located in the bottom right corner of the window.

Sending a file

You can send a file to another NetMeeting user by following these steps:

1. Call up another NetMeeting user.

See the section "Placing a NetMeeting call" earlier in this chapter.

2. Click the Transfer Files button.

Or, if clicking buttons makes you belch, try using Tools⇨File Transfer instead. Or just press Ctrl+F. However you go about it, the File Transfer dialog box shown in Figure 11-13 appears. You use this dialog box to first build a list of files you want to send, and then to actually send the files.

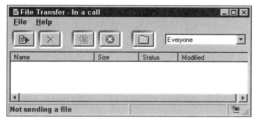

Figure 11-13:
Sending files to other NetMeeting participants.

3. Click the Add Files button.

A dialog box appears that allows you to select the file you want to add to the list of files to be sent.

4. Select the file you want to send, and then click Add.

You may have to navigate through the folders on your hard drive to find the file you want to send. When you click Add, you are returned to the File Transfer dialog box. The file you selected appears in the list of files to send.

5. Repeat Steps 3 and 4 for any other files you want to send.

You can send as many files as you want.

6. If more than one person is in your NetMeeting call, choose the person to whom you want to send the file or files from the drop-down list that appears in the upper right portion of the File Transfer dialog box.

By default, the file or files are sent to everyone in the call.

7. Click the Send All button.

The files are sent.

8. When the transfer is finished, close the File Transfer dialog box by clicking its Close button.

You are returned to the main NetMeeting window.

If someone sends you files, the File Transfer dialog box appears on your screen automatically. When the transfer is finished, you can retrieve the files that were sent to you by clicking the View Received Files button.

Sharing an application

One of NetMeeting's coolest features is that it enables you to share programs on the Internet with other NetMeeting users. For example, if you are discussing your marketing budget in a NetMeeting conference, you can call up Microsoft Excel, open the budget spreadsheet, and let everyone in the conference see and even edit the spreadsheet.

To share an application, just follow these steps:

1. **Start the application you want to share.**

   If you want to share a particular document, open it, too.

2. **In the NetMeeting window, click the Share Program button.**

   If your mouse button is broken, choose Tools⇨Sharing instead. Or press Ctrl+S. One way or another, a dialog box appears listing the programs that are currently running on your computer.

3. **Select the application you want to share from the list of programs, and then click Share.**

   The program appears on the screens of the other people in your NetMeeting call.

4. **Use the application as you normally would.**

   Anything you do in the application is visible to the other members of the NetMeeting conference. However, other conference participants cannot take over and use the application until you complete the next step.

5. **Click the Allow Control button.**

   This button enables other users to take over and use the program you have shared. When another user takes over your application, you see your mouse pointer move magically by itself, with the other user's initials tacked onto the bottom of the mouse pointer so you can tell who's driving. You can wrest control away from the other user at any time by simply clicking the mouse.

   Note that when you click the Allow Control button, the name of the button changes to Prevent Control. You can then click the Prevent Control button to prevent people from playing with your program. (The button then changes back to Allow Control.)

6. **To stop sharing the program, select the program in the Sharing dialog box, and then click the Unshare button.**

Beware of security problems when you share a program — especially when you use the Allow Control button. When you give someone access to your application from across the Internet, that person can delete files, open sensitive documents, and even plant macro viruses on your computer. You should use the Allow Control feature only with users you trust. And never leave your computer unattended — even for a moment — with Allow Control enabled.

Chapter 12

Accessing Newsgroups with Outlook Express

In This Chapter

▶ Figuring out how newsgroups work

▶ Browsing newsgroups with Outlook Express

▶ Reading and writing newsgroup messages

▶ Downloading pictures and other binary files from newsgroups

*B*esides handling Internet e-mail, the Outlook Express program that comes with Internet Explorer 5.5 can also access *newsgroups,* the Internet equivalent of a bulletin board. This chapter explains the ins and outs of using Outlook Express to access newsgroups.

Introducing Newsgroups

A *newsgroup* is a place where you can post messages (called *articles*) about a particular topic and read messages that others have posted about the same topic. People with similar interests visit a newsgroup to share news and information, find out what others are thinking, ask questions, get answers, and generally shoot the breeze.

The Internet has thousands of newsgroups — *tens* of thousands — on topics ranging from astronomy to the Civil War. You can find a newsgroup for virtually any subject that interests you.

Newsgroups come in two basic types:

 ✔ **Moderated newsgroup:** In a moderated newsgroup, one person is designated as a moderator and has complete control over what appears in the newsgroup. All new articles are submitted to the moderator for his or her review. Nothing is actually posted to the newsgroup until the moderator approves it.

The moderator establishes the criteria for which articles get posted to the newsgroup. For some newsgroups, the criterion is simply that the article must be somehow related to the subject of the newsgroup. Other newsgroups use more stringent criteria, enabling the moderator to be more selective about what's posted. As a result, only the best postings actually make it into the newsgroup. This supervision may seem stifling, but in most cases, the monitoring dramatically improves the quality of the newsgroup articles.

✔ **Unmoderated newsgroup:** In an unmoderated newsgroup, anyone and everyone can post an article. Unmoderated newsgroups are free from censorship, but they're also often filled with blatant solicitations, chain letters, and all sorts of noise, such as articles that have nothing to do with the newsgroup topic.

Using Usenet

The term *Usenet* refers to a collection of newsgroups that are distributed together to computers that run special software called *news servers*. Each Internet service provider (ISP) provides its own news server so that you can access the newsgroups that are part of Usenet. For example, my ISP, MediaOne, has a news server named nntp.we.mediaone.net.

In theory, Usenet servers share their new postings with one another, so that all the servers contain the most recent postings. In practice, Usenet servers are never really quite up-to-date, nor are they always in sync with one another. When you post an article to a newsgroup, a day or so may pass before your article propagates through Usenet and appears on all servers. Likewise, replies to your articles may take a while to show up on your server.

Each Usenet site decides which Usenet newsgroups to carry. As a result, you may find that a particular newsgroup isn't available from your Internet service provider.

Because the content of some newsgroups, particularly the renegade alt newsgroups, is sometimes a bit offensive, your Internet service provider may not automatically grant you access to all newsgroups. If you find yourself locked out of these groups, consult your ISP to find out how to gain access.

Understanding Usenet newsgroup names

Usenet has literally tens of thousands of newsgroups. Each newsgroup has a unique name that consists of one or more parts separated by periods. For example, `soc.culture.assyrian` is a newsgroup that discusses Assyrian culture, `sci.polymers` contains information on the scientific field of polymers, and `rec.food. drink.beer` is a place to discuss your favorite brew.

The first part of a newsgroup name identifies one of several broad categories of newsgroups, as I describe in the following list:

- `comp`: Newsgroups that start with `comp` contain discussions about computers. Many of the participants in the `comp` newsgroups wear pocket protectors and glasses held together by tape.

- `news`: These newsgroups contain discussions about Usenet itself, such as help for new Usenet users, announcements of new newsgroups, and statistics about which newsgroups are most popular.

- `rec`: Recreational topics, such as sports, fishing, basket weaving, model railroading, and so on, are discussed in `rec` newsgroups.

- `sci`: Look to the `sci` newsgroups for discussions about science.

- `soc`: In the `soc` newsgroups, people gather to shoot the breeze or to discuss social issues.

- `talk`: These newsgroups favor long-winded discussions of topics such as politics and religion.

- `misc`: These newsgroups are for topics that don't fit into any of the other categories.

- `bit`: Bitnet is the network that supports Internet mailing lists. (A *mailing list* is like a newsgroup, except that all messages are exchanged via e-mail.) *bit newsgroups* are bitnet mailing lists presented in newsgroup form.

- `biz`: This prefix denotes a business-related newsgroup.

- `bionet`: Newsgroups with this prefix discuss topics related to biology.

- **Regional newsgroups:** Newsgroups that share regional interests are indicated by a short prefix (usually two or three letters), such as `aus` (Australia) or `can` (Canada). Most states have regional newsgroups designated by the state's two-letter abbreviation (`CA` for California, `WA` for Washington, and so on).

- `alt`: Hundreds of newsgroups using this prefix discuss topics that range from bizarre to X-rated to paranoid. These newsgroups are not officially sanctioned by Usenet, but some of the more popular newsgroups fall into the `alt` category. The most visited of the `alt` newsgroups are those with an `alt.binaries` designation. These newsgroups contain binary files (such as pictures, sounds, and actual programs) that are specially encoded to be sent via Usenet's text-only messages. Fortunately, Internet Explorer is able to automatically decode these attachments, so you don't have to worry about using a separate program to do so.

The Microsoft Public Newsgroups

Microsoft sponsors several dozen newsgroups that provide official online support for various Microsoft products. These newsgroups all have names that begin with the words microsoft.public, followed by the name of a Microsoft product (or an abbreviation of it). Here are a few of the Microsoft newsgroups that are dedicated to supporting users of Internet Explorer 5.5 and related products:

- ✔ microsoft.public.inetexplorer.ie55
- ✔ microsoft.public.inetexplorer.ie55.browser
- ✔ microsoft.public.inetexplorer.ie55.outlookexpress
- ✔ microsoft.public.inetexplorer.ie55.setup

These newsgroups are available on most news servers. If you can't find them on your Internet service provider's list of newsgroups, you can access them via Microsoft's public news server, msnews.microsoft.com.

You can launch Outlook Express as a newsreader from within Internet Explorer in the following ways:

- ✔ Click the Mail icon and select the Read News command from the pop-up menu that appears.
- ✔ Choose Tools⇨Mail and News⇨Read News.
- ✔ Click a link to a newsgroup. (Newsgroup addresses begin with news:. For example, news:rec.backcountry refers to the newsgroup named rec.backcountry.)

Accessing Newsgroups

Outlook Express can handle Internet news just as easily as it can handle e-mail. To read Internet newsgroups, follow these steps:

1. **Start Outlook Express by clicking the Launch Outlook Express button that appears in the Windows taskbar.**

   Or click the Start button and then choose Programs⇨Internet Explorer⇨ Outlook Express.

2. Click the <u>Read News</u> link, which appears near the center of the main Outlook Express window.

Assuming you have not previously subscribed to any newsgroups, Outlook Express responds by displaying the dialog box shown in Figure 12-1.

Figure 12-1:
Outlook
Express
complains
that you
have not
subscribed
to any
newsgroups.

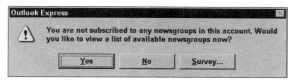

If you do not have a <u>Read News</u> link in your Outlook Express window, click the <u>Set Up a Newsgroups Account</u> link instead. Then, follow the instructions that appear to set up your news server.

3. Click Yes.

Outlook Express displays a list of all of the newsgroups that are available on your news server, as shown in Figure 12-2.

Figure 12-2:
Outlook
Express
displays a
list of
newsgroups.

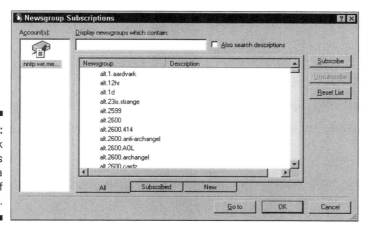

You can scroll through this list to find the newsgroup you want to access, but that will take awhile: On most servers, the list contains thousands of servers. (Mine lists more than 43,000.)

4. **Type a word or phrase in the Display Newsgroups Which Contain text box.**

For example, to find newsgroups that pertain to *Star Trek,* type **startrek** in the text box. Outlook Express narrows the newsgroup listing to just those newsgroups that contain the word or phrase you typed, as shown in Figure 12-3. (It may take a few moments for Outlook Express to find the newsgroups you requested. Be patient.)

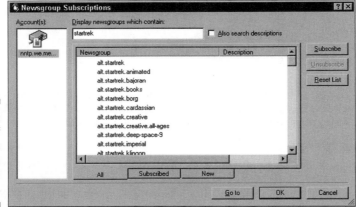

Figure 12-3:
A list of
newsgroups
that contain
the word
startrek.

You may have to try several different spellings of the word or words you are looking for. Or, if you are looking for two words (such as Star Trek), try the words mushed together or separated with periods (for example, try both **startrek** and **star.trek**).

5. **Click the newsgroup you want to read and then click Go To.**

The newsgroup opens. You may have to wait a few moments while Outlook Express downloads the subject headers for the newsgroup.

When you arrive at a newsgroup, Outlook Express displays a list of the messages that are currently available on the newsgroup, as shown in Figure 12-4. You can sort the message list by subject, author, or date by clicking the appropriate header above each column. The bottom portion of the Outlook Express window shows a preview of the currently selected message.

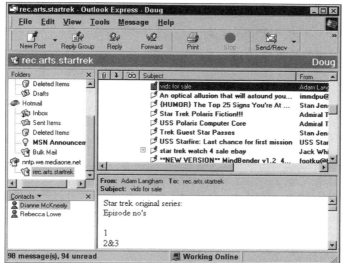

Figure 12-4:
A
newsgroup.

Subscribing to a Newsgroup

If you find a newsgroup that you want to visit frequently, you should subscribe to it. *Subscribing* to a newsgroup adds the newsgroup to a list of newsgroups that appears in the folders list at the left side of the Outlook Express
window — so you can access it quickly.

To subscribe to a newsgroup, find the newsgroup you want to subscribe to
following the procedure described in the section "Accessing Newsgroups"
earlier in this chapter. Click the newsgroup in the list of newsgroups to select
it and then click the Subscribe button. Or just double-click the newsgroup
you want to subscribe to.

After you have subscribed to a newsgroup, that newsgroup appears along
with any other newsgroups you have subscribed to when you click the Read
News link in the main Outlook Express window, as shown in Figure 12-5.

You can call up the list of newsgroup subscriptions shown in Figure 12-5 at
any time by clicking the name of the news server that appears in the folder
tree at the left side of the Outlook Express window. Each newsgroup you've
subscribed to is listed in the folder tree beneath the news server. Just
double-click a newsgroup in the folder tree to go directly to that newsgroup.

First come, first server

If you use more than one news server, the servers appear in the folders list at the left side of the Outlook Express window. To switch to another news server, just click its icon. Each news server has a different set of newsgroups, so some newsgroups may not be available on every server.

If you need to configure Outlook Express to work with a different news server, choose Tools⇨Accounts and click the News tab. You can find buttons that enable you to add a new server, delete a server, or change the properties of a server.

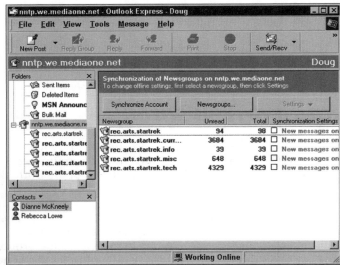

Figure 12-5:
Newsgroups you have sub-scribed to.

You can also view a list of subscribed newsgroups by clicking the Newsgroups button and then clicking the Subscribed tab that appears at the bottom of the dialog box that appears. From this dialog box, you can then remove a newsgroup from your subscription list by selecting the newsgroup and clicking the Unsubscribe button.

Reading Threads

A *thread* is a newsgroup article plus any articles that were posted as replies to the original article, articles posted as replies to the replies, and so on. Outlook Express groups together all the articles that belong to a thread. A plus sign next to a message title indicates that the article has replies.

To expand a thread, click the plus sign that appears next to the article. You see all the replies to the articles, as well as replies to the replies, replies to the reply replies, and so on. The plus sign on the original message turns into a minus sign to indicate that you are seeing an expanded thread.

To collapse the thread — that is, to hide all replies and list only the original message — click the minus sign.

Reading an Article

To read an article, double-click the article's title. The article appears in a separate window, as shown in Figure 12-6. After you finish reading the article, click the article window's Close button to close the window.

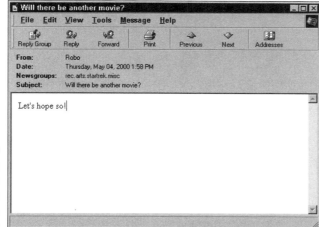

Figure 12-6:
A
newsgroup
article.

To save an article to your computer, choose File⇨Save As or click the Save button. Then, select the folder you want to save the article in and the format (you can save it as a newsgroup message or as a plain text file) and click Save.

To print an article, choose File⇨Print or click the Print button.

You can go to the next or previous articles by clicking the following buttons:

   ✔ Read the next article

   ✔ Read the previous article

Replying to an Article

To reply to a newsgroup posting, follow these steps:

1. **Count to ten and then reconsider your reply.**

   Keep in mind that replying to a newsgroup is not like replying to e-mail. Only the intended recipient can read an e-mail reply. Anyone on the planet can read your newsgroup postings. If you don't really have anything to add to the discussion, why waste your time?

2. **After reading the article you want to reply to, click the Reply to Group button in the toolbar.**

   A new message window appears with the subject line already filled in.

3. **Type your reply.**

4. **Click the Send button.**

   Your article is posted to the newsgroup.

5. **You've become a published writer.**

By default, the complete text of the original message is added to the end of your reply. If the message is long, you may want to delete some or all of the original text. If you don't want the original message text to be automatically added to your replies, choose Tools⇨Options, click the Send tab, and deselect the Include Message in Reply option.

Déjà vu all over again

If you hang around newsgroups long enough, sooner or later you're going to want to find a newsgroup post that you remember seeing way back when. Or maybe one of your friends will tell you that he saw a really great post on a newsgroup last year that you should check out. Unfortunately, because news servers do not have unlimited amounts of disk storage, they periodically delete older newsgroup posts. So that old message you want to retrieve may not be available on your news server.

The good news is that you can find a huge archive of old newsgroup postings at Deja.com.

At the time I wrote this, Deja.com's archive held more than 300 million posts from over 45,000 newsgroups, dating back to March of 1995. The only thing Deja.com does not archive is binary attachments. So you can't use Deja.com to retrieve pictures, videos, and other binary posts.

To use Deja.com, just point Internet Explorer to www.deja.com/usenet. You can then search Deja.com's archives for newsgroup messages by keywords in the message subject, the newsgroup name, the author of the message, and the date the message was posted.

If you want to reply to several specific points of an article, you can intermingle your responses with the original message. The original message appears after greater-than signs, setting it off from your insightful responses.

If you want to send a private e-mail reply directly to the author of a newsgroup article rather than post your reply to the entire newsgroup, click the Reply button rather than the Reply Group button.

Writing a New Article

When you have finally mustered the courage to post an article of your own to a newsgroup, follow these steps:

1. **Open the newsgroup in which you want to post a new article.**

2. **Click the New Post button.**

   A new message window appears.

3. **Type a subject for the article in the Subject box.**

   Make sure that the subject you type accurately reflects the topic of the article — or prepare to get flamed. (Being *flamed* doesn't mean that your computer screen actually emits a ball of fire in your direction, singeing the hair off your forearm. It refers to getting an angry — even vitriolic — response from a reader.) If your subject line is misleading, at least one Internet user is sure to chew you out for it.

4. **Type your message in the message area.**

5. **If you're worried about your vice-presidential prospects, click the Spelling button.**

   If clicking buttons makes you dizzy, choose Tools⇨Spelling instead. Either way, the spell checker dutifully examines each and every word in your message to find any potentially embarrassing misspellings, giving you the opportunity to correct your boo-boos. (For more information about spell checking in Outlook Express, refer to Chapter 8.)

6. **Click the Send button when you're satisfied with your response.**

Using Stationery and HTML Formatting

Just as it does with e-mail, Outlook Express allows you to create fancy stationery and HTML formatting options for your newsgroup postings. Stationery and HTML formatting let you create messages with fancy background designs, use fonts for your text, and add emphasis with bold, italic, or colored text and more.

The procedure for creating stationery for newsgroup articles is the same as the procedure for e-mail messages, so I humbly refer you back to Chapter 9 for the steps required to do so.

Dealing with Attachments

Originally, Internet newsgroups did not allow you to include binary files (such as programs, pictures, and sound files) in newsgroup postings. Internet users are very resourceful, however, and they long ago figured out a way to get around this dilemma. They invented a technique, called *encoding,* that converts a nontext file into a series of text codes that you can post as a newsgroup article. Such an article looks completely scrambled when you see it. However, you can save the article to a file on your hard drive and then run the saved file through a special decoding program that converts it back to its original form — whether it's a program, picture, or sound file.

With Outlook Express, the decoding routine is built in, so you don't need a separate program. All you have to do is open the message. If the message contains an image attachment, the image is decoded and displayed right in the body of the message. Other types of attachments (such as sounds) display an icon in the Attach line above the message body. Double-click the icon to play the attachment.

To save a binary file that has been attached to a newsgroup article, right-click the icon in the Attach line that appears above the message body, and then choose the Save As command that appears in the pop-up menu. A Save As dialog box appears. Choose the folder where you want to save the file and then click Save.

Some attachments are too large to be posted in a single message. Instead, the binary attachment is broken apart and posted to several messages. Outlook Express lets you combine and decode such messages to re-create the attachment. Just follow these steps:

1. **Hold down the Shift key and click each of the messages that contains a part of the attachment.**

   You can usually tell which messages contain a split-up attachment by looking at the message subjects. For example, if you see a series of messages with subjects such as "monkey.mpg [01/04]," "monkey.mpg [02/04]," and so on, each of the messages contain one part of a four-part attachment. Hold down the Shift key and select all four of the messages.

2. **Choose <u>M</u>essage⇨Com<u>b</u>ine and Decode.**

   A dialog box similar to the one in Figure 12-7 appears.

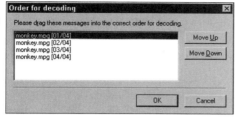

Figure 12-7:
Combining a
multi-
message
attachment.

3. **If necessary, adjust the order in which the messages are listed.**

   To move a message in the list, select the message you want to move and then click the Move Up or Move Down button.

4. **Click OK.**

   The messages are downloaded and combined. A dialog box is displayed to show the progress of the download.

5. **Get a cup of coffee.**

   The download may take a while.

6. **Save the attachment if you want.**

   Outlook Express displays the combined message when the download completes. You can then save the attachment by right-clicking the icon in the Attach line above the message body and choosing Save As from the menu that appears.

Working Offline

Outlook Express lets you access newsgroups you have subscribed to even when you're not connected to the Internet. To work offline, you should first set the synchronization settings for each of your subscribed newsgroups. To do so, click your news server in the Folders pane to display the newsgroups you have subscribed to (refer to Figure 12-5).

To set the synchronization setting for a newsgroup, first click the newsgroup to select it. Then, click the Settings button and choose one of the four options that appear:

   ✔ **Don't Synchronize:** Doesn't download messages for offline reading. Select this option if you do not want to synchronize the newsgroups for offline reading.

   ✔ **All Messages:** Downloads all articles for the newsgroup.

✔ **New Messages Only:** Downloads only those articles that have been posted to the newsgroup since you last synchronized.

✔ **Headers Only:** Downloads the message headers but not the text of the articles. If you select this option, you won't be able to read the articles offline because you have not downloaded the article bodies.

After you've selected the synchronization settings you want to use, click the Synchronize Account button to download the newsgroup articles from your news server. You can then disconnect from the Internet and read the articles offline.

If you decide to reply to any articles or post new articles, click the Synchronize Account button again. Outlook Express connects to the Internet and posts your articles.

Part IV
Customizing Your Explorations

The 5th Wave · By Rich Tennant

"No Stuart, I won't look up 'rampaging elephants' on the Internet. We're studying plant life and right now photosynthesis is a more pertinent topic."

In this part . . .

This is the part to turn to when you're tired of working with Internet Explorer the way it runs out-of-the-box and you want to customize it to more closely suit your working style. These chapters show you how to customize Internet Explorer's toolbars, start page, and other options, how to set up parental controls to ensure that your kids have a safe and sane Internet experience, how to use Internet Explorer's security options, and how to create a login script so that you won't have to type your user ID and password every time you connect to the Internet.

Chapter 13

Doing It Your Way: Personalizing Internet Explorer

In This Chapter

▶ Customizing the toolbars
▶ Fiddling with options
▶ Personalizing your home page

*I*nternet Explorer 5.5 has a bushel of configuration options that affect the way you browse the World Wide Web. Of course, Internet Explorer can't help you with your *real* preferences, such as playing golf instead of toiling with your computer. But you can do stuff that's almost as much fun, such as rearranging the buttons on the toolbar, changing the colors used to display links you already visited, or personalizing your default start page.

Read this chapter after you become comfortable with the out-of-the-box version of Internet Explorer and you're ready to find out what all those options really do. This chapter describes the most useful options, but more importantly, it tells you which options you can safely ignore so that you (unlike some people I know — me, for example) can catch up on your golf.

Note: I am aware, of course, that for some people golf is a more frustrating pastime than using your computer. And for some, golf is more boring than reading the online help feature of Internet Explorer. If you're one of those poor, unenlightened souls, feel free to substitute your favorite non-golf pastime — and may I recommend *Golf For Dummies,* 2nd Edition, by Gary McCord (published by IDG Books Worldwide, Inc.)?

Toiling with the Toolbars

Internet Explorer includes four built-in toolbars, which contain helpful buttons that let you perform common tasks. The four toolbars are as follows:

✔ **Standard Buttons:** Displays buttons for navigating the Internet, stopping long downloads, going back to your home page, and so on.

✔ **Address:** Includes a field in which you can type a Web address and the Go button, which you click to go to a Web page.

✔ **Links:** Contains buttons that you can click to quickly call up your favorite Web pages.

✔ **Radio:** Includes controls for listing to online radio broadcasts.

The following sections show you how to show or hide any of these toolbars in Internet Explorer and how to change the buttons that appear on the Standard Buttons toolbar.

Playing hide and seek with the toolbars

Normally, Internet Explorer displays the Standard Buttons, Address, and Links toolbars on separate lines at the top of the screen and hides the Radio toolbar until you need it. This default arrangement of toolbars takes up a lot of screen space. Fortunately, Internet Explorer lets you hide the toolbars that you don't use or rearrange the toolbars into a less intrusive arrangement. For example, if you never use the Links toolbar, you can hide it, leaving more room on your screen to view Web pages.

To show or hide a toolbar, follow these steps:

1. Choose the View⇨Toolbars command.

The Toolbars menu appears, as shown in Figure 13-1. A check mark appears next to the toolbars, which are currently visible.

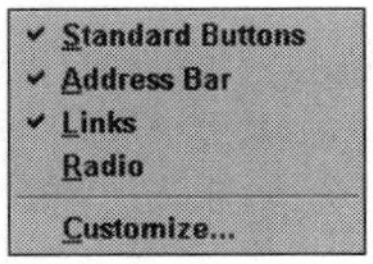

Figure 13-1:
The
Toolbars
menu.

✔ Standard Buttons
✔ Address Bar
✔ Links
  Radio

  Customize...

2. Click the menu option for the toolbar that you want to show or hide.

If the toolbar is visible, clicking the menu option makes it disappear. Likewise, if the toolbar is hidden, clicking the menu option makes it reappear.

Here are a few points to ponder when you play hide and seek with toolbars:

✔ If you don't like the position of the toolbars at the top of the Internet Explorer window, you can rearrange them by dragging the Move Handle, the vertical bar that appears near the left edge of each toolbar.

✔ You can arrange toolbars so that they are side-by-side rather than on top of each other. Just grab the Move Handle of one of the toolbars and then drag that toolbar on top of one of the other toolbars. You can also drag the Move Handle left or right to adjust how much of each toolbar is visible in a side-by-side arrangement.

Figure 13-2 shows how I like to arrange the toolbars when I use Internet Explorer. As you can see, I've placed all three toolbars side-by-side to free up more room to view Web pages. The Standard toolbar buttons I use most are visible on the left, the Address toolbar is in the middle, and the Links toolbar is squeezed in on the right.

✔ Another way to summon the Toolbars menu is to right-click on any visible toolbar.

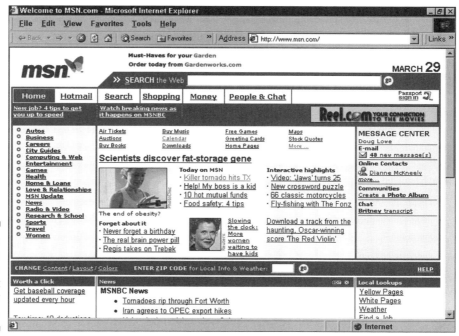

Figure 13-2:
One way to arrange the Internet Explorer toolbars.

Customizing the Standard Buttons toolbar

The good people at Microsoft who created Internet Explorer did their best to anticipate which buttons you would use most, putting those buttons in plain view on the Standard Buttons toolbar. However, after stuffing the Standard Button toolbar to the gills with buttons, they had a few buttons left over that they didn't know what to do with. So they decided to throw them into a Customize Toolbar dialog box, which you can use to add extra buttons to your Standard Toolbar if you wish.

Table 13-1 lists the extra buttons that you can add to the Standard Buttons toolbar. Note that the first four buttons — Up, Map Drive, Disconnect, and Folders — are useful when you use Internet Explorer to browse folders on your hard drive or a network server.

Table 13-1		Extra Buttons You Can Add to the Standard Buttons Toolbar
Button	**Name**	**What It Does**
	Up	Moves up one level when you are navigating folders on your hard drive or on an FTP server.
	Map Drive	Lets you assign a drive letter to a folder on a network file server.
	Disconnect	Disconnects a mapped network drive.
	Folders	Shows a tree-like display of folders in the left portion of the Internet Explorer display.
	Full Screen	Switches to full-screen view.
	Size	Lets you select the size used to display text on Web pages.
	Cut	Cuts the selected portion of the Web page to the clipboard.
	Copy	Copies the selected portion of the Web Page to the clipboard.
	Paste	Pastes the contents of the clipboard at the current cursor position.
	Encoding	Lets you select a different language.

Button	Name	What It Does
![Print Preview icon]	Print Preview	Lets you preview how a page will appear when printed before sending the page to the printer.
![Related icon]	Related	Automatically searches for Web pages on related topics.

To add these buttons to your Standard Buttons toolbar, follow these steps:

1. **Summon the View⇨Toolbars⇨Customize command.**

   The Customize Toolbar dialog box appears, as shown in Figure 13-3. The right side of this dialog box shows the buttons that are already contained in your Standard Buttons toolbar. The left side of the dialog box lists the extra buttons that you can add.

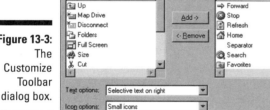

Figure 13-3:
The
Customize
Toolbar
dialog box.

2. **Click the button you want to add in the Available Toolbar Buttons list on the left side of the Customize Toolbar dialog box.**

3. **Click the button in the Current Toolbar Buttons list that you want to insert the button you selected in Step 2 next to.**

   If you want the button you selected in Step 2 to be the last button in the toolbar, click Separator at the very bottom of the Current Toolbar Buttons list.

4. **Click Add.**

   The button that you selected in Step 2 is removed from the Available Toolbar Buttons list and added to the Current Toolbar Buttons list above the button you selected in Step 3.

5. **Repeat Steps 2 through 4 to add more buttons.**

   Add all the buttons if you want.

6. After you finish, click Close.

The Customize Toolbar dialog box is dismissed.

Here are a few additional thoughts about the Customize Toolbar dialog box:

✔ You can remove buttons from the Standard Buttons toolbar by selecting the button that you want to remove in the Current Toolbar Buttons list and clicking Remove. The button is removed from the Current Toolbar Buttons list and added to the Available Toolbar Buttons list.

✔ If you get your toolbar all jumbled up, you can restore it to its original, pristine condition by clicking Reset.

✔ You can use the Move Up and Move Down buttons to rearrange the order in which the toolbar buttons appear. Just select the button you want to move in the Current Toolbar Buttons list and then click Move Up or Move Down to change the button's position.

✔ If you have a lot of buttons on your toolbar, you can insert one or more separator lines to visually divide the buttons into groups. The Separator is listed at the top of the Available Toolbar Buttons list. You can add it to the toolbar the same way that you add a button.

✔ You can use the Text Options and Icon Options controls to change the way the toolbar buttons appear. The Text Options control lets you select whether descriptive text appears below each button, to the right of just certain buttons, or not at all. And the Icon Options control lets you choose whether to display small or large buttons.

Tweaking Internet Explorer's Options

Internet Explorer has about a gazillion options that let you customize everything from what color hyperlinks appear in to whether you want to allow Java programs to run on your computer. You can access all of these options by selecting the Tools⇨Internet Options command. Be prepared, however. The Tools⇨Internet Options command summons a killer dialog box that has tabs out the wazoo (whatever a *wazoo* is). Each of the tabs has a set of controls. To switch from one tab to another, just click the tab label at the top of the dialog box.

Here's the lowdown on the six tabs that appear in the Internet Options dialog box:

✔ **General:** Contains options that affect the general operation of Internet Explorer.

✔ **Security:** Enables you to indicate whether you want to be warned before doing something that may jeopardize your security. (See Chapter 15.)

✔ **Content:** Enables you to filter out pages with questionable content. (See Chapter 14.)

✔ **Connections:** Indicates which dial-up connection to use to establish a connection to the Internet.

✔ **Programs:** Enables you to indicate which programs to use to read Internet mail and newsgroups and do other necessary chores.

✔ **Advanced:** Holds a number of options that just didn't fit anywhere else.

To set any of the preceding options, follow this general procedure:

1. **Choose Tools⇨Internet Options.**

   The Internet Options dialog box appears.

2. **Click the tab that contains the option that you want to set.**

   If you're not sure which tab to click, just cycle through all the tabs until you find what you're looking for.

3. **Set the options however you want.**

   Most of the options are simple check boxes that you click to select or deselect. Some require that you select a choice from a drop-down list, and some have the audacity to require that you actually type something as proof of your keyboard proficiency.

4. **Repeat Step 3 until you've exhausted your options (or yourself).**

   You can set more than one option with a single use of the Tools⇨Internet Options command.

5. **Click OK.**

   You're done!

The following sections explain the options that appear on each of the tabs in the Options dialog box.

Saluting the General options

Back in the days of Internet Explorer 1.0, the options on the General tab were lowly Private options. But they reenlisted for version 2.0 and eventually decided to become Career options. Now, with Internet Explorer 5.5, they boast the rank of General. I suggest you snap-to whenever you call up these options, which are shown in Figure 13-4.

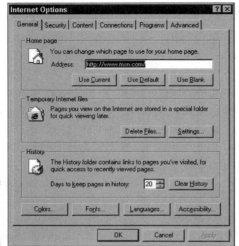

Figure 13-4:
The General
options.

The General options comprise the following three categories:

- ✔ **Home Page:** Enables you to set the location of the page that displays when you first start Internet Explorer or when you click the Home button. For example, if the only Internet site you're really interested in is David Letterman's Top Ten List, you can set the Top Ten List site to be your home page.

  The easiest way to set your home page is to first navigate your way to the page that you want to use as your home page. Then call up Tools➪Internet Options and click the Use Current button. For more information about changing your home page, see the section "Changing Your Home Page."

- ✔ **Temporary Internet Files:** Lets you manage the temporary files that Internet Explorer downloads to your hard drive. Whenever you visit a Web page, Internet Explorer keeps a copy of the page and any graphics that appear on the page in a special folder on your hard drive. That way, if you revisit the same page, Internet Explorer can quickly retrieve the information from your hard drive rather than from the Internet.

  You can click the Settings button to bring up the dialog box shown in Figure 13-5. This dialog box lets you change how often Internet Explorer should check for newer versions of pages stored in the temporary folder, how much space Internet Explorer is allowed to use for temporary files, and the location of the folder used to store temporary files.

  You can empty the Temporary Internet Files folder by clicking the Delete Files button. But be warned that deleting these files causes delays because Internet Explorer must then download files that were previously stored on your disk.

Figure 13-5:
The Settings
dialog
box for
temporary
Internet
files.

🮤 **History:** This option enables you to specify how many days of history information you want to retain. Also, you can click the Clear History button to remove all the files from the History folder.

The four buttons at the bottom of the General tab bring up dialog boxes that let you change several other aspects of how Internet Explorer works:

🮤 **Colors:** Lets you change the colors used to display text and hyperlinks

🮤 **Fonts:** Lets you change the default font used to display text

🮤 **Language:** Lets you specify which language to use for Web pages that display information in two or more languages

🮤 **Accessibility:** Allows you to force Internet Explorer to use the colors and font selections you made via the Color and Fonts buttons

Serenading the Security options

Figure 13-6 shows the Security options, which are designed to protect you from Internet sites that contain offensive content, to protect your privacy, and to warn you about potential security problems. To bring up these options, you can click the Security tab at the top of the Internet Options dialog box.

For complete information about how to use these options, refer to Chapter 15.

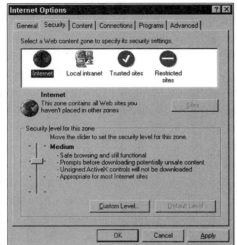

Figure 13-6:
The Security
options.

Cruising with the Content options

The Content tab lets you fiddle with the Internet Explorer Content Advisor,
which is designed to block access to offensive Web sites. Figure 13-7 shows
the Content options.

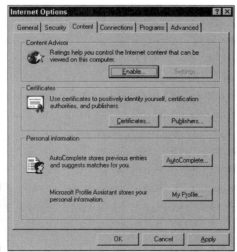

Figure 13-7:
The Content
options.

You can find a complete rundown on the Content Advisor in Chapter 14, so I
won't discuss it further here.

Cajoling the Connections options

The Connections options, shown in Figure 13-8, enable you to specify which dial-up connection you use to connect to the Internet. You may find yourself turning to this tab frequently if you have more than one Internet service provider and you often switch from one to another. You should also visit this tab if you decide to change providers.

Figure 13-8:
The
Connections
options.

If you've yet to create a dial-up connection for your Internet provider, click the Add button. The Make a New Connection Wizard comes to life to create a connection for you after you answer basic questions, such as the phone number you dial and your user ID.

If more than one connection is listed in the Connections options, choose the connection that you want to use when you access the Internet. You can use the buttons beneath this list box to create an additional connection (Add), delete an existing connection (Remove), or modify an existing connection (Settings).

Perusing the Programs options

The Programs tab, shown in Figure 13-9, contains options that enable you to tell Internet Explorer what programs you want to use to read your e-mail, access newsgroups, and handle Internet calls. The default settings are Outlook Express for e-mail and news and Microsoft NetMeeting for Internet calls.

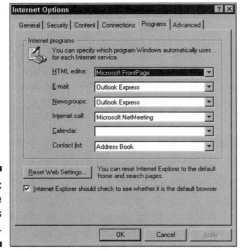

Figure 13-9:
The
Programs
options.

The other settings on the Programs tab enable you to choose the program to use for Internet phone calls, your Calendar, and Address Book. You should leave these settings alone.

Achieving Advanced options

The Advanced options, shown in Figure 13-10, enable you to set several features that govern Internet Explorer's operation. Wow, there are a lot of options in this dialog box! So many, in fact, that Microsoft uses an unusual method of enabling you to set them. Rather than spew a bunch of check boxes onto the Advanced options dialog box, all the options are shown in a big scrollable list box. To set any of the options, scroll down the list until you find the option you want to set and then click the option.

The Advanced options fall into the following categories:

- **Accessibility:** Options that make Internet Explorer easier to use for those users with disabilities.

- **Browsing:** These options control basic aspects of how the Internet Explorer browser works, such as whether it uses the AutoComplete feature to finish typing Web addresses for you and whether it uses fancy smooth scrolling. (If you have a slower computer, you may want to disable smooth scrolling.)

- **HTTP 1.1 settings:** Steer clear of these options unless you know what HTTP 1.1 is and know you want to use it.

✔ **Microsoft VM:** If you're a Java guru, you may want to look at these options. Otherwise, try not to step in them.

✔ **Multimedia:** You can indicate whether graphics, sounds, and video are downloaded automatically whenever you go to a Web page. Disabling any or all of these options improves Internet Explorer's performance over phone-line connections.

✔ **Printing:** Enables you to include background colors and textures when you print a Web page. If you have a color printer, this option can be nice. But otherwise, you should leave it off. (In fact, you should probably leave it off even if you have a color printer unless you want each page to be filled with the background color. Expect to go through a lot of ink cartridges if you turn this option on.)

✔ **Search from the Address bar:** These options let you configure Internet Explorer so that if you type an Internet address that doesn't exist, Internet Explorer can look for other similar addresses using different domain suffixes. For example, if you type www.whitehouse.com, Internet Explorer can automatically find the White House for you by using the correct address, which is www.whitehouse.gov.

✔ **Security:** Yep, there are still more security options that didn't fit in the Security tab. Fortunately, you don't have to worry about them.

If you mess up the Advanced options settings, you can restore them all to their original factory settings by clicking Restore Defaults.

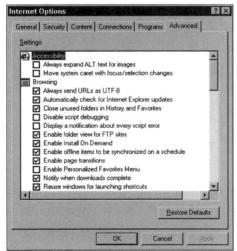

Figure 13-10:
The
Advanced
options.

Changing Your Home Page

Your *home page* is the page that Internet Explorer automatically displays each time you begin an exploration of the World Wide Web. This section shows you how to designate any page on the Web as your home page.

Note: Your Internet Explorer home page is not the same as a home page that you can set up for other Web users to see. When you designate a page as your Internet Explorer home page or if you customize your home page, only *you* can see the home page and the custom options that you select. If you want to create a home page that other Web users can see, you must make arrangements with your Internet service provider to place your home page on its Web server.

A home page is often referred to as a *portal,* because it is the page from which you access the rest of the Internet.

Normally, Internet Explorer defaults to msn.com (www.msn.com) as its home page. If you obtain your copy of Internet Explorer from a company other than Microsoft, Internet Explorer may be configured with a different home page. Whatever your home page currently is, Internet Explorer enables you to designate *any* page on the Web as the first one you see.

The home page is also the page that pops up when you click the Home button on the Standard toolbar.

To change your home page, follow these steps:

1. **Navigate your way to the page you want to use as your new home page.**

   See Chapter 3 for details about getting around on the Web.

2. **Choose View⇨Internet Options.**

   The Internet Options dialog box appears (refer to Figure 13-4).

3. **Click the Use Current button.**

   The home page is now set to the current page.

4. **Click OK to dismiss the Internet Options dialog box.**

   You're done!

You can change back to the default home page by choosing View⇨ Internet Options and clicking the Use Default button. And if you prefer to have no home page at all, click Use Blank. That way, Internet Explorer simply displays a blank page when you start it.

If you can't find a Web page that you want to use as your home page, you can always create your own home page. Just use FrontPage Express to create a Web page that contains links to the pages you visit most often along with any other information you want to appear on your home page. Save this page to your computer's hard drive. Then call up the View⇨Internet Options command to set the home page to the page you created. (For more information about using FrontPage Express, see Chapter 18.)

Customizing msn.com

One of the great things about the msn.com (www.msn.com) home page is that you can customize it to include information that you're interested in seeing every time you access the Internet. For example, you can add or delete sports scores, daily news, weather reports, hyperlinks to your favorite Internet locations, and other useful information.

This section shows you how to customize msn.com to include just the information you want to see. If you choose to use some page other than msn.com as your home page, you can skip the rest of this chapter.

Information you can add

Microsoft designed the msn.com home page to be the ideal jumping-off point to other information on the Internet. The msn.com home page is filled with links to other useful msn.com pages as well as a search box that lets you find Web pages on any subject imaginable.

However, the msn.com home page is more than a search service and a collection of links: The msn.com home page has snippets of useful information, such as the major news headlines of the day, current stock quotes, sports scores, and so on. Microsoft refers to these snippets as *clips*.

Clips are what enable you to create your own customized msn.com home page. The generic msn.com home page — the one you see by default when you visit www.msn.com — has just a few clips on it: Today on MSN, E-mail & Chat, News, and Personal Finance. However, you can create your own customized version of the msn.com home page by adding additional clips of your own choosing.

In all, you have about 90 clips to choose from when creating your own personalized msn.com home page. The following is a list of some of the clips you can include when you personalize your msn.com home page:

✔ **Today on MSN:** Shows the day's top news stories as well as great bargains for online shopping and new programs you can download.

✔ **Business & Careers:** For the latest business news from the likes of *Forbes* and *The Wall Street Journal*.

✔ **Computing & Web:** Get the latest technology news from sources, such as Computing Central, Microsoft TechNet, *Wired*, and more.

✔ **Daily Diversions:** Fun things to include on your page, such as a quote of the day and a daily horoscope.

✔ **Entertainment:** For fun and games, you can include MSN Gaming Zone, MSNBC Entertainment, MTV, and other entertainment features.

✔ **Health:** For health information, include MSNBC Health, the Mayo Clinic, and Prevention's Healthy Ideas.

✔ **Home and Family:** Include information for home and family from sources, such as MSN HomeAdvisor, Disney's Family.com, and Parent Soup.

✔ **Local information:** If you provide your zip code, your home page can include local information, such as a local weather forecast and local news headlines. You can also include the Sidewalk City Guide for your favorite city.

✔ **News:** You can display news headlines from online news services, such as MSNBC, CBS, CNN, Fox News, and more.

✔ **People & Chat:** You can include a link to Hotmail, MSN's free e-mail service, on your msn.com home page as well as links to several popular MSN Chat rooms.

✔ **Personal Finance:** You can display quotes for specific stocks or stock indexes, as well as financial information from the likes of Charles Schwab, Forbes, and Merrill Lynch.

✔ **Radio & Video:** Listen to the radio or watch TV from your computer using sites, such as Yahoo! Broadcast (`www.broadcast.com`) or CBS Events.

✔ **Reference:** Get the information you need from reference sources, such as the Discovery Channel and Merriam-Webster.

✔ **Shopping:** Keep tabs on daily specials from MSN's online merchants.

✔ **Sports:** You can get sports news from sources, such as MSNBC Sports, CBS Sportsline, and Fox Sports, and include the latest scores for several popular sports (including baseball, football, hockey, and basketball) right on your MSN home page.

✔ **Travel:** Include travel information from Expedia.

✔ **Your links:** This section enables you to add up to four hyperlinks of your own to your home page.

Customizing your home page

Now that you know what clips are available, you're ready to create your own customized msn.com home page to add the information you're interested in. To do so, follow these steps:

1. **Go to the msn.com home page.**

   The address is `www.msn.com`. Just click the Home button.

2. **Click Change Content in the navigation bar.**

   The page illustrated in Figure 13-11 appears. You can do your home page customization from this page.

3. **Type your zip code in the Zip Code text box and select your time zone from the drop-down list.**

   Typing in your zip code enables msn.com to display local information, such as movie times and weather forecasts on your home page.

4. **To add a clip to your home page, click one of the categories that appears on the left side of the page and then click the check box for the clip that you want to include.**

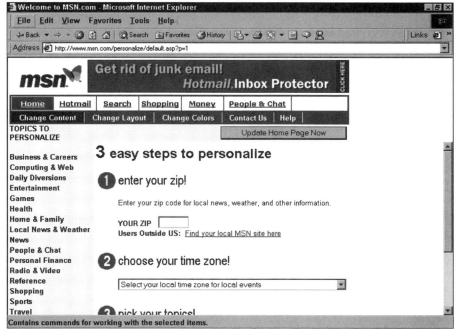

Figure 13-11:
Customizing
the
msn.com
home page.

When you select a category, one or more clip items will be displayed. For example, Figure 13-12 shows the clips that are available under the Business & Careers category. To add one or more of these clips to your msn.com home page, just click the appropriate check boxes.

5. **To change the order in which your items appear on-screen, click Change Layout in the navigation bar near the top of the screen.**

   The page shown in Figure 13-13 appears.

6. **Select one of the clips listed in the Content column. Then click the up or down arrow in the Position column to change the position of the clip on your home page.**

7. **When you are finished making changes, click the Update Home Page Now button.**

   Your custom msn.com home page is built for you with the features that you selected.

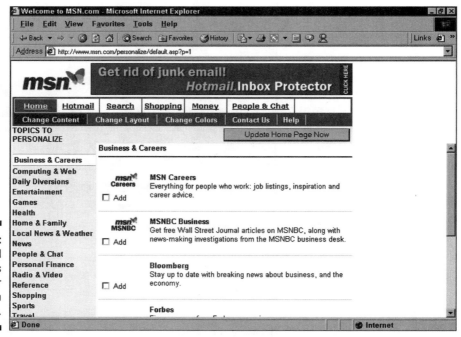

Figure 13-12: Add cool things to your msn.com home page.

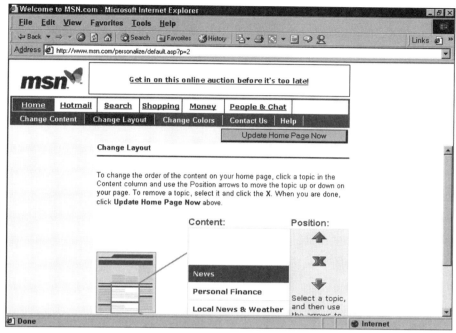

Figure 13-13:
Changing
the layout
of clips
on your
msn.com
home page.

Here are some topics to wonder about while you lay awake at night wondering about customizing your msn.com home page:

✔ When you customize your msn.com home page, the clips you select will be displayed only when you view the customized home page from the same computer that you used to customize the page. If you visit msn.com from someone else's computer, your personal settings will not be in effect.

✔ Another way to customize the msn.com home page is to scroll through your msn.com home page to a section that you want to customize and then click the Edit button that appears in the heading for that section. This action takes you directly to the part of the Personalize page that lets you customize that section.

✔ If you are unable to customize your msn.com home page, it could be because your security settings are too strict. Call up the Tools⇨ Internet Options command, click the Security tab, and set the Security level to Medium, Medium-Low, or Low.

Chapter 14

Using the Content Advisor to Make Sure That Your Kids Surf Safely

In This Chapter

▶ Determining your blush threshold

▶ Activating the Content Advisor feature of Internet Explorer

▶ Picking a secret password

▶ Requiring password access to restricted sites

*A*lthough the Internet can be a great resource for kids, it's also a notoriously unsafe place for kids to hang out unsupervised. For every museum, library, and government agency that springs up on the Internet, a corresponding adult bookstore or sex shop seems to appear. What's a parent to do?

Fortunately, Internet Explorer has a built-in feature called the *Content Advisor,* which enables you to restrict access to many off-color Internet sites. The Content Advisor uses a system of ratings similar to the ratings system used for motion pictures. Although this system isn't perfect, it goes a long way toward preventing your kids from stumbling into something that they shouldn't.

About Internet Ratings

Internet ratings work much like motion picture ratings: They let you know what kind of content you can expect at a given Internet site. The ratings are assigned voluntarily by the publisher of each individual Internet site.

Although motion picture ratings give you an overall rating for a movie (G, PG, PG-13, R, or NC-17), the ratings system doesn't give you a clue about *why* a movie receives a particular rating. For example, does a PG-13 rating mean that a movie is filled with foul language, almost-explicit sex, or excessive violence? It could be any of these — or all of them.

By contrast, Internet ratings give specific information about several categories of potentially offensive material. Several different ratings systems are currently being developed. The system that Internet Explorer uses was created by a nonprofit organization called the Recreational Software Advisory Council, or RSAC, and was originally designed for rating computer games.

When used to rate Internet sites, the RSAC rating system is sometimes referred to as RSAC*i* (the *i* stands for *Internet*). The RSAC*i* rating system is managed by a nonprofit organization known as the Internet Content Rating Association (also known as ICRA).

RSACi assigns a rating of 0 to 4 for each of the following four categories:

✔ Violence

✔ Nudity

✔ Sex

✔ Language

Table 14-1 shows the specific meaning for each rating number in an RSAC rating.

Table 14-1	What the RSAC Ratings Mean			
Rating	**Violence**	**Nudity**	**Sex**	**Language**
4	Rape or wanton, gratuitous violence	Frontal nudity (qualifying as a provocative display)	Explicit sexual acts or sex crimes	Crude, vulgar language or extreme hate speech
3	Aggressive violence or death to humans	Frontal nudity	Nonexplicit sexual acts	Strong language or hate speech
2	Destruction of realistic objects	Partial nudity	Clothed sexual touching	Moderate expletives or profanity

Rating	Violence	Nudity	Sex	Language
1	Injury to human being	Revealing attire	Passionate kissing	Mild expletives
0	None of the above or sports-related	None of the above	None of the above or innocent	None of the above

With Internet Explorer, you can set a threshold value for each of the four categories. If any attempt is made to access a Web site that has a rating higher than the threshold value, Internet Explorer blocks the user from viewing the Web site.

For more information about RSAC*i* ratings, check out the ICRA Web site at `www.icra.org`. Figure 14-1 shows the ICRA Web page, where you can learn more about RSAC; if you're a Web publisher, you can find out how to provide a rating for your site.

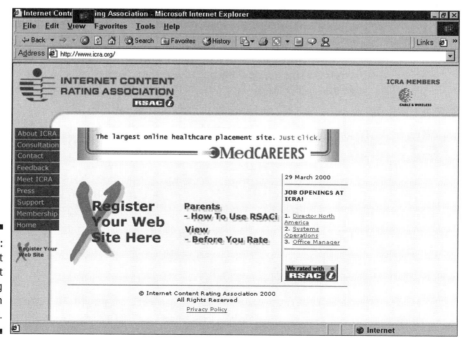

Figure 14-1: The Internet Content Rating Association home page.

Limitations of Internet Ratings

Before I show you how to activate and configure the Internet Explorer Content Advisor, I want to be sure that I don't lull you into a false sense of security, thinking that after you activate the Ratings feature, you won't have to worry about your kids getting into trouble on the Internet. Just to be sure, here are a few of the limitations of the RSAC rating system:

✔ Ratings are voluntary. Many sites are not rated at all. And for those sites that are rated, there is no guarantee that the Web site publisher has rated his or her site accurately.

✔ Internet Explorer's Ratings feature applies only to the World Wide Web. However, some of the nastiest Internet content is found not on the Web, but in Usenet newsgroups.

✔ Not all Web sites are rated. In fact, most are *not* rated. Internet Explorer enables you to either ban all unrated sites or allow full access to unrated sites. Neither option is good: If you ban unrated sites, you ban most of the Web. If you allow access to unrated sites, you let some garbage in. Sigh.

✔ Another area where kids get into trouble on the Internet is in chat rooms. Unfortunately, ratings do not apply to chat rooms.

✔ Kids are clever, and you can rest assured that some kids figure out a way to bypass the ratings feature altogether. No security system is totally secure.

Activating the Content Advisor

When you first install it, Internet Explorer does not check for Web site ratings. To screen out offensive Web sites, you must first activate the Content Advisor. Just follow these steps:

1. **Choose <u>V</u>iew⇨Internet <u>O</u>ptions.**

   The Internet Options dialog box appears.

2. **Click the Content tab.**

   The Content options dialog box appears, as shown in Figure 14-2.

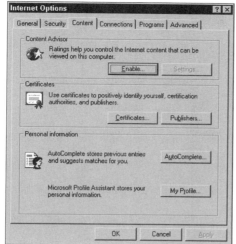

Figure 14-2:
The Content
options
dialog box.

3. **Click the Enable button in the Content Advisor area of the dialog box.**

   The Content Advisor dialog box appears, as shown in Figure 14-3.

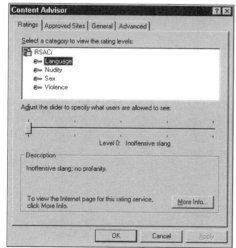

Figure 14-3:
The Content
Advisor
dialog box.

4. **Set the rating for each category by clicking the category and then
   adjusting the slider bar for the rating that you want to use.**

   Notice that a description of each rating level appears beneath the slider
   bar; this description changes as you move the slider bar.

5. **After you have set the ratings to appropriate levels for your kids, click OK.**

   Internet Explorer asks you to create a supervisor password by display-ing the dialog box shown in Figure 14-4.

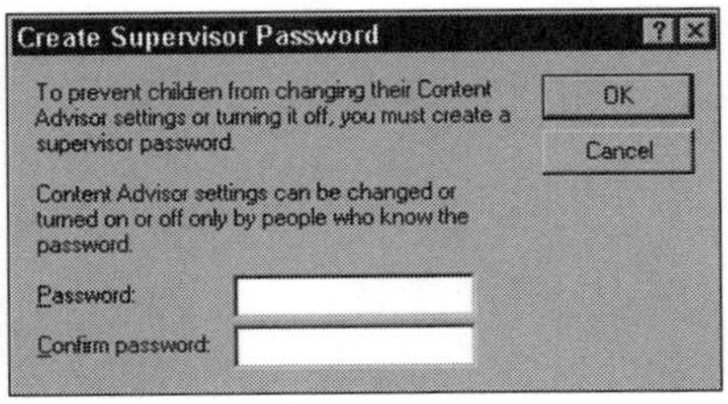

Figure 14-4:
The Create
Supervisor
Password
dialog box.

6. **Think up a good password.**

   Read the sidebar "Open sesame" later in this chapter for guidelines on creating a good password.

7. **Type the password twice.**

   The password is not displayed on-screen as you type it. Therefore, Internet Explorer requires you to type your password twice, just to make sure that you don't make a typing mistake. Type the password once in the Password text box and then type it again into the Confirm Password text box.

8. **Click OK.**

   The informative dialog box shown in Figure 14-5 appears.

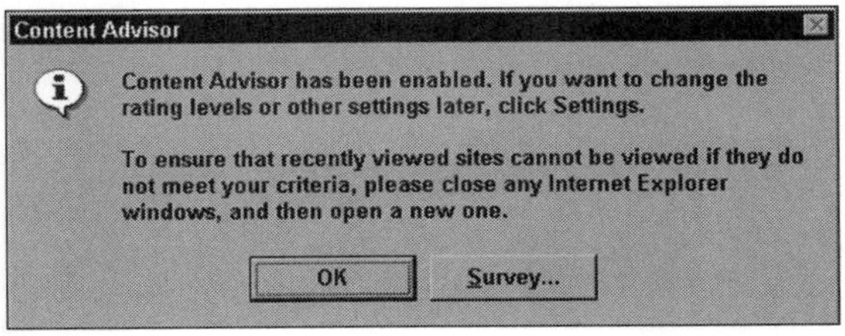

Figure 14-5:
Internet
Explorer
tells you
that the
Content
Advisor
has been
turned on.

9. **Click OK to return to the Internet Options dialog box; then click OK again to dismiss the dialog box.**

   Finally! You're finished!

After the Content Advisor is in place, the dialog box shown in Figure 14-6 appears whenever someone attempts to access a site that your ratings do not allow.

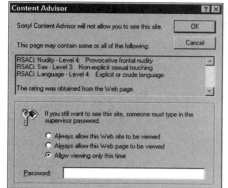

Figure 14-6:
Caught in
the act!

You can deactivate the Content Advisor at any time by calling up the Content options (choose View⇨Internet Options and then click the Content tab) and clicking the Disable Ratings button. You are, of course, required to enter your password in the process.

If you turn off the Content Advisor so that you (a consenting adult) can use Internet Explorer without restriction, don't forget to turn it back on after you're finished!

Open sesame

The Internet Ratings feature is only as good as the password you pick. Thus, you must make sure that you don't pick a password that your kids can easily figure out. Here are some passwords to avoid:

- Your name or your kids' names

- The names of your pets

- The name of your boat

- Your birthday or anniversary

- Your car license plate number

- The password you use to access the Internet

- Any other word or number that's important to you and that your clever kids could come up with on their own

The best passwords are random combinations of letters and numbers. Of course, these are also the hardest to memorize. Next best passwords are a combination of two or three randomly chosen words. Just flip open the dictionary to a random page, pick a short word on the page, and flip to another random page and pick another short word. Jam the words together to create your password.

Above all, do *not* write the password down on a stick-on note attached to the computer monitor! If you must write the password down, put it in a secure place where only *you* can find it.

Dealing with Unrated Sites

Internet ratings are a great idea. Unfortunately, not all the sites on the Net have yet rated themselves. When you enable the Content Advisor, Internet Explorer bans access not only to sites whose ratings are above the threshold you set, but also to any site that's not rated.

Fortunately, Internet Explorer enables you to ease the ban on unrated sites. Here's the procedure:

1. **Choose View⇨Internet Options and click the Content tab.**

   The Content options appear (refer to Figure 14-2).

2. **Click the Settings button.**

   You're asked for your password. Type the password and then click OK. The Content Advisor dialog box appears.

3. **Click the General tab.**

   You see the General Content Advisor options, as shown in Figure 14-7.

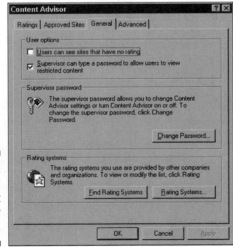

Figure 14-7:
The General
Content
Advisor
options.

4. **Check the Users Can See Sites That Have No Rating check box.**

5. **Click OK to dismiss the Content Advisor dialog box.**

   You return to the Internet Options dialog box.

6. **Click OK to dismiss the Internet Options dialog box.**

Now you can view unrated sites without the constant `Sorry! Your ratings do not allow you to see this site` message.

To restrict access to unrated sites once again, repeat the procedure, but check (rather than uncheck) the Users Can See Sites That Have No Rating check box in Step 4.

Note that the General tab of the Content Advisor dialog box also enables you to change the supervisor password. Simply click the Change Password button. A dialog box into which you can type a new password appears. (As before, you must type the password twice to make sure that you don't make any typing errors.)

You can disable the dialog box that allows a user to type the supervisor password to view a site that the Content Advisor has restricted by entering the supervisor password. Just uncheck the Supervisor Can Type a Password to Allow Users to View Restricted Content option.

Banning or Allowing Specific Sites

Internet Explorer 5.5 lets you control access to specific sites on a site-by-site basis using a feature known as *Approved Sites*. This enables you to ban access to a site that you find offensive, even if the site slips by the ratings that you have chosen for the Content Advisor. You can also allow access to a site that the Content Advisor might otherwise restrict if you find that the site is acceptable.

To ban or allow access to a site, follow these steps:

1. **Determine the Web address of the page or site you want to ban or approve.**

2. **Choose Tools⇨Internet Options and then click the Content tab.**

   The Content options are shown (refer to Figure 14-2).

3. **Click the Settings button in the Content Advisor section of the Options dialog box.**

   A dialog box appears, asking you to enter the Supervisor password.

4. **Type the password in the text box and then click OK.**

   The Content Advisor dialog box comes to life (refer to Figure 14-7).

5. **Click the Approved Sites tab.**

   This action takes you to the Approved Sites options shown in Figure 14-8.

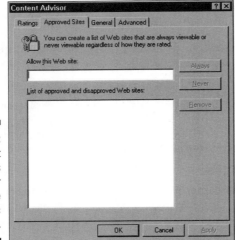

Figure 14-8:
Internet
Explorer lets
you ban or
approve
specific
sites.

6. **Type the address of the site you want to ban or approve in the Allow This Web Site text box.**

7. **Click the Always button to approve access to the site or click the Never button to ban access to the site.**

   The Web site is added to the list of banned or approved sites.

8. **Repeat Steps 6 and 7 for any other Web sites that you want to ban or approve.**

   You can also remove a Web site from the list of banned or approved sites by clicking the site you want to remove and then clicking the Remove button.

9. **Click OK to dismiss the Content Advisor dialog box.**

   You return to the Options dialog box.

10. **Click OK again to dismiss the Options dialog box.**

   You're done!

Chapter 15

Lowering the Cone of Silence: Using Internet Explorer's Security Features

In This Chapter

▶ Some security issues that you should worry about

▶ Working with secure sites

▶ Setting up the Internet Explorer security options

*I*f Internet Explorer had been designed by Maxwell Smart, Secret Agent 86 from the popular '60s television series *Get Smart*, it would have a Tools⇨Cone of Silence command that you could use whenever you were about to send private information over the Internet. Of course, the computer you were trying to send your private information to wouldn't be able to see the information either, just as the Chief could never hear what Max was saying whenever Max insisted that they use the Cone of Silence.

The Cone of Silence from *Get Smart* illustrates well the dilemma of Internet security: balancing usability with security. The more usable the Internet is, the less secure it is. The more secure we try to make the Internet, the less usable it becomes. The trick to Internet security is to use enough security features to give users confidence that private information (such as a credit card number) won't be intercepted by criminals over the Internet, but not so much security that users have to jump through hoops to access a simple Web page.

This chapter lays out the security features of Internet Explorer 5.5, which attempt to manage this balancing act for you.

Security Issues to Worry About

The following sections summarize the basic security issues that all Internet users are exposed to and should therefore be concerned about.

Sending information over the Internet

Suppose that you want to purchase something over the Internet. When you type your name, address, and credit card information in the online order form, that information is sent over the Internet to the Web site. Without the right security measures, it isn't difficult at all for criminals to intercept that information and steal your credit card number.

You shouldn't be overly alarmed about the risk of using your credit card over the Internet. After all, your credit card number can also be stolen if you use it over the phone, through the mail, or in person at a retail store. However, your credit card numbers can be stolen if you send them over the Internet without using proper security, so you should think twice before using your credit card when ordering products online.

Before you send your credit card number or any other information to a Web site, make sure that the Web site you are sending information to uses a security measure known as *SSL*. If the site doesn't, get the 800 number and phone in your order instead. For more information about SSL (such as how to tell if a Web site uses SSL), see the section "Scrambling: It's Not Just for Breakfast Anymore" later in this chapter.

Downloading programs over the Internet

A common danger when downloading a program over the Internet is that the program you download may not do what it claims to do. For example, instead of playing a game of chess, the program may instead erase everything on your hard disk. Or the program may plant a virus on your computer that can not only damage your computer but also infect other computers that are attached to a local area network or that you share disks with.

Internet Explorer uses a scheme known as *certification* to help prevent you from mistakenly downloading malicious programs. Check out the section "Certifying Your Security" later in this chapter for more information about how certification works.

Viewing Web pages that do more than meets the eye

In the early days of the World Wide Web, all a Web page could do was display information on your screen. Now, with programming tools, such as Java and ActiveX, and scripting languages, such as JavaScript and VBScript, a Web page can do more than display information: The page itself can act like a computer program. For the most part, this is good: It enables Web pages to come alive by displaying fancy animations and responding interactively to your mouse movements. But it also entails risk: An unscrupulous Web programmer can set up a Web page that displays a smiley face while it secretly erases files on your hard drive.

Preventing a Web page from doing damage is simple enough. The trick is to prevent a malicious Web page from doing damage without restricting a friendly Web page from doing good. Internet Explorer uses *security zones* to help manage the security restrictions that are placed on different Web sites. For more information, see the section "Zoning Out" later in this chapter.

Scrambling: It's Not Just for Breakfast Anymore

One of the most important methods of providing security on the Internet is to scramble information that is sent so that those who intercept the information cannot use it. Internet Explorer 5.5 uses the latest scrambling technology, known as *Secure Sockets Layer,* or *SSL.* SSL effectively scrambles your information before sending it over the Internet and unscrambles it at the other end. The scrambling is done in such a way that other users who might intercept your message cannot unscramble it.

With SSL, sending credit card numbers and other personal information over the Internet is safe — provided that the party to whom you are sending the private information also uses SSL. And herein lies the rub: Not everyone on the Internet is using SSL. So before you send any sensitive information over the Internet, make sure that the party you're sending the information to uses SSL to protect your data.

Most companies that are using SSL are happy to brag about the fact that they offer secure communications. For example, Figure 15-1 shows a page from the popular shopping site Amazon.com (`www.amazon.com`) that assures customers that they can safely place online orders without worrying about someone stealing their credit card numbers. Most sites that use SSL include similar pronouncements. If you don't see such an assurance, don't send sensitive information to the site.

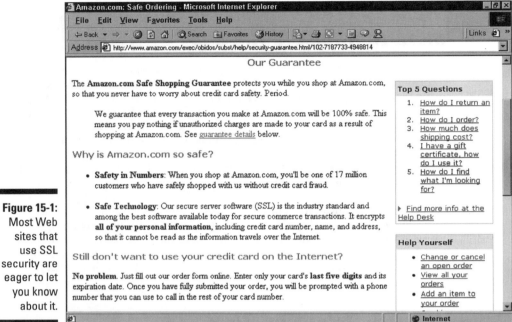

Figure 15-1:
Most Web sites that use SSL security are eager to let you know about it.

 Of course, any Web site can claim to use a secure connection without actually being secure. Fortunately, Internet Explorer helps you verify a Web site's security claim by displaying the dialog box shown in Figure 15-2 whenever you enter a secured site. In addition, a Lock icon (shown in the margin) is displayed in the status bar when you connect to a secure site. As long as the Lock icon is displayed, you can safely send credit card numbers and other private information over the Internet.

Figure 15-2:
Internet Explorer lets you know when you are entering a secure site.

Whenever you leave the protection of a secure site, Internet Explorer displays a similar dialog box informing you that you are about to leave the secure connection.

Do *not* send private information, such as credit card numbers, if the Lock icon does not appear in the status bar.

Zoning Out

One of the more useful security tricks of Internet Explorer is its ability to divide the Internet into different zones. Each zone enforces a different level of security procedures. Internet Explorer uses four basic security zones:

- ✔ **Local intranet:** If your computer is connected to a local area network (LAN), this zone encompasses files or Web pages that reside on the local network rather than on the Internet. Internet Explorer assumes that these Web pages are completely safe, so it imposes very few security precautions on pages that live in this zone.

- ✔ **Trusted sites:** This zone involves sites that you have deemed fully trustworthy. Security for sites in this zone is relaxed.

- ✔ **Restricted sites:** This zone comprises sites that you think are not safe. Whenever you enter a site that is in the restricted zone, Internet Explorer insists on lowering the Cone of Silence.

- ✔ **Internet:** This zone is for sites that you don't know whether or not you should trust. Internet Explorer imposes modest security restrictions for sites in the Internet zone.

When you first install Internet Explorer, both the Trusted Sites and Restricted Sites zones are empty. That means that every Internet site you visit is placed in the Internet zone, where modest security measures are imposed. If you decide that a site can be elevated to Trusted status or dumped in the Restricted sites zone, you must do so yourself.

To add a site to the Trusted sites or Restricted sites zone, complete the following steps:

1. **Choose the Tools⇨Internet Options command.**

   The Internet Options dialog box appears.

2. **Click the Security tab.**

   This displays the Security options, shown in Figure 15-3.

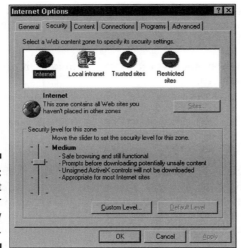

Figure 15-3:
The Internet
Explorer
Security
options.

3. **Click the icon for the zone you want to add a site to.**

4. **Click the Sites button.**

   This summons a dialog box that allows you add a Web site to the zone you selected in Step 3.

5. **Type the address of the page that you want to add to the zone.**

   Unfortunately, you have to type the full Internet address of the Web site you want to add to the zone. It would be nice if Internet Explorer would fill in the address of the page you were viewing when you called up the Security options, but it doesn't.

6. **Click the Add button.**

   The site you entered in Step 5 is added to the list of sites for the zone.

7. **Click OK.**

   This returns you to the Internet Options dialog box.

8. **Click OK.**

You can also use the dialog box that appears in Step 4 to remove a page from a security zone if you decide you misjudged the page.

Certifying Your Security

Another method Internet Explorer uses to ensure security is the use of certificates. A *certificate* is the computer equivalent of your driver's license. Certificates help guarantee that you are who you say you are and, more importantly, that the Web sites you send information to are what they say they are.

A complete explanation of how certificates work would span pages and require you to take a couple of Maalox before reading. But the basic concept is that an independent company, called a *certification authority,* issues two different types of certificates:

- ✔ **Personal:** This certificate identifies you so that you can access Web sites that require positive identification (such as banks that allow online transactions).

- ✔ **Sites:** These certificates ensure that the site you are visiting is not a fraud. Internet Explorer automatically checks site certificates to make sure that they're valid.

Internet Explorer has a very interesting dialog box that shows all the certificates you have accumulated during your Web explorations, as shown in Figure 15-4. You can get to this dialog box by summoning the Tools⇨ Internet Options command, clicking the Content tab, and then clicking the Certificates button. However, there's little reason to visit this dialog box, other than to brag about the number of certificates you have accumulated.

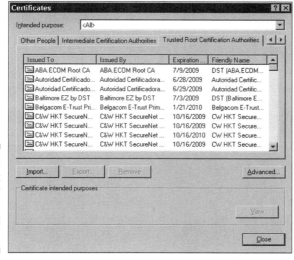

Figure 15-4:
Internet
Explorer
loves to
collect
certificates.

Security Options You Should Leave Alone

Thought you'd had your fill of security options? But wait, there's more. Figure 15-5 shows some additional security options you can get to by choosing the Tools⇨Internet Options command, clicking the Advanced tab, and scrolling down to the Security options section.

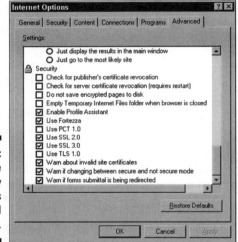

Figure 15-5:
Some
security
options
you should
leave alone.

You probably shouldn't mess with these security settings unless you have a Ph.D. in Advanced Computer Security and want to play. I show them here only so that you will know that if you happen to stumble into this dialog box, you should click Cancel as quickly as possible.

Chapter 16

Creating a Login Script

• •

In This Chapter

▶ Getting to know scripts

▶ Planning your own Dial-up Networking Script

▶ Creating a script file

▶ Using script commands

▶ Attaching a script to a connection

• •

*S*cripting is a feature of Windows Dial-up Networking support that I hope you don't have to use. It's the type of feature that requires you to don a pocket protector and assume the role of a computer geek. But after you have it set up, a Dial-up Networking Script can simplify your Internet sign-on procedures dramatically.

Scripting is designed for those users whose Internet service providers require them to go through a complicated login sequence whenever they access the Internet. If, when you dial up your ISP, a terminal window pops up and greets you with a message such as User-ID: and a cold, blinking cursor, then you should consider creating a Dial-up Networking Script. If your Internet service provider launches you straight into Internet Explorer, you can fall down on your knees, give thanks, and skip this chapter.

What Is a Dial-up Networking Script?

A *Dial-up Networking Script* is a special file that contains text and commands that are automatically typed in for you when you log in to a computer network. If the computer system you use to connect to the Internet requires you to manually enter information before it sends you to the Net, you can create a Dial-up Networking Script to automate the process.

Some Internet service providers display a terminal window similar to the one shown in Figure 16-1, in which you are required to enter your user ID and password. In some cases, you may also be required to choose which of the provider's several systems you need to log in to before you are connected to the Internet.

Figure 16-1:
Some
service
providers
require you
to sign in on
a screen
like this.

By using a script, you can have the computer do the typing for you. The script can wait for your provider to ask for your user ID and then type the user ID. Then it can wait for the password prompt and type your password. All you have to do is sit back and enjoy a sip of coffee while the script does all the work.

Unfortunately, you have to write the script yourself. The script is a simple text file that can be edited with ease, but it must contain certain commands, which I describe in the section "Working with Script Commands," later in this chapter. In addition, you have to attach the script to the Dial-Up Connection so that Windows knows to run your script when you dial in. I describe the procedure for attaching the script in the section "Attaching the Script to a Dial-Up Connection," later in this chapter.

Planning a Script

The first step in creating a script file is to plan the contents of the script. Get a piece of paper and label two columns *Computer Types* and *I Type.* Then sit down at your computer and log in to your Internet service provider. As you do, carefully write down in the *I Type* column everything you must type. Make sure you get the capitalization right and indicate when you must press the Enter key. In addition, enter in the *Computer Types* column the last thing that you see displayed on-screen before anything you must type, such as `User id:` or `Password:`.

Windows 95 users: Don't panic!

Windows 98 and Windows Millenium come with scripting support built in. Windows 95 also comes with Dial-Up Scripting support, but unlike Windows 98 or Windows Millennium, Windows 95 does not install Dial-Up Scripting automatically. As a result, if you are a Windows 95 user, you may have to pull out your Windows 95 CD and install Dial-Up Scripting before you can use it. Just follow these steps:

1. Insert your Windows 95 CD in your CD-ROM drive. If the Windows 95 setup program doesn't automatically start up, double-click My Computer and then double-click the icon for the CD drive.

2. Click the Add/Remove Software button.

3. Scroll through the list of Windows 95 components to find and select SLIP and Scripting for Dial-up Networking. If this option doesn't appear on your list, click the Have Disk button and then click Browse and locate the folder \admin\apptools\dscript on your CD-ROM drive. Click OK and then check SLIP and Scripting for Dial-up Networking.

4. Click OK. The Dial-Up Scripting tool is installed.

For example, here's what I wrote down to create the script for my provider:

Computer Types	*I Type*
Username:	user ID (Enter)
Password:	my password (Enter)

The purpose of your script is to automatically type the information for you so that you don't have to type it yourself. The script includes special commands that wait for the computer to ask the questions that you list in the *Computer Types* column and that automatically type the correct responses that you list in the *I Type* column.

Creating a Script

To create a script, you must use a text editor, such as Notepad. Here's the procedure for creating a script file:

1. **Click Start on the Windows taskbar and choose Programs⇨ Accessories⇨Notepad.**

   Notepad appears in its own window.

2. **Type whichever commands you need to type to establish your Internet connection.**

   Use the information you gathered in the previous section ("Planning a Script") as a guide. The commands vary depending on your service provider's requirements. Figure 16-2 shows the script I use for my provider. I describe each of the commands in this script in the section "Working with Script Commands," later in this chapter.

```
cvip.scp - Notepad
File  Edit  Search  Help
proc main

        waitfor "Username:"

        transmit $USERID
        transmit "^M"

        waitfor "Password:"
        transmit $PASSWORD

        transmit "^M"

endproc
```

Figure 16-2:
The script I
wrote to log
in to my
service
provider.

3. **Choose File⇨Save As to save the file.**

   Choose a filename that ends in .scp and save the file in \Program Files\Accessories.

4. **Choose File⇨Exit to quit Notepad.**

Your script filename must end in .scp, and your script must reside in the \Program Files\Accessories folder.

Working with Script Commands

The hard part of creating a script is knowing which commands to include in the script file. Table 16-1 lists the most commonly used scripting commands, and the sections that follow describe the commands that I used for the script in Figure 16-2. For a complete list of all the commands that you can use in a script file, run WordPad (available by choosing Start⇨Programs⇨Accessories⇨ WordPad) and then open the script.doc file located in your Windows folder.

Table 16-1	Dial-Up Scripting Commands	
Command	*What It Does*	*Explanation*
`proc main`	Begins the script	The script begins running at the main procedure and stops at the end of the main procedure. (Every script must start with `proc main`.)
`endproc`	Marks the end of the script	When your computer reaches this command, Dial-up Networking starts PPP or SLIP.
`delay`	Pauses the script for n seconds before executing the next command	For example, `delay 4 <n seconds>` pauses for four seconds.
`waitfor "<string>"`	Waits until the computer you are connecting to has received the specified characters	*String* refers to the words your Internet service provider uses to prompt you for information (from the *Computer Types* column). Note that the string is not case sensitive.
`transmit "<string>"`	Sends the specified characters to the computer to which you are connecting	*String* refers to the words you type as you log in to your Internet service (from the *I Type* column).
`transmit $USERID`	Sends the user ID obtained from the Connect To dialog box	
`transmit $PASSWORD`	Sends the password obtained from the Connect To dialog box	
`set screen keyboard on	off`	Enables or disables keyboard input to the terminal window	
`getip <optional index>`	Reads an IP address and uses it as the workstation address	

(continued)

Command	What It Does	Explanation
	Table 16-1 *(continued)*	
halt	Causes Dial-up Networking to stop running the script but leaves the terminal window open so that you can enter additional information manually	
;	Indicates a comment	All text after the semicolon is ignored — comments are for your reference only.

Beginning and ending with proc main and endproc

Every script must begin with a line that says proc main and end with a line that says endproc. It's a programming thing, required probably because the programmers at Microsoft who created the Dial-Up Network Scripts tool were in a bad mood that day and figured, hey, because we have to type stuff like proc main and endproc all day, everyone should have the opportunity to enjoy the same wonderful experience.

So the first thing you do when creating a script is add these two lines, as follows:

```
proc main

endproc
```

Notice that I left a blank row between these two lines. This space is where the meat of the script goes.

Waiting for stuff: waitfor

Before your script can type anything to the computer, it must wait until the computer is ready to accept the information. To tell the script to wait, you must make note of the text that's displayed as a prompt and then use a waitfor command to tell the script to wait until that text appears on the screen.

For example, the following line tells the scripting tool to wait until the prompt Username: appears:

```
waitfor "Username:"
```

The only trick in using a waitfor command is to make sure that the text you specify is unique — it doesn't occur anywhere else during your login procedure.

The script in Figure 16-2 uses two waitfor commands. In both cases, I used the text that I had written down in the *Computer Types* column when I planned the script.

Typing text: transmit

To send text to the computer, you use a transmit command. There are several variations of this command that you may need to use:

- transmit $USERID: This command transmits the user ID that I enter into the Connect To dialog box. By using this command in your script, you don't have to actually type your user ID into the script.

- transmit $PASSWORD: This command sends the password I enter into the Connect To dialog box. Once again, typing your command this way enables you to send the password without actually having to type your top-secret password into the script.

- transmit "^M": This cryptic command is equivalent to pressing the Enter key.

- transmit "some text": This command transmits some text as if you had typed it at the keyboard. Note that if the text includes ^M, the Enter key is sent as well.

^M is but one example of several special characters that you can send as part of a text string. Table 16-2 lists all the special characters that you can include in strings.

Table 16-2	Special Characters for Strings
Character	*Description*
^M	Carriage return (Enter — same as <cr>)
<cr>	Carriage return (Enter — same as ^M)
<lf>	Line feed
\"	Includes the quotation mark as part of the string

(continued)

Table 16-2 *(continued)*

Character	Description
\ '	Includes the apostrophe as part of the string
\ ^	Includes the caret (^) as part of the string
\ <	Includes the less-than sign as part of the string
\ \	Includes the backslash as part of the string

Attaching the Script to a Dial-Up Connection

After you create your script, you must attach it to a dial-up connection so that the script plays automatically each time you start the connection. Here's the procedure for attaching a script:

1. **Click Start on the Windows taskbar and choose Settings➪Dial-up Networking.**

   The Dial-up Networking folder appears, as shown in Figure 16-3.

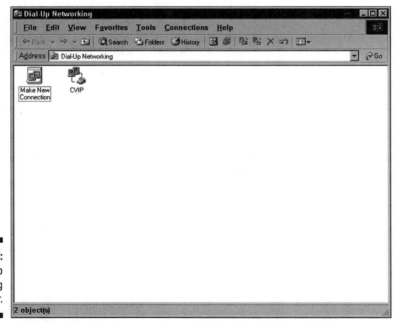

Figure 16-3:
The Dial-up Networking folder.

2. **Select the connection to which you want to attach the script.**

3. **Choose File⇨Properties.**

   Or right-click the connection to which you want to attach the script and choose the Properties command from the pop-up menu that appears. Either way, a Properties dialog box similar to the one shown in Figure 16-4 appears.

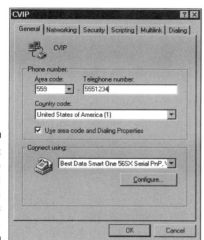

Figure 16-4:
The Dial-up
Networking
Connection
Properties
dialog box.

4. **Click the Scripting tab to display the script settings.**

   Figure 16-5 shows the script settings that appear in the Properties dialog box.

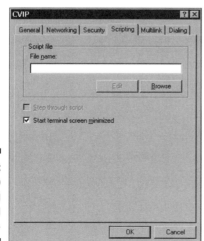

Figure 16-5:
Dial-up
Networking
Scripting
settings.

5. **Click Browse.**

   An Open dialog box appears.

6. **Select the file you want to use as the script.**

   You may have to use the Open dialog box's navigation controls to find the correct drive and folder.

7. **Click the Open button.**

8. **Back in the Properties dialog box, make sure the Start terminal screen minimized check box is selected.**

9. **Click OK.**

You're almost there. You need to make one more change in order for the script to work: You must turn off the terminal window that's displayed automatically after you start the connection. To suppress the terminal window, follow these steps:

1. **Click Start and choose Settings⇨Dial-up Networking.**

   This command brings up the Dial-up Networking window, which lists your connections.

2. **Right-click the icon for the connection you attached the script to and then choose Properties from the pop-up menu.**

   The properties dialog box appears (refer to Figure 16-4).

3. **Click the Configure button.**

   The dialog box shown in Figure 16-6 appears.

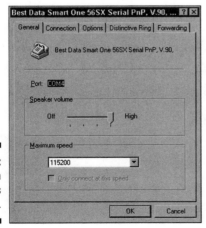

Figure 16-6:
The modem
Properties
dialog box.

4. Click the Options tab.

The modem options appear, as shown in Figure 16-7.

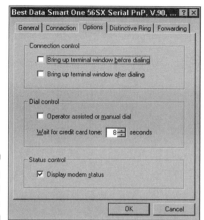

Figure 16-7:
The modem
options.

5. Uncheck both of the Connection control options.

If necessary, click to make sure both the Bring Up Terminal Window
Before Dialing and Bring Up Terminal Window After Dialing options are
unchecked.

6. Click OK to dismiss the Modem Properties dialog box.

7. Click OK again to dismiss the Connection Properties dialog box.

8. Close the Dial-up Networking window.

Now, at long last, you're ready to run the script. When you open the Dial-Up
Network connection, the script should run automatically. As the script runs,
watch it carefully to make sure that it appears to be running correctly. If it
doesn't run properly, double-check the script to make sure that you're transmitting the correct information and, just as importantly, waiting for the correct text before transmitting information.

Part V

Grow Your Own Web Pages

The 5th Wave — By Rich Tennant

"YOU KNOW KIDS — YOU CAN'T BUY THEM JUST ANY WEB AUTHORING SOFTWARE."

In this part . . .

This part covers the ins and outs of creating your own Web pages. The first three chapters in this part show you how to create simple Web pages using a free Microsoft program called FrontPage Express and how to publish those pages using Microsoft's Web Publishing Wizard. You'll also learn how to set up a nifty little program called Personal Web Server, which can turn your own computer into a miniature Web server so that you can display your Web pages on your computer.

Chapters 20 and 21 are where the technical stuff comes out. In these chapters, I show you how to use the new DHTML features that Microsoft has introduced for Internet Explorer 5.5, including such features as element behaviors, ViewLinks, and new style attributes. Chapters 20 and 21 are a bit on the technical side, however. You'll want to avoid them if you don't already have a fairly solid understanding of HTML.

Chapter 17

So You Want Your Own Web Site

In This Chapter

▶ Determining what type of information to put on your Web site

▶ Finding a Web server to host your Web site

▶ Choosing the software to use to create a Web site

*S*ooner or later you're going to grow weary of being an Internet spectator. After you've made the momentous decision to create your own Web site, you may need some help. This chapter can guide you through the steps involved in setting up your first Web site — deciding what to put on your Web site, finding a place to put your Web site, registering your own domain name, and obtaining the software programs you need to create a Web site.

As you would expect, IDG Books Worldwide, Inc. offers plenty of books on creating Web sites. Seeing as how I have three teenage daughters who are going to college soon, naturally I'll recommend my own *Creating Web Pages For Dummies Quick Reference,* 2nd Edition, first. In addition to that, there is *Creating Web Pages For Dummies,* 4th Edition, by Bud Smith and Arthur Bebak, *HTML 4 For Dummies,* 2nd Edition, by Ed Tittel and Natanya Pitts, and *FrontPage 2000 For Dummies* by Asha Dornfest.

Clarifying Some Familiar Terminology

Before I get far into this chapter, I want to clarify a few terms that you are probably already familiar with. A *Web page* is a single page that you can view with a Web browser such as Internet Explorer. A *Web site* is a collection of one or more pages that are linked together so that you can move from one page to another. A *home page* is the top page in a Web site — that is, the page that most users view first when they visit a Web site.

Many people (myself included) tend to use these three terms interchangeably. For example, if I tell you that I just set up a home page for my company, what I probably really mean is that I set up a company Web site with a home page and several other Web pages.

Deciding What to Put on Your Web Site

Before you even begin, you must decide what type of Web site you want to create and what information you want to put on the site. The following sections describe three of the most common types of Web sites: personal home pages, special interest Web sites, and business Web sites.

Personal home pages

The Internet is stuffed to the gills with personal home pages. Personal home pages provide you with a place to put up pictures of your family vacation to the Grand Canyon; a list of your hobbies, your pet peeves, and your kid's soccer accomplishments; links to your favorite Web sites; and anything else that suits your fancy. Most personal home page sites consist of just one Web page.

Just about anyone with access to the Internet can create a home page. In fact, most Internet Service providers offer you a limited amount of space on their Web servers for personal home pages. And if your ISP doesn't, you can choose from any of several free Web hosting services (which I describe later in this chapter, in the section "Getting a free site").

Here are some other ideas for what to put on your home page:

- A family photo album featuring pictures of you, your kids, and your pet turtle
- Your résumé
- The first chapter of your soon-to-be-published novel
- Voluminous tomes detailing your children's exploits in school and sports
- Your e-mail address so that people can send you comments about your Web page
- A discussion area so that people can leave comments that can be read by other visitors

Special interest Web sites

Many of the most interesting Web sites are devoted to special interests. For example, if you are involved with a youth soccer league, you may want to create a Web page that includes team rosters, schedules, and standings. Or if you are one of those annoying neighbors who decorates his or her house with 100,000 lights at Christmastime, you can create a Web page that focuses on Christmas decorating. The possible topics for a special interest Web site are limitless.

Business Web sites

By now, just about every major company has created an elaborate Web site, and many smaller companies ranging from custom cabinetmakers to mom-and-pop pizza parlors are putting up Web pages. The simplest corporate Web sites provide basic information about a company, such as a description of the company's products or services, phone numbers, and so on.

A more elaborate corporate Web site can include any or all of the following:

- ✔ An online catalog that enables Internet users to see detailed information about products and services. If you want, the catalog can include pictures and prices.

- ✔ Online ordering, which enables Internet users to actually place orders, pay for products, and arrange for shipment.

- ✔ A customer survey so that you can find out whether customers are satisfied with your products and services.

- ✔ Lists of frequently asked questions about the company's products and services.

- ✔ Online support, where a customer can leave a question about a problem he or she is having with one of your products and receive an answer within a day or two.

- ✔ Articles and reviews about your company's products and services.

- ✔ Press releases.

- ✔ Biographies of company employees.

- ✔ Company policies, such as equal opportunity statements and hiring practices.

- ✔ Employment opportunities.

Finding a Home for Your Web Site

To publish a Web site on the Internet, you must have access to a *Web server*. A Web server is a special computer that's connected to the Internet and runs special Web server software that enables the computer to store Web page files that other Internet users can view on their computers.

A Web server is also known as a *Web host*.

This section gives you some ideas for where to find Web server space to host your Web site.

Internet service providers

If you access the Internet through an Internet service provider (ISP), you probably already have space set aside to set up a small Web site. Most ISPs give each of their users a small amount of disk space for Web pages included in their monthly service fee. The space may be limited to a few megabytes, but that should be enough to set up a modest Web site with several pages. You can probably get additional disk space if you need it for a small monthly fee. Some service providers also limit the amount of traffic your Web site receives. In other words, you can't host a wildly popular site that receives millions of visits per day on your ISP account.

Your ISP should be able to give you step-by-step instructions for copying your Web pages to the ISP's Web server. Visit the help section of your ISP's home page for more information.

Web hosting services

A Web hosting service is a company that specializes in hosting Web sites on its own server computers. Unlike ISPs, which include limited Web hosting features as a part of their normal fee for Internet access, a Web hosting service charges you for hosting your Web site. However, Web hosting services offer much more than an ISP: your own domain name for your Web site, more disk space for your Web site and a larger traffic allowance, technical support for your Web server, help designing and creating your Web site, and support for advanced Web server features.

Of course, you have to pay for all of this, and the cost varies from one service to the next. A typical Web hosting package includes the following:

✔ Your own domain name so that you can pick the Web address users will use to access your site. The Web hosting service may register this name for you, or you can register it yourself. For more information, see the sidebar "Obtaining a domain name."

If you let the hosting service register the domain name for you, make sure that you are listed as the owner of the name so that you can take the name with you to another Web hosting service if you decide to switch later. The best way to make sure that you own the domain name is to register it yourself.

✔ A limited amount of disk storage on one of the hosting company's Web server computers — typically from 15MB to 50MB for a basic package, with more space available at additional charge.

✔ A high-speed connection to the Internet for your Web site, with a relatively high limit on the amount of traffic, such as 1GB or 2GB per month.

If your Web site becomes very popular, you may have to pay extra for the increased traffic. On the other hand, some Web host services provide unlimited traffic even with their basic packages.

A claim of unlimited traffic can be misleading — the Web host service may not have the equipment necessary to allow an unlimited amount of traffic for all of their customers with acceptable speed. To find out, try accessing a few Web sites hosted by the Web host service you are considering to see how long it takes to access the Web pages.

✔ A Web server that runs Windows NT, Windows 2000, or UNIX. Some Web hosting services let you choose the operating system and other software for the server.

✔ One or more e-mail accounts using your domain name. You can get additional e-mail accounts for a small fee, typically $1 per month per account.

Getting a free site

If you can't find a home for your Web site at your Internet service provider and you don't want to pay for a Web hosting service, you can opt for one of the many free Web servers to host your Web site. You won't be able to create a huge site on a free server, but most will give you several megabytes of Web server space free of charge — enough to set up a few pages at least.

What's the catch? Advertising. Users who visit your Web site have to put up with advertisements that pop up in their own windows or appear as banners on your pages. If you don't mind the advertisements, a free Web server can be an easy way to get started creating Web pages.

Obtaining a domain name

The best part about using a Web hosting service is that you get to register your own domain name. With an ISP-hosted Web page, your Web page address is based on a combination of your user ID and your ISP's domain name. For example, if your user ID is wilbur and your ISP's Web domain name is www.myditzyprovider.com, your Web page would have an address, such as www.myditzyprovider.com/~wilbur. But if you host your page with a Web hosting service, you can register your Web site under a name of your choosing, such as www.myveryowncompany.com.

Registering a domain name is inexpensive — $70 for the first two years and $35 each year after that to keep the name active. You can easily register a name yourself by going to the Network Solutions Web site at www.networksolutions.com. From there, you can search for a domain name that hasn't been taken yet. When you find a name that isn't already in use, you can sign up over the Web by providing the contact information for the domain name and a credit card number for payment.

If you don't want to mess with HTML or Web page editors, such as FrontPage, most free Web servers include simple fill-in-the-blank tools that make it easy to create basic Web pages. For example, you can create a basic home page by selecting one of several templates, typing the page title and information that you want on the page, such as your name and a description of your family, hobbies, or interests, and uploading pictures you want to appear on the page.

The following are some of the more popular free home page sites:

- ✔ **MSN Home Pages:** Microsoft's msn.com site gives you up to 30MB of disk space to create a Web site. msn.com provides templates that let you build Web sites that include advanced features such as a photo album, file cabinet, discussion board, and chat room.

- ✔ **Yahoo! GeoCities:** Yahoo! GeoCities (geocities.yahoo.com) is one of the best-known free home page services, hosting more than 1 million home pages. Each free site can use up to 15MB of disk space, and you can increase the allocation to 25MB for a mere $4.95 per month.

- ✔ **America Online:** AOL offers up to 15MB of space for home pages, and you don't have to be an AOL subscriber. Just visit hometown.aol.com to sign up.

Many other free home page services are available. Some cater to specific types of home pages, such as artists pages, churches, chambers of commerce, and so on. Others are for general use. You can find a good directory of free home pages services by going to Yahoo! (www.yahoo.com) and searching for *Free Web Pages*.

Software for Creating Web Sites

Before you begin to create your Web site, you need to acquire the right software for creating and editing Web pages. Walk the aisles of any store that sells computer software, and you quickly discover that you have many options to choose from.

If you want to create a professional quality Web site, are computer savvy, and are willing to spend the time it takes to learn how to use complicated but powerful software, you may want to invest in a professional-quality Web development program, such as Macromedia Dreamweaver 3, Microsoft Visual InterDev Professional 6, or Adobe GoLive 5. These programs (which cost $300 and up) let you incorporate advanced Web design features, such as templates and style sheets, to give the pages in your site a consistent look; navigation bars to automatically link the pages in your site; and special effects, such as buttons that change shape or color when the user points at them with the mouse.

If your budget and needs are more modest, you can choose an inexpensive (under $150) Web site development program such as Microsoft FrontPage 2000, (which you can purchase separately or as a part of Microsoft Office 2000) Adobe PageMill 3, or HotDog Professional 6 from Sausage Software. These programs don't have as many advanced features as their more expensive counterparts, but you can use them to create great looking Web sites.

If you're just getting started with Web design, you may want to start with a free Web page editor: Microsoft's FrontPage Express. FrontPage Express is a scaled-down version of FrontPage that was included free with Internet Explorer 5. Unfortunately, Internet Explorer 5.5 does not include FrontPage Express. However, you can still obtain it from Microsoft's download site. For more information about using FrontPage Express, see Chapter 18.

Chapter 18

Creating Web Pages with FrontPage Express

- -

In This Chapter

▶ Using FrontPage Express to produce simple Web pages

▶ Using the Personal Home Page Wizard to create a home page

▶ Formatting your Web page

▶ Placing hyperlinks on your page

▶ Adding interesting items such as lines, graphics, and background pictures

▶ Viewing the HTML source code for a Web page

- -

*F*rontPage Express is a scaled-down version of the Microsoft FrontPage Web publishing program that you can get from Microsoft free of charge. With FrontPage Express, you can create your own Web pages, and you can publish them on the Web for all the world to see. You can think of FrontPage Express as a word processor for Web pages. It enables you to create, edit, and save documents in the Web's special HTML document format.

The good news is that you don't have to learn a whit about HTML to use FrontPage Express. If you've put off creating a home page because you hesitate to face the prospect of learning HTML, expect to fall head over heels in appreciation for FrontPage Express. What are you waiting for? Jump right in and get that home page started! Your friends may think that you're a genius when they spot your home page on the Web.

Installing FrontPage Express

FrontPage Express was distributed as a part of Internet Explorer 5. However, Microsoft decided not to include FrontPage Express with Internet Explorer 5.5. As a result, you may have to jump through a few hoops to get FrontPage Express installed on your computer.

If you are using Windows 98 (first or second edition), you probably already have FrontPage Express because FrontPage Express is automatically installed as a part of the full Windows 98 installation. If you can't find FrontPage Express, you can install it by calling up the Control Panel (Start⇨Settings⇨Control Panel), double-clicking Add/Remove Programs, and choosing Windows Setup. Then click Internet Tools, click the Details button, check the FrontPage Express check box, and click OK.

If you are using Windows 95, you may also already have FrontPage Express. Click the Start button and look for FrontPage Express under Programs⇨ Internet Explorer or Programs⇨Accessories⇨Internet Tools.

If you cannot locate FrontPage Express anywhere on your computer, you can download FrontPage Express from the Windows Update Web site at www.windowsupdate.com.

If you are using Windows Millennium, installing FrontPage Express is a bit trickier. If you have upgraded to Windows Millennium from an older version of Windows, you may be in luck. Choose Start⇨Programs⇨Accessories⇨ Internet Tools to see if FrontPage Express is there. If it isn't, follow these steps to download and install it:

1. **Start Internet Explorer and go to the Corporate Windows Update Web site.**

   The correct URL is corporate.windowsupdate.microsoft.com.

   The Corporate Windows Update site is one of the stranger Microsoft Web sites you'll come across. Corporate Windows Update requires that your security settings be to its liking, and you'll be told to change your security settings if necessary. In addition, the first time you use Corporate Windows Update, a program called WU Corporate Catalog will be downloaded to your computer.

2. **Click the Product Updates link.**

   The page shown in Figure 18-1 appears.

3. **Click the Filter & Sort button.**

   The page shown in Figure 18-2 appears.

4. **Type** FrontPage Express **in the Specific Search Item text box and then click the Display Results button.**

   The search results page appears, as shown in Figure 18-3.

5. **Click the check box next to the second FrontPage Express link.**

   The second FrontPage Express link indicates that it is for Windows 98 and Internet Explorer 5, but it works fine with Windows Millennium and Internet Explorer 5.5.

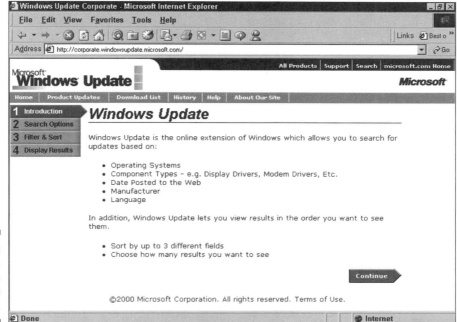

Figure 18-1:
The
Corporate
Windows
Update site.

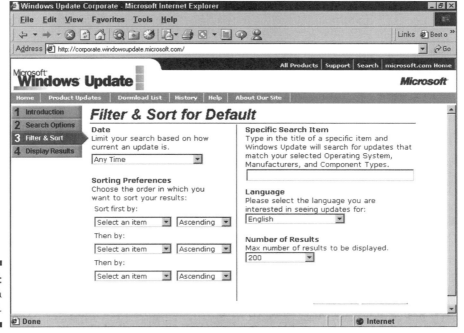

Figure 18-2:
The Filter &
Sort page.

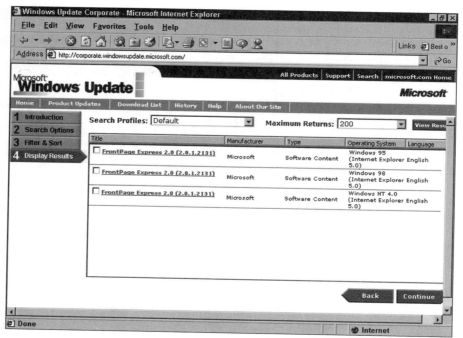

Figure 18-3:
The search
results.

Do not click the FrontPage Express link itself. If you do click the link, you stumble into a bug in the Corporate Windows Update site, and you won't be able to download FrontPage Express. If that happens, start the whole procedure again back at Step 1.

6. Click the Continue button located at the bottom of the page.

Another page appears to confirm the file that you have selected to download (see Figure 18-4).

7. In the Download To . . . box, specify the folder on your hard drive to which you want to download the FrontPage Express installation program.

For example, you can specify **C:\Windows\Desktop**.

8. Click the Download button.

A license agreement appears in a separate dialog box.

9. Read the license agreement and then click Yes.

The FrontPage Express file begins to download. When the download finishes, you are taken to a download summary page that indicates the file was successfully downloaded.

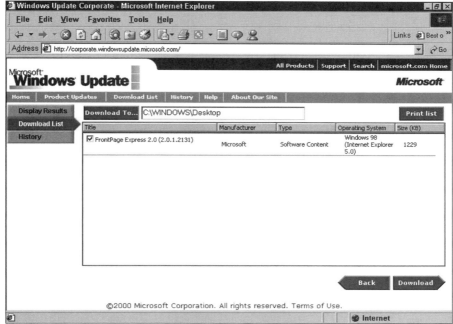

Figure 18-4:
The
Download
List page.

10. **Close Internet Explorer.**

Click the Close button or choose the File➪Close command.

11. **Open the download folders on your desktop to locate the FrontPage Express setup program.**

To get to the FrontPage Express setup program, you'll have to work your way through three folders. First, double-click the Software folder on your desktop. Then, double-click the En folder that appears in the Software folder. Finally, double-click the W98IE5 folder that appears in the En folder.

12. **Double-click the FrontPage Express icon that appears in the W98IE5 folder.**

FrontPage Express starts its installation program, which brings up an Install Confirmation dialog box.

13. **Click OK to install FrontPage Express.**

Your computer grinds and whirs for a moment as it installs FrontPage Express. When the installation is finished, a final Install Results dialog box appears to notify you that the installation was successful.

14. **Click OK.**

   You're done!

Starting FrontPage Express

If FrontPage Express is installed on your computer, you can start FrontPage Express by clicking the Start button and then choosing Programs⇨ Accessories⇨Internet Tools⇨FrontPage Express. (If you can't find FrontPage Express there, try Programs⇨Internet Explorer⇨FrontPage Express instead.)

When FrontPage Express springs to life, it displays the screen shown in Figure 18-5, ready for you to begin editing.

If FrontPage Express starts up in a minimized window, I suggest you maximize the window by clicking the Maximize button (the button with the rectangle icon in the upper-right corner of the FrontPage Express window). That way, you have the entire screen on which to view and edit your Web pages.

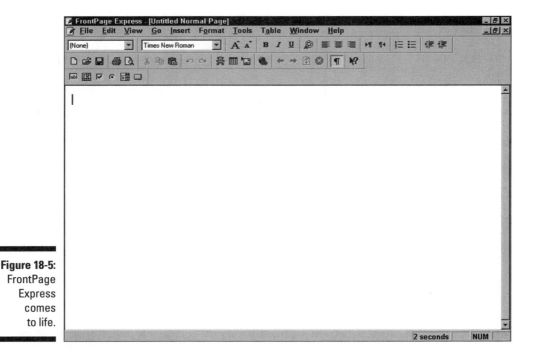

Figure 18-5:
FrontPage
Express
comes
to life.

Using the Personal Home Page Wizard

The easiest way to begin creating a Web page with FrontPage Express is to use the built-in Personal Home Page Wizard. This wizard asks you a bunch of questions about the information you want to include in your home page, and then it automatically generates a simple home page for you. You can edit the page as you see fit, save it to your hard drive, and then use the Web Publishing Wizard (described in Chapter 19) to upload the home page to your Internet service provider's Web server.

If you prefer, you can start from a blank Web page. When you start FrontPage Express from the Start➪Programs menu, a blank page is automatically loaded for you, so you can just begin editing. If you start FrontPage Express from Internet Explorer and you want a blank page, choose File➪Close to close the current page. Then choose File➪New to create a new blank Web page. Either way, you can skip the rest of this section because you won't be using the Personal Home Page Wizard.

The following procedure shows you step-by-step how to use the Personal Home Page Wizard to create your own home page:

1. **Start FrontPage Express.**

   FrontPage Express comes to life. (If you don't remember how to start FrontPage Express, refer to the section "Starting FrontPage Express" earlier in this chapter.)

2. **Choose File➪New.**

   The New Page dialog box appears, as shown in Figure 18-6.

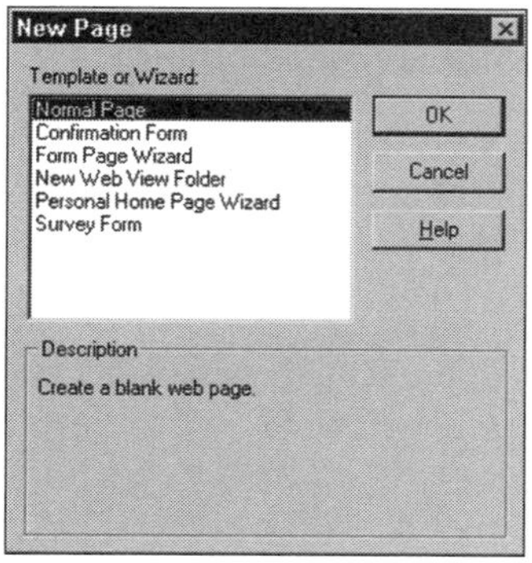

Figure 18-6:
The New
Page
dialog box.

3. **Select Personal Home Page Wizard from the Template or Wizard list and then click OK.**

   The Personal Home Page Wizard appears, as shown in Figure 18-7.

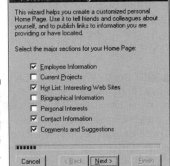

Figure 18-7:
The
Personal
Home Page
Wizard.

4. **Choose the major sections you want to include in your home page.**

   The wizard offers seven choices for sections to include: Employee Information, Current Projects, Hot List: Interesting Web Sites, Biographical Information, Personal Interests, Contact Information, and Comments and Suggestions. You can select any or all of these sections to include in your own home page.

   Note: If you want to include a section that doesn't appear in this list, don't worry. You can always manually add that section when the wizard is finished.

5. **Click Next.**

   The wizard displays the dialog box shown in Figure 18-8.

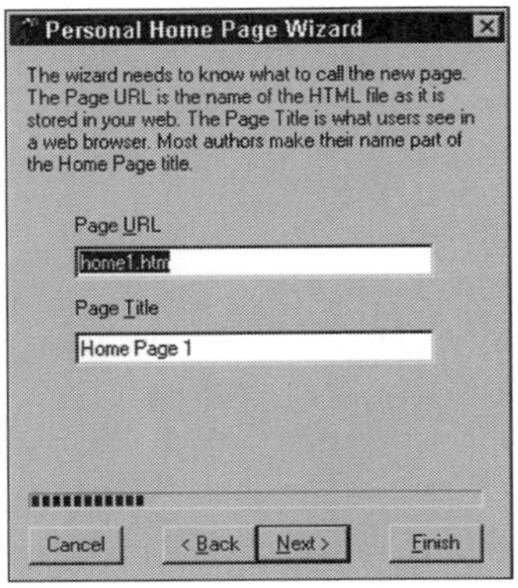

Figure 18-8:
What do you
want to call
your home
page?

6. Type a filename and title for your home page.

Type the filename in the Page URL text box and then type the title in the Page Title text box. You can use any filename and title you want.

7. Click Next.

The wizard requests information about the first section of your home page, as shown in Figure 18-9.

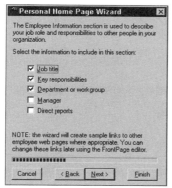

Figure 18-9:
Tell the wizard about the information you want in the Employee Information section.

8. Select the items you want to include in the first section of your home page and then click Next.

The wizard displays a dialog box for the next section of your home page.

9. Repeat Step 8 for each section you selected in Step 4.

For each section you choose to include in your home page, a slightly different dialog box appears and asks you what type of information you want to include in the section.

After you complete all the sections, the dialog box shown in Figure 18-10 appears.

10. Click Finish.

FrontPage Express whirs and spins for just a moment and then spits out a skeleton home page similar to the one shown in Figure 18-11.

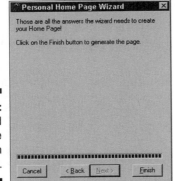

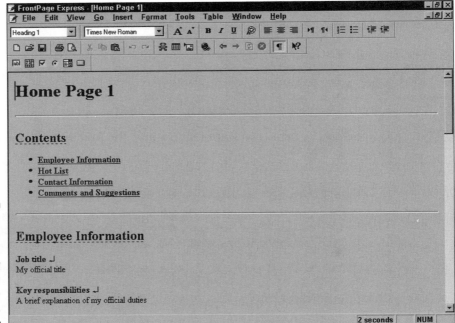

11. **Make whatever changes you want to the document, filling in the blanks left by the Personal Home Page Wizard.**

    The page created by the wizard includes text such as *My Job Description* and *Sample Site 3*. This text serves only as a placeholder for the actual text you want to appear on your Web page. You undoubtedly want to type some more-meaningful text to replace these placeholders and add new information of your own.

12. **Save the document.**

> To save the document as an HTML file, choose the File⇨Save command and then click the Save As File button.

After your home page is finished, you can use the Web Publishing Wizard to upload the page to your Web server. See Chapter 19 for more information about how to publish your Web page.

Formatting Text in a Web Document

FrontPage Express lets you apply formatting to the text in a Web page much the same way a word processor lets you format text in a document. FrontPage Express doesn't have all the text formatting abilities of an expensive word processing program, such as Microsoft Word, but it offers enough text formatting to enable you to create good-looking Web pages.

Applying a style

Every paragraph of text in a FrontPage Express Web document must have a *style* that governs the basic formatting for the text. To apply a style to a paragraph, place the insertion point anywhere in the paragraph and then choose a style from the Style drop-down list that appears on the toolbar.

Styles are most commonly used to create headings for Web pages. FrontPage Express enables you to create up to six levels of headings using Heading 1, Heading 2, and so on, up to Heading 6. The regular paragraph text of your document should be formatted using the Normal style.

Other styles enable you to create various types of lists (Bulleted List, Numbered List, Definition List, Directory List, and Menu List) or to create specially formatted paragraphs (Address and Formatted).

Applying text formatting

To change the font used for text, select the text you want to change and then select a font from the Font drop-down list that appears in the Standard toolbar next to the Style drop-down list.

You may wonder where the Font Size drop-down list is. Unfortunately, there isn't one. Instead, you control the size of your text by clicking one of the following two buttons:

  ✔ Increases the text size

  ✔ Decreases the text size

Only seven different point sizes are used in HTML documents. Your text can be 8, 10, 12, 14, 18, 24, or 36 points; no other sizes are allowed. Clicking the Increase Text Size or Decrease Text Size buttons increases or decreases the text size to the next allowable size. (Of course, most browsers let the viewer change the text size. You can't do anything about that.)

You can apply bold, italic, and underline formats by using the following buttons or keyboard shortcuts:

Bold	**B**	Ctrl+B
Italic	*I*	Ctrl+I
Underline	U	Ctrl+U

You can also change the text color by clicking the Text Color button. When you click this button, you see a dialog box that contains each of the standard colors that you can apply to text. Choose the color you want and click OK to apply the color.

Another way to apply text formatting is to summon the Format⇨Font command, which brings up the Font dialog box, shown in Figure 18-12. This dialog box enables you to control all the font formatting options from one convenient place.

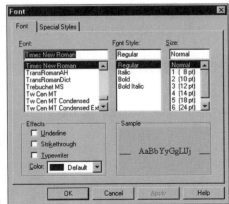

Figure 18-12:
The Font
dialog box.

As you can see, the Font dialog box has controls that enable you to set the font, font style (regular, italic, bold, or bold italic), size, underline, and color. You can also apply two effects that are not available via toolbar buttons: strikethrough and typewriter.

If you click the Special Styles tab in the Font dialog box, the additional font controls, shown in Figure 18-13, appear. These controls enable you to apply special text styles that are unique to HTML and to create subscripts and superscripts. You probably won't need to use these styles for most of your Web pages, but they're available if you need them.

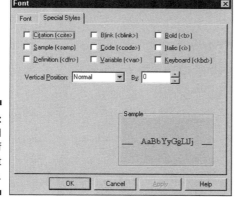

Figure 18-13:
The Special Styles tab of the Font dialog box.

Aligning and indenting text

FrontPage Express lets you set the alignment and indentation for text by using the following buttons:

Align left

Center

Align right

Increase indent

Decrease indent

Creating bulleted and numbered lists

By clicking one of the following buttons, you can create lists in which each paragraph in the list is marked by a bullet character or a number:

Bulleted list

Numbered list

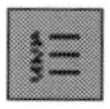

However, for more precise control over the format of your list, use the Format⇨Bullets and Numbering command. Choosing this command brings up the dialog box shown in Figure 18-14.

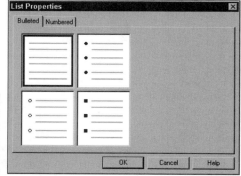

Figure 18-14:
The List
Properties
dialog box.

The Bulleted tab, which is pictured in Figure 18-14, enables you to choose from one of four different styles of bullet characters. To create a numbered list, click the Numbered tab to reveal the numbered list options, shown in Figure 18-15. Here, you have the option of using Arabic numbers, Roman numerals, or letters. You can pick the starting number for the list by using the Start At control.

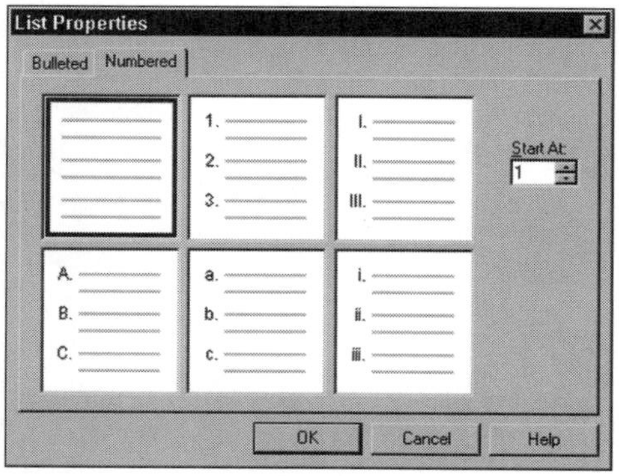

Figure 18-15:
The
Numbered
list options
in the List
Properties
dialog box.

Creating a Hyperlink

A *hyperlink* is a bit of text that, when clicked, sends users to another page. The link can be to another location in the current Web page, another page at the same Web site, or a page at a different Web site somewhere else on the Internet.

To add a hyperlink to a FrontPage Express Web page, follow these steps:

1. Type some text that you want to turn into a link.

For example, type `click here to go to my home page`.

If you prefer, you can insert a picture and turn it into a link. See the section "Inserting a picture" later in this chapter for more information.

2. Highlight the text you want to turn into a link.

3. Choose Insert⇨Hyperlink.

The Create Hyperlink dialog box appears, as shown in Figure 18-16.

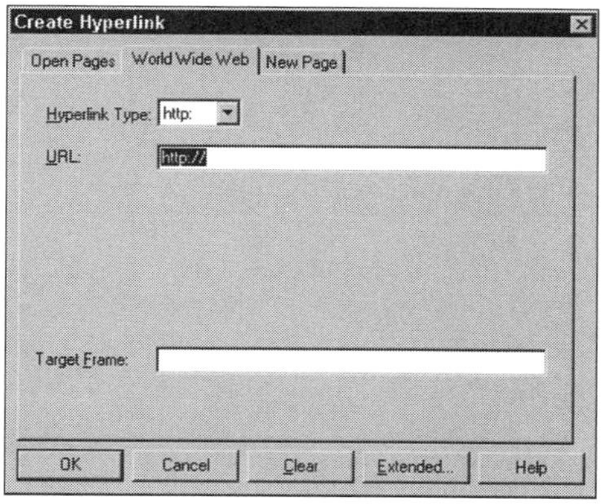

Figure 18-16:
The Create
Hyperlink
dialog box.

4. Type the address of the Web page you want to link to in the URL field.

If the page is intended to reside at your own Web site, you don't have to type the complete URL. Instead, just type the filename for the HTML document that you want to link to.

5. Click OK.

Your selected text is transformed into a link. To indicate that the text is a link, FrontPage Express displays it in blue underlined text. When Web users view your page on the Web, they can jump to the page referred to in the link by clicking the underlined text.

If an address change is in order for a linked page, you can update your hyper-link in FrontPage Express by selecting the link text and choosing Edit⇨Hyperlink. Choosing this command brings up the Edit Hyperlink dialog box, which is identical to the Create Hyperlink dialog box. Change the address in the URL field and then click OK to update the link.

Spicing Up Your Page with Graphics

FrontPage Express enables you to improve the appearance of your page by adding graphics, as I describe in the following sections.

Inserting a horizontal line

One of the commonly used formatting features in Web pages is the horizontal line, which is drawn across the page to visually separate groups of information. Figure 18-17 shows a Web page with two types of horizontal lines on it.

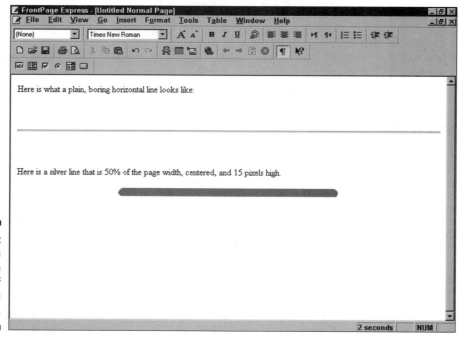

Figure 18-17:
A Web page with two types of horizontal lines.

To insert a horizontal line, follow these steps:

1. **Position the insertion point where you want to insert the horizontal line.**

2. **Choose Insert⇨Horizontal Line.**

   A plain, rather boring horizontal line is inserted into your document. For example, have a look at the first line shown in Figure 18-17.

3. **Click the line to select it.**

4. **Choose the Edit⇨Horizontal Line Properties command.**

   The dialog box shown in Figure 18-18 appears.

Figure 18-18:
Changing the properties of a horizontal line.

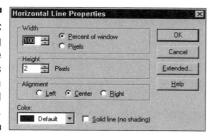

5. **Set the line properties to something more interesting.**

   For example, to create the second line in Figure 18-17, I set the line width to 50 percent of the page, its height to 15 pixels, its alignment to Centered, and its color to Silver.

6. **Click OK.**

   The line is formatted.

To remove it later on, select the line by clicking anywhere on it and then press the Delete key.

Inserting a picture

Pictures attract attention, and nearly all Web pages are crafted with at least a few graphics. In some cases, the pictures are actual scanned photographs, but more often, the pictures are small graphic images created by a drawing program, such as Windows Paint (the free drawing program that comes with Windows).

Before you can insert a picture on your Web page, of course, you must first obtain the graphic file for the picture you want to add. Good news — there are plenty of Internet sites from which you can download pictures to include on your Web pages. Just search for "Images" or "Pictures" using Yahoo! or any other search service. Here are a few of the better sources for pictures to use on your Web site:

✔ Microsoft's Images library (msdn.microsoft.com/downloads/images) is a gallery of arrows, backgrounds, banners, rules, and clip art. When you first visit this page, click the Show TOC button to reveal the table of contents that lists the images in the library.

✔ Yahoo! Picture Gallery (gallery.yahoo.com) has thousands of photographs you can download and use.

✔ The Library of Congress (www.loc.com) has several large collections of historical photographs you can use.

To insert a picture into a FrontPage Express Web page, follow these steps:

1. Move the insertion point to the position where you want the picture inserted.

2. Choose the Insert⇨Image command.

Or just click the Insert Image button in the Standard toolbar. Either way, an Image dialog box like the one in Figure 18-19 appears.

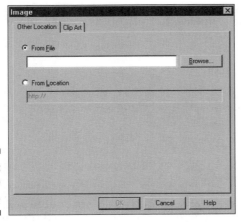

Figure 18-19: The Image dialog box.

3. Click the Browse button.

Clicking this button summons the Image dialog box, shown in Figure 18-20.

Figure 18-20:
Selecting an image.

4. **Find and select the image you want to insert.**

   You may have to navigate through the various folders on your hard disk to find the file.

5. **When you find the image you want, click Open.**

   The image is inserted into your Web page.

Be careful about inserting large graphics in your Web pages. The larger your graphic, the more time it takes to download when a Web user views your page. If the page takes too long to download, expect the Web user to curse under his or her breath and vow to never visit your page again.

Also, make sure you don't break any copyright laws — use graphics only with permission from the creator or owner.

Inserting a marquee

A *marquee* is a bit of text that scrolls across the screen from one side to the other. To create a marquee in your Web page, choose the Insert⇨Marquee command. Choosing this command brings up the dialog box shown in Figure 18-21. You can play with the various settings in this dialog box to set the text that you want to scroll, the direction and speed with which you want the text to scroll, the size of the area in which the text scrolls, and whether you want the text to scroll just once or to repeat in a loop.

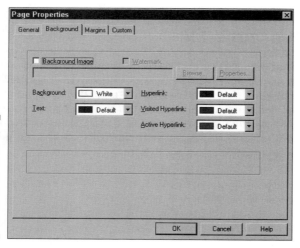

Figure 18-21:
Creating a
scrolling
marquee.

Adding a background image

Many Web pages use a background graphic that makes the page more attractive. You can add a background image to your Web page by following these steps:

1. **Choose Format⇨Background.**

   The Page Properties dialog box appears, as shown in Figure 18-22.

2. **Select the Background Image option.**

Figure 18-22:
The
Background
options in
the Page
Properties
dialog box.

3. **Click the Browse button.**

   A Select Background Image dialog box appears, as shown in Figure 18-23.

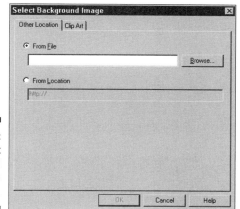

4. **Click Browse.**

   This summons another dialog box that enables you to search your files and folders for the image that you want to use.

5. **Locate the graphic file you want to use for your background image.**

6. **Click Open.**

   You return to the Page Properties dialog box.

7. **Click OK.**

   The image you selected becomes the background image for your page.

Viewing HTML Source Code

Normally, FrontPage Express displays your Web pages pretty much as they appear when displayed by a Web browser such as Internet Explorer. However, there are occasions when you may want to view the actual HTML codes that compose your Web page. To do so, just call up the View⇨HTML command. The HTML file for your Web page is displayed in a separate window, as shown in Figure 18-24.

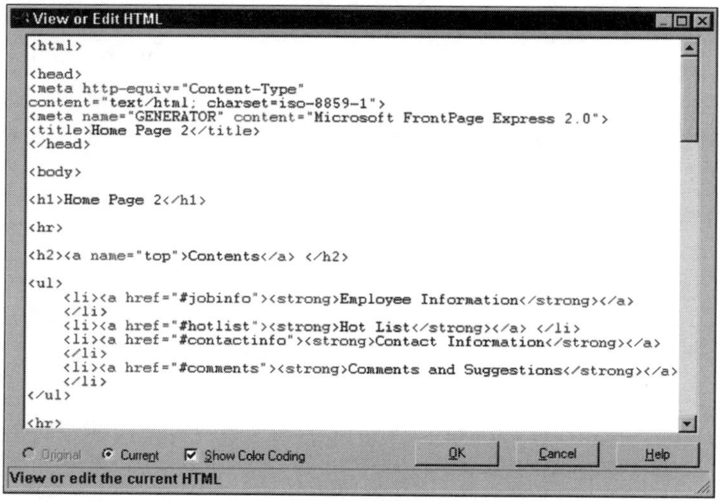

Figure 18-24:
Viewing the
HTML for a
Web page.

If you want to, you can actually edit the HTML in this window. Just click anywhere and start typing. Or if you have better judgment, just look at the HTML
for a moment, gasp in amazement that some people are actually interested in
such arcane subjects, and click OK to close the HTML window.

Chapter 19

Publishing Your Web Pages

● ●

In This Chapter

▶ Uploading your Web pages using the Web Publishing Wizard

▶ Using Personal Web Server to set up a Web server on your own computer

● ●

*A*fter you use FrontPage Express or some other Web page editor to create your Web pages, go ahead and plunge right into copying those pages from your computer to a Web server. A Web server hosts your Web site on the Internet. This chapter shows you how to accomplish that feat using the Microsoft Web Publishing Wizard, which works for most Web servers.

This chapter also shows you how to turn your own computer into a mini–Web server using a handy little program called Personal Web Server that lets you view and test your Web pages on your own computer.

Using the Web Publishing Wizard

The Web Publishing Wizard is designed to automate the task of copying HTML files from your computer to the Web server computer that hosts your Web site. Before you can use the Web Publishing Wizard, you need to know the following details:

- ✔ The Web address that people on the Internet will use to access your Web page. For example, www.myserver.com.

- ✔ The name of the folder on your computer's hard drive where your Web pages are stored.

- ✔ The method your Internet service provider wants you to use to upload the files to its Web server. The choices are FTP, HTTP Post, and CRS. (You don't need to know what any of those acronyms stand for, just which one your ISP uses.)

- ✔ The name of the folder on your Internet service provider's Web server where you're supposed to upload your files.

After you have this information, you can follow the procedure in the next section, "Using the Web Publishing Wizard for the first time," to set up the Web Publishing Wizard for your Web server. After you set up the Web Publishing Wizard, you can use the procedure I describe under "Updating your Web files" to upload your HTML files to the Web server whenever necessary.

Using the Web Publishing Wizard for the first time

The first time you use the Web Publishing Wizard, you have to supply the wizard with the information it needs to configure itself for the Web server that hosts your Web page. To do so, follow these steps:

1. **Click the Start button in the Windows taskbar and then choose the** **P**rograms⇨**Accessories**⇨**Internet Tools**⇨**Web Publishing Wizard** **command.**

   The Web Publishing Wizard appears, as shown in Figure 19-1.

Figure 19-1:
The Web
Publishing
Wizard
springs
to life.

2. **Click Next to get started.**

   The Web Publishing Wizard displays the dialog box shown in Figure 19-2, asking you to provide the location of the HTML files you want to upload to the Web server.

3. **Indicate the location of the file or files you want to upload to the Web** **server.**

   To upload a single HTML file, type the name of the file (along with the drive and the folder that contains it) in the File or Folder Name field. Or click the Browse Files button, select the file you want to upload in the dialog box that appears and then click Open.

To upload an entire folder of files, either type the name of the folder in the File or Folder Name field or click the Browse Folders button, select the folder in the dialog box that appears, and click OK.

If you want to include files from any subfolders contained within the folder you specify, check the Include Subfolders check box.

Figure 19-2:
The Web
Publishing
Wizard
wants to
know what
files you
want to
upload to
your Web
server.

4. **Click Next.**

The dialog box shown in Figure 19-3 appears. The Web Publishing Wizard asks you to provide a name for the Web server that you want the files uploaded to.

Figure 19-3:
The Web
Publishing
Wizard
needs a
name for the
Web server.

5. **Type a name for your Web server in the Descriptive Name field.**

You can use any name you want. If you can't think of anything better, type My Web Server.

6. **Click the Advanced button.**

You see the dialog box shown in Figure 19-4.

7. **Choose the connection method your Internet service provider uses to upload files to the Web server from the drop-down list.**

The choices are FrontPage Extended Web, FTP, HTTP Post, and Microsoft Content Replication System (also known as CRS). You have to ask your ISP which method it uses. Mine relies on FTP, so that's the method I illustrate for the remainder of this procedure. (The other methods are similar, but the wizard asks for specific information based on the method you select.)

8. **Click Next.**

The dialog box shown in Figure 19-5 appears.

9. **Type the address for your Web page in the URL or Internet Address field.**

For example, if the address for your home page is www.mycompany.com/me, that's what you type into the URL or Internet Address field.

10. **Click Next.**

The Web Publishing Wizard now asks for information that depends on the connection method you selected in Step 7. For FTP, the dialog box resembles the one shown in Figure 19-6. The dialog box is somewhat different if you choose FrontPage Extended Web, HTTP Post, or CRS.

Figure 19-5:
The wizard needs to know the URL for your page.

Figure 19-6:
The wizard now needs information about the FTP connection.

11. Type the FTP server name and the name of the subfolder on the FTP server that will contain your files.

You have to find out this information from your Internet service provider.

12. Click Next.

The wizard displays its final dialog box, as shown in Figure 19-7.

13. Click Finish.

The Enter Network Password dialog box appears, as shown in Figure 19-8.

14. Type your username and password; then click OK.

The Web Publishing Wizard connects to your Web server and begins to copy the files from your computer to the server. A progress dialog box similar to the one shown in Figure 19-9 is displayed as the files are copied.

After the files are copied, the dialog box shown in Figure 19-10 appears.

Figure 19-7:
The wizard is ready to publish your files.

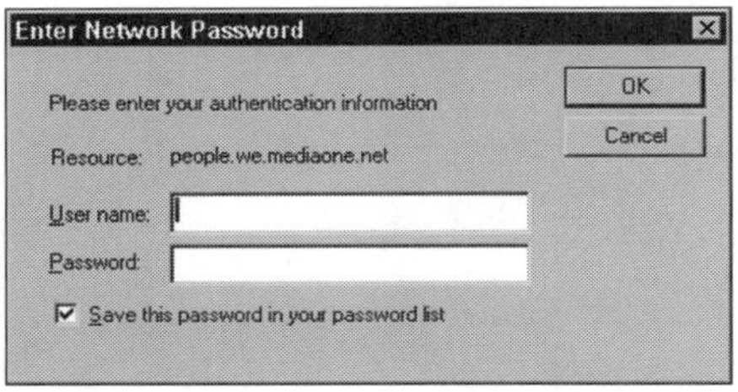

Figure 19-8:
Enter your username and password.

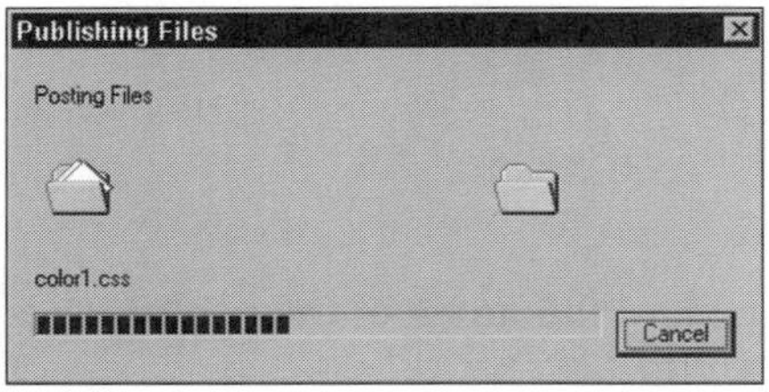

Figure 19-9:
Now we're making progress.

15. Click OK.

The wizard vanishes. Your files have now been successfully copied from your computer to the Web server.

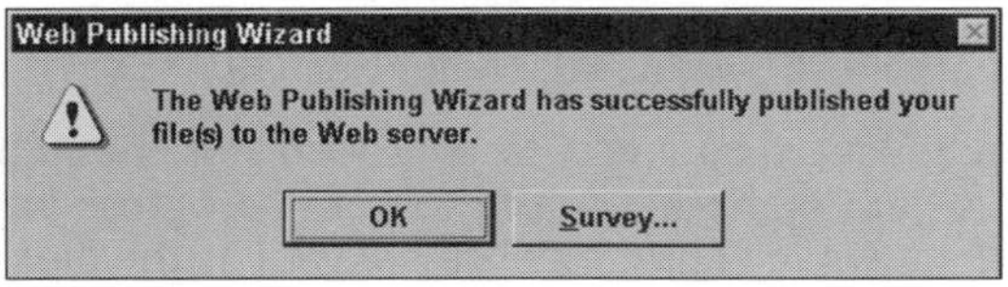

Figure 19-10:
Success!

Updating your Web files

The Web Publishing Wizard keeps track of almost everything it asks of you when you run it the first time. As a result, after you post your Web pages to your Web server once, you can upload updates quickly, without having to muddle through most of the Web Publishing Wizard screens.

The following procedure shows how easy it is to upload Web pages to your Web server after you've configured the Web Publishing Wizard:

1. **Start the Web Publishing Wizard by choosing Start⇨Programs⇨ Accessories⇨Internet Tools⇨Web Publishing Wizard.**

   The Web Publishing Wizard appears. (You can take a look at the starting dialog box in Figure 19-1.)

2. **Click Next.**

   The Web Publishing Wizard asks which file or folder you want to upload. The wizard defaults to the file or folder you uploaded the last time you ran the wizard, so you don't have to do anything if you want to upload the same files again.

3. **Click Next.**

   The wizard asks which server to use. Again, the default is set for the same server you used the last time you ran the wizard.

4. **Click Next.**

   The wizard displays its final screen (the one that I show in Figure 19-7).

5. **Click Finish.**

   The wizard connects to the server, uploads the files, and then displays a confirmation dialog box advising you that the files' upload is a rousing success.

6. **Click OK.**

   That's all there is to it!

Serving It Up with Personal Web Server

To publish a Web page on the Internet, you need a server computer that has a high-speed Internet connection and runs special Web server software. If you don't want to set all this stuff up yourself and your Internet service provider doesn't provide a Web server for you, you can use a Microsoft program called Personal Web Server (PWS) to set up a group of Web pages that can run on your own computer or over a small network.

Starting Personal Web Server

To start Personal Web Server, choose Programs⇨Accessories⇨Internet Tools⇨Personal Web Server⇨Personal Web Manager from the Windows Start button. Doing this launches a program called Personal Web Manager, which lets you control the operation of Personal Web Server. Figure 19-11 shows the main Personal Web Manager window.

Figure 19-11:
The main Personal Web Manager window.

Notice in Figure 19-11 that Personal Web Manager indicates whether or not the Web server is active. Web publishing is on indicates that PWS is active, so anyone who has access to your computer via a network can access the Web pages you have published to PWS.

You can disable the PWS server by clicking the Stop button. When you do, the message changes to Web publishing is off, and the Stop button changes to a Start button. Click this Start button to reactivate the server.

 After Personal Web Server starts, the icon shown in the margin appears in the Windows taskbar. You can double-click this icon at any time to summon Personal Web Manager.

 Personal Web Server comes with a set of Web pages that serve as Help files to give you an overview of how the Web server works and how you can manage it. To access these help files, start Personal Web Manager and then choose Help⇨Personal Web Server Topics.

Publishing a Web page to Personal Web Server

Publishing your HTML files to Personal Web Server is easy. After you do, you can view them using Internet Explorer from your computer or from another computer connected to your local area network. Personal Web Server uses a folder named `C:\Inetpub\wwwroot` as the root directory for your Web pages. To post an HTML file to Personal Web Server, all you have to do is save the file in the `C:\Inetpub\wwwroot` folder.

To save a file in FrontPage Express, just choose the File➪Save As command. When the Save As dialog box appears, navigate your way to `C:\Inetpub\wwwroot` and then click Save to save the HTML file.

Alternatively, you can use Personal Web Server's built-in Publishing Wizard to publish Web files to your PWS folders.

Accessing a Web page on Personal Web Server

To access a page stored in Personal Web Server, you need to know the Internet address for your Personal Web Server root directory. To find out, start Personal Web Manager. The Internet address of your PWS home page is shown in the Personal Web Manager dialog box. For example, in Figure 19-11, the address for the PWS home page is shown as `http://douglowe`.

When PWS is active, you can display your PWS home page in Internet Explorer by typing the home page address in Internet Explorer's address bar and pressing the Enter key. This action retrieves the document named default.html in your home page directory (C:\Inetpub\wwroot). For example, since my PWS home page address is `douglowe`, I can just type **douglowe** in the Address bar and press Enter to display my home page.

To display an HTML file other than default.html, type the filename after the Internet address that's separated by a slash. For example, to display a page named softball.html, I type **douglowe\softball.html**.

The Internet address that Personal Web Server uses is based on your Windows computer name that you create when you first install Windows on your computer. If you want to change this name, open the Control Panel and double-click the Network icon. Doing this reveals the Network dialog box. Click the Identification tab and then type a new computer name in the Computer Name field. After you click OK, your computer restarts, and then you can use the new name for your Personal Web Server Internet address.

Chapter 20

Ain't Misbehavin'
(Or, Creating and Using
DHTML Behaviors)

In This Chapter

▶ Understanding DHTML behaviors

▶ Reviewing styles, scripts, and custom tags — stuff you have to know before messing with behaviors

▶ Creating simple behaviors

▶ Creating custom tags that have built-in behaviors

▶ Creating behaviors that expose properties, methods, and custom events

*I*n the battle for Web browser dominance, both Microsoft and Netscape continually introduce new HTML features for their browsers. Microsoft and Netscape both hope that you and thousands of other Web page developers can't resist a full-fledged commitment to using their unique HTML features.

Microsoft's latest volley in this HTML war is a new feature called *Dynamic HTML (DHTML) behaviors*. The idea of DHTML behaviors is to completely separate a Web page's content from the script elements that implement dynamic behavior that the content exhibits. One of the most popular uses of DHTML behaviors is to create rollover effects, where an element such as a bit of text, a button, or a graphic changes its appearance when the user moves the mouse over the element.

DHTML behaviors were first introduced with Internet Explorer 5. With Internet Explorer 5.5, Microsoft has expanded the abilities of DHTML behaviors to enable you to create *element behaviors*. When you use an element behavior, you create a custom tag and assign a DHTML behavior to it. Whenever you use the custom tag in an HTML document, the behavior that is associated with the tag always is in effect.

Here are a few warnings and caveats to be aware of before you continue to read this chapter:

✔ This chapter assumes that you have a basic understanding of how Web pages are developed, including at least a rudimentary knowledge of *Hypertext Markup Language* (HTML), the programming language behind all Web pages. If you're new to Web page creation or you're just starting out with HTML, check out *HTML 4 For Dummies,* Second Edition, by Ed Tittel and Natanya Pitts (published by IDG Books Worldwide, Inc.), for some really great tips on creating Web pages. And for detailed information about Dynamic HTML, you can get a copy of *Dynamic HTML For Dummies,* Second Edition, by Michael I. Hyman (also published by IDG Books Worldwide, Inc.).

✔ This chapter also assumes that you have some general knowledge of scripting, either in JScript (Microsoft's version of JavaScript) or VBScript (which is based on Visual Basic). Although the scripts I present in this chapter are not too complicated, a basic understanding of programming concepts goes a long way as you plow through this chapter.

✔ Also, be warned that the Dynamic HTML features described in this chapter work only when your pages are viewed with Internet Explorer 5 or later, and the element behavior features work only with Internet Explorer 5.5. If you use these features and someone views your pages using a different Web browser (including an earlier version of Internet Explorer), he or she won't be able to see the cool new features you worked so hard to put on your pages.

Understanding DHTML Behaviors

With Internet Explorer 4, Microsoft introduced Dynamic HTML, which let you create Web pages with elements that can sing and dance. Among other things, Dynamic HTML lets you precisely control the placement of elements on the page and lets you create scripts that can handle events such as mouse movements for all the elements on the page.

One of the most popular uses of Dynamic HTML has been to create rollover effects, in which a text or graphical element changes when the user points the mouse at it. For example, to create a heading that turns red when the user moves the mouse over it, you can use HTML such as this:

```
<h1 onmouseover="this.style.color='red'">
Don't Make Me Angry!
</h1>
```

The trouble with this type of Dynamic HTML is that you have to intermingle the content that you want displayed (in this case, the text "Don't Make Me Angry!") with the scripting elements that control the content's behavior.

That's exactly the problem the DHTML behaviors feature is designed to correct. DHTML behaviors let you *encapsulate* the behavioral aspects of your HTML coding, which is a $64 way of saying that you can separate the script from the content. The script that causes the text to turn red when the mouse points to it is kept in a totally separate file from the HTML that contains the content you want to display.

There are several reasons why separating the script from the content is a good idea:

- ✔ It lets the Web page developer focus on the content of the Web page and the dynamic behavior of the Web page separately. In fact, different people or even teams of people can work on these tasks.

- ✔ It lets you reuse complicated behaviors without having to recode them every time you need them. After a script has been implemented as a behavior, you can use it on any page that needs the behavior without rewriting the script. This feature also makes it easy to create consistent effects that appear throughout your Web site.

- ✔ It makes updating Web page content without running the risk of messing up the scripts easier because the scripts are kept separate from the content.

- ✔ It makes changing a behavior or correcting an error in a behavior easier because the script for the behavior is isolated in one location, even if the behavior is used in many places throughout a Web site.

Scripts, Styles, and Custom Tags: A Little Review (Yuck!)

To get the full effect of dynamic behaviors, you have to create scripts using the VBScript or JScript scripting language. You also have to know how to use Cascading Style Sheets (also known as CSS) and how to create your own custom tags. The following sections present a brief (and I mean brief!) review of scripts, styles, and custom tags.

Scripts

A *script* is a program that can be embedded in an HTML document. Internet Explorer enables you to choose one of two scripting languages to create scripts: VBScript, which is based on Microsoft's Visual Basic, and JScript, which is based on Netscape's JavaScript. In this chapter, I use JScript.

Using the <script> tag

A script can be inserted into an HTML document within a pair of `<script>` and `</script>` tags, as in this example:

```
<script language='JScript'>
       window.alert("Hello world!");
</script>
```

This script displays a dialog box containing the message "Hello world!" when the page is loaded. A script such as this can be added to the `<head>` or `<body>` section of an HTML document.

You can also associate a procedure with a form control, such as a button. Then the procedure is usually coded inline with the form control, like this:

```
<form name='myform'>
  <input name='button1' type='button' value='button1'>
  <script language='JScript' for='button1'
  event='onclick'>
     window.alert("That tickles!")
  </script>
</form>
```

In this case, the procedure is triggered when the user clicks the button1 button. The script then displays a dialog box containing the message `That tickles!`

Intrinsic events

Intrinsic events enable you to attach scripts to the elements of your Web page and have those scripts executed whenever certain events occur. You can use intrinsic events in virtually any HTML tag. For example, you can use `onclick` in an `<h1>` tag to specify a script that runs whenever the heading is clicked. Or you can use `onmouseover` in an `<img>` tag to trigger a script whenever the mouse moves over an image.

Table 20-1 lists the most commonly used intrinsic events.

Table 20-1	Intrinsic Event Attributes
Event	*Explanation*
onclick	The user clicks the mouse on the element.
ondblclick	The user double-clicks the mouse on the element.
onmouseover	The user moves the mouse pointer over the element.
onmouseout	The user moves the mouse pointer away from the element after first moving the pointer over the element.
onmousedown	The user presses down the mouse button when the mouse pointer is over the element.
onmouseup	The user releases the mouse button while the mouse pointer is over the element.
onmousemove	The user moves the mouse while the mouse pointer is over the element.
onfocus	The element receives input focus by pointing or by tabbing.
onblur	The element loses focus (see onfocus).
onkeypress	The user presses and releases a key while the element has input focus.
onkeydown	The user presses down a key while the element has input focus.
onkeyup	The user releases a key while the element has input focus.
onload	Internet Explorer finishes loading the page or frame (used only with <body> or <frameset>).
onunload	Internet Explorer unloads the page or frame (used only with <body> or <frameset>).

Here's a simple example that demonstrates how to create a script that modifies the appearance of a text element when the user moves the mouse pointer over the text:

```
<h1 onmouseover="this.style.color='red'">
Don't Make Me Angry!
</h1>
```

In this example, the script consists of a single line:

```
this.style.color='red'
```

This line causes the style color attribute of the current object (this) to be set to red. The script runs whenever the user moves the mouse pointer over the text. Thus, the text *Don't Make Me Angry!* turns red when the user points to it with the mouse.

Pay attention to the confusing syntax that's required when you embed a script within an HTML tag. The script must be contained within quotation marks in the HTML tag. But what if the script itself requires quotation marks? To avoid confusion, I use apostrophes rather than quotation marks within the script. But be careful: It's easy to forget to add the closing quotation mark at the end of the script. If you do, your page won't work properly, but you probably won't see any error messages either. So always double-check the closing quotation marks.

How do you make the text turn back to black when the user moves the mouse pointer away from the text? By adding a second script to the <h1> tag, like this:

```
<h1 onmouseover="this.style.color='red'"
    onmouseout="this.style.color='black'">
Don't Make Me Angry!
</h1>
```

Now, whenever the user moves the mouse pointer out of the heading text, the onmouseout script is run, and the color is set back to black.

Using functions

If a script requires more than one line, you can separate the lines with semi-colons. However, for longer scripts, you can instead create functions that you can call up whenever you need them. Place these functions in the <head> section of the HTML document.

The trick to using functions for handling intrinsic events is knowing how to refer to the HTML element that triggered the event. When you code the script directly in the HTML tag, you can use this to refer to the current element. When you create a function, this won't work. Instead, you use the arcane but functional construct window.event.srcElement. To set the color of the element that triggered the procedure, you use window.event.srcElement.style.color.

Listing 20-1 contains an example that uses functions to change the color and size of text when the mouse pointer moves over the text and then to set the color and size back when the mouse pointer leaves the text.

Listing 20-1	Creating a Mouseover Effect

```
<head>
<script language='JScript'>
function TurnItOn() {
    window.event.srcElement.style.color="red";
    window.event.srcElement.style.fontSize="48";
}
function TurnItOff() {
    window.event.srcElement.style.color="black";
    window.event.srcElement.style.fontSize="24";
}
</script>
</head>
<body>
<h1 onmouseover="TurnItOn()" onmouseout="TurnItOff()">
Don't Make Me Angry!
</h1>
</body>
```

Here, the `TurnItOn` function sets the color to red and the font size to 48. The `TurnItOff` function restores the color to black and the font size to 24.

Style sheets

HTML applies only rudimentary formats by using *paragraph tags* that associate a paragraph with a particular format. For example, higher-level headings (h1, h2, and h3) are formatted using tags such as `<h1>`, `<h2>`, and `<h3>`; block quotations are formatted with `<blockquote>` tags; and normal paragraphs are formatted with `<p>` tags.

All Web browsers apply simple, basic formatting to your Web page text based on these HTML tags. For example, headings are always displayed with a larger type size than normal text. A *style sheet,* however, enables you to add additional formatting information to these standard HTML tags.

For example, with a style sheet, you can create a Web page in which all first-level headings (using the `<h1>` and `</h1>` tags) are centered on the page and appear in 26-point Arial Bold font. Or you can create regular paragraphs (using the `<p>` and `</p>` tags) that are formatted as 9-point Century Schoolbook font with a first line indent of 1/2 inch. You can make your text different colors, italicize words you want to emphasize, or highlight sections of your Web page — you can really make your Web pages come alive using style sheets.

I object to the object model!

The cornerstone of Dynamic HTML is the HTML object model, which enables you to access each and every element of an HTML document from a script written in VBScript or JScript.

Unfortunately, object models are troublesome to learn — especially if you're new to object programming. The good news is that the HTML object model is relatively straightforward. Most of the objects correspond directly to HTML elements you already know (well, assuming you already know some HTML). For example, you use the style object to access the `style` attributes of an element. Within the `style` object are additional objects that correspond to each `style` attribute. For example, `style.color` is used for an element's color.

Here are a few tricks you need to know:

✔ Object names are case sensitive and use mostly lowercase letters.

✔ If an attribute name includes a hyphen, drop the hyphen and capitalize the first letter that follows the hyphen. For example, `font-face` becomes `fontFace` and `font-size` becomes `fontSize`.

✔ To access a specific page element, use the `id` attribute in the element's HTML tag. Then, in the script, use the object `document.all` followed by the `id` you gave the element. For example, if you create a heading paragraph with the tag `<H1 id=MyHeading>`, you refer to it in your script as `document.all.MyHeading`.

✔ If the script is included directly in an HTML tag (for example, in an `onmouseclick` attribute), you can use `this` to refer to the element itself.

✔ If you use a sub or function procedure in an HTML file, you can refer to the element that triggered the procedure by using the `window.event.srcElement` object.

To give your Web pages life, color, and personality, Internet Explorer enables you to choose from more than a dozen formatting attributes that can be included in your HTML style sheets. For example, you can set the font using the `font-family` attribute, and you can set the point size using the `font-size` attribute. And the `color` and `background` attributes enable you to set the text color or the background color.

You can apply style sheets to your HTML documents in the following three ways. Each method is appropriate in different situations.

✔ Embedded style sheets

✔ Linked style sheets

✔ Inline styles

Embedded style sheets

The first type of style sheet is an *embedded style sheet*, which you include in the `<head>` section of your Web document. The embedded style sheet contains codes that specify the formats that should be applied to all text marked with a specific tag. This method enables you to apply consistent text formatting throughout an entire HTML document. For example, if you specify in an embedded style sheet that headings (`<h1>` tags) should be formatted in 36-point Arial font, then *all* `<h1>` headings in a Web document are formatted in 36-point Arial font.

Here's an example of an embedded style sheet:

```
<style>
    H1 {font-family: Arial; font-size: 36pt}
    H2 {font-family: Times New Roman;
        font-size: 24pt; color: Red}
</style>
```

With this style sheet placed at the beginning of the document (in the `<head>` section), any `<h1>` heading appears in 36-point Arial and any `<h2>` appears in 24-point red Times New Roman.

Linked style sheets

A *linked style sheet* contains a set of style definitions and exists as a separate file with a `.css` filename extension. You use a `<link>` tag in an HTML document's `<head>` section to link the Web document to the style sheet.

For example, suppose that you store your style sheet in a file named `styles.css`, located at `http://freedonia.gov/styles.css`. The `style.css` file looks like this:

```
H1 {font-family: Arial; font-size: 36pt}
H2 {font-family: Times New Roman;
    font-size: 24pt; color: Red}
```

Notice that the `<style>` and `</style>` tags aren't required in the `.css` file.

To link an HTML document to the `style.css` style sheet, you include the following lines between the `<head>` tags of the HTML file:

```
<head>
<title>This document uses a linked style sheet</title>
<link rel=stylesheet
href="http://freedonia.gov/styles.css" type="text/css">
</head>
```

That's all there is to it. The `rel` attribute indicates that the `link` applies to a style sheet, and the `href` attribute supplies the filename for the style sheet to be used. As a result, this Web document is formatted using the style definitions found in the `styles.css` file.

Inline styles

Occasionally, you may want to override one of the formatting options provided by the embedded style sheet or the linked style sheet. For example, suppose that your style sheet formats `<h1>` headings as 36-point text, but you have one heading that you want to emphasize by displaying it as 44-point text. You can override the style sheet settings by applying an *inline style*. You first apply an `<h1>` tag to the heading and then add an inline `style` attribute. This code overrides the `font-size` attribute of the `<h1>` tag (which is specified in the embedded style sheet, for example) and specifies the new, larger type size.

To override a formatting attribute for a tag, you add a `style` attribute to the tag, as in this example:

```
<h1 style="font-size: 44pt">
```

Notice that the `style` attribute's value is a standard style definition enclosed in quotation marks. Thus, any of the formatting properties that can be used in a style sheet can also be used in a `style` attribute on *any* HTML tag.

The override formatting specified by an inline `style` attribute applies *only* to the tag in which the attribute appears. In the preceding example, for instance, all subsequent `<h1>` headings appear in the font size designated in the style sheet (that is, 36-point text).

To apply formatting to only a portion of a paragraph, you can use the `<span>` tag along with a `style` attribute. For example, suppose that you want to change the background color of a few words of text to yellow in order to give the text a highlighted appearance. You can format a portion of text using the `<span>` tag, as shown in the following code:

```
This is <span style="background: yellow">
    some text</span> that has been highlighted.
```

In the preceding code, the `<span>` tag includes a `style` attribute that changes the background color to yellow for the words "some text."

The `style` attribute is also used in a `<div>` tag to apply a style to a section of a document or in the `<body>` tag to apply a style to the entire body of your Web page. In addition, you can use styles with many other types of tags, including `<img>` (used to insert an image), `<iframe>` (used to create a floating frame), and `<table>` (used to create a table).

Custom tags

Wouldn't it be great if you weren't limited to the tags that are part of standard HTML but could create your own custom tags? For example, suppose you want to create a `<red>` tag that displays text in red and a `<blue>` tag that creates blue text. Then you could use your new tags like this:

```
This is <red>red</red>.<br>
This is <blue>blue</blue>.<br>
```

With Internet Explorer, you can do this — almost. The only trick is that the custom tags you create must reside in their own little world known as a *namespace,* and you must include the namespace as a part of the tag name. For example, if you create the `<red>` and `<blue>` tags in a namespace called `color`, you can use them like this:

```
This is <color:red>red</color:red>.<br>
This is <color:blue>blue</color:blue>.<br>
```

In other words, you can't create a `<red>` tag, but you can create a `<color:red>` tag, which is almost as good.

To create your own tags, you must start by creating a namespace for them. To do that, drop the `xmlns` attribute into the `<html>` tag for the document, like this:

```
<html xmlns:color>
```

Doing this creates a namespace named `color`.

Next, you create the new tags using a style sheet. Start each new tag that you want to define with the namespace, followed by a backslash, a colon, and the new tag. For example, define the `<red>` tag like this:

```
color\:red {color: red}
```

A complete embedded style sheet that defines `<color:red>` and `<color:blue>` tags looks like this:

```
<style>
  color\:red {color: red}
  color\:blue {color: blue}
</style>
```

Putting everything together, Listing 20-2 contains an HTML document that defines a namespace called `color`, creates custom `<color:red>` and `<color:blue>` tags, and then uses them in the body of the document.

Listing 20-2	Using XML to Create Custom Tags

```
<html xmlns:color>
<head>
<style>
  color\:red {color: red}
  color\:blue {color: blue}
</style>
</head>
<body>
This is <color:red>red</color:red>.<br>
This is <color:blue>blue</color:blue>.<br>
</body>
</html>
```

Creating a DHTML Behavior

Okay, enough reviews — on to creating DHTML behaviors. Suppose you want to create a behavior that causes text to become angry by changing its color to red and its size to a 48-point font whenever the user moves the mouse pointer over the text. When the user moves the mouse pointer away, the text calms down by reverting to its original size and color. I'll call this behavior "Angry."

To create and use a DHTML behavior, you must do two things: Create a special file known as an HTC file, and use the behavior in an HTML file. The following two sections explains these tasks.

Creating an HTC file

The first step in creating a behavior is to create a file known as an *HTML component*, or *HTC* for short. As you might guess, the HTC file has a filename extension of htc. Start by creating a skeleton of the HTC file, using the following bare-bones tags:

```
<public:component>

<script language="JScript">

</script>

</public:component>
```

Save the file under the name angry1.htc.

Now, add a `<public:attach>` tag for each event you want the behavior to handle. The `<public:attach>` tag indicates the name of the event to be handled and the name of the script function that will handle the event. To set up a function named Angry to handle the onmouseover event and a function named CalmDown to handle the onmouseout event, add these lines immediately after the `<public:component>` line:

```
<public:attach event="onmouseover"
    onevent="Angry()" />
<public:attach event="onmouseout"
    onevent="CalmDown()" />
```

Next, add any variable declarations your script requires to the beginning of the `<script>` portion of your HTC file. The Angry behavior requires two variables to store the initial settings for the text color and size, and it must handle two events: onmouseover and onmouseout. So you should add the following line immediately after the `<script>` tag:

```
var savedColor, savedSize;
```

Next, create the script for the Angry function.

```
function Angry() {
    savedColor = style.color;
    savedSize = style.fontSize;
    style.color="red";
    style.fontSize=48;
}
```

This function executes whenever the user moves the mouse pointer over the HTML object that the behavior is attached to. The function begins by saving the current color and font size of the element in the savedColor and savedSize variables. Then it sets the color to "red" and the font size to 48. In this script, runtimeStyle.color and runtimeStyle.fontSize refer to the HTML object to which the behavior is attached.

Finally, create the script for the CalmDown function:

```
function CalmDown() {
    style.color=savedColor;
    style.fontSize=savedSize;
}
```

This function, which executes whenever the user moves the mouse pointer away from the HTML object the behavior is attached to, restores the HTML object's color and font size to their saved values.

Listing 20-3 shows the complete angry1.htc file.

Listing 20-3	The angry1.htc Script

```
<public:component>
<public:attach event="onmouseover"
    onevent="Angry()" />
<public:attach event="onmouseout"
    onevent="CalmDown()" />

<script language="JScript">

var savedColor, savedSize;

function Angry() {
  savedColor = style.color;
  savedSize = style.fontSize;
  style.color = "red";
  style.fontSize = "48";
}

function CalmDown() {
  style.color = savedColor;
  style.fontSize = savedSize;
}

</script>

</public:component>
```

Applying a behavior

After you create the HTC file for a behavior, applying the behavior to an element in an HTML document is easy. All you have to do is specify the URL of the HTC file via the `behavior` style attribute.

If you specify just the filename for the HTC file, Internet Explorer will attempt to retrieve the HTC file from the same folder as the HTML file for the page that uses the behavior. If you want to store the HTC file in some other folder, you should specify the complete URL or the HTC file, such as `www.mysite.com/scripts/angry1.htc`.

You can apply a behavior to a specific element by using an inline style, like this:

```
<h1 style="behavior: url(angry1.htc)">
Don't Make Me Angry!
</h1>
```

In this case, the text *Don't Make Me Angry* is displayed using the usual <h1> formatting. When the user moves the mouse pointer over the text, the text color changes to red and the font size changes to 48 point. And when the user moves the mouse pointer away from the text, the color and size are restored to their original settings.

Alternatively, you can set the behavior in the <style> section of the document. For example, here is how you can apply the Angry behavior to all <h1> paragraphs:

```
<style>
    h1 {behavior: url(angry1.htc)}
</style>
```

Yet another method is to create a style class that references the behavior. Any element to which you assign the class adopts the behavior. In the <style> section, list the name of the class you create preceded by a period, like this:

```
<style>
    .angry {behavior: url(angry1.htc)}
</style>
```

Then specify class=angry in any HTML tag to apply the behavior. For example:

```
<a href="hulk.htm" class=angry>Don't make me angry!</a>
```

In this example, the text "Don't make me angry!" is displayed as a link and also adopts the Angry behavior.

Creating Custom Tags with Behaviors

With Internet Explorer 5.5, you can create HTC files that are tied to custom tags. When you use the custom tag, the behavior you created for the tag is automatically applied. A DHTML behavior that implements a custom tag is known as an *element behavior.* (For more information about creating custom tags, refer to the section "Custom tags" earlier in this chapter.)

Creating an element behavior is similar to creating a regular DHTML behavior, with one key difference: You must list the name of the custom tag on the tagName attribute of the <public:component> tag. For example, to create an element behavior that implements a custom tag called angry, you want to code the <public:component> tag like this:

```
<public:component tagName="angry">
```

Listing 20-4 contains a complete HTC file named `angry2.htc` that implements a custom `angry` tag that changes the size and color of text when the mouse passes over the text, and then changes the size and color back when the mouse leaves. Except for the `<public:component>` tag, this HTC file is identical to the `angry1.htc` file I presented in the section "Creating an HTC file" earlier in this chapter.

Listing 20-4	The angry2.htc Script

```
<public:component tagName="angry">
<public:attach event="onmouseover"
    onevent="Angry()" />
<public:attach event="onmouseout"
    onevent="CalmDown()" />

<script language="JScript">

var savedColor, savedSize;

function Angry() {
   savedColor = style.color;
   savedSize = style.fontSize;
   style.color = "red";
   style.fontSize = "48";
}

function CalmDown() {
   style.color = savedColor;
   style.fontSize = savedSize;
}

</script>

</public:component>
```

To use the custom tag that is implemented by an element behavior, you must include several things in your HTML file:

✔ The `<html>` tag must use an `xmlns` attribute to provide the name of the namespace that will be used for the custom tag.

✔ You must use an `<?import>` tag with a `namespace` attribute that indicates the name of the namespace for the custom tag and an `implementation` tag that names the HTC file.

✔ To use the custom tag, you must include the namespace before the custom tag name, separating the two with a colon.

The following bit of HTML puts these elements together to use the custom angry tag:

```
<html xmlns:hulk>
<?import namespace="hulk" implementation="angry2.htc">
<body>
<hulk:angry>Don't make me angry!</hulk:angry>
</body>
</html>
```

In this example, the text between the `<hulk:angry>` and `</hulk:angry>` tags changes size and color when approached by the mouse.

You can also use a style sheet to create a style format for the element behavior's custom tag. Here's an example that does so using an embedded style sheet:

```
<html xmlns:hulk>
<?import namespace="hulk" implementation="angry2.htc">

<style>
   hulk\:angry {font-family: Arial; font-size: 24pt}
</style>

<body>
<hulk:angry>Don't make me angry!</hulk:angry>
</body>
</html>
```

Using Behavior Properties, Methods, and Events

Because DHTML behaviors are themselves objects, behaviors can have their own properties, methods, and events. You can therefore create sophisticated behaviors that interact with HTML page elements. The following sections explain how to expose properties, methods, and events in your own DHTML behaviors. To keep things simple, these sections create simple DHTML behaviors. But the same techniques work as well for element behaviors.

Exposing properties

The Angry behavior described in the section "Creating a DHTML Behavior" always changes the text color to red and the size to 48. To make the Angry behavior more useful, you can give the behavior properties that enable you to change the color and size from the HTML that references the behavior. You can think of properties as script variables that have been exposed to the outside world so that they can be examined and modified from HTML documents that use the behavior.

To expose behavior properties, you must add a `<public:property>` tag for each property you want to expose. Place these tags right after the `<public:component>` tag, like this:

```
<public:component>
<public:property name="angryColor" />
<public:property name="angrySize" />
```

Replace the hard-coded *red* and *48* in the `Angry` function with references to the properties instead.

```
function Angry() {
   savedColor = style.color;
   savedSize = style.fontSize;
   style.color=angryColor;
   style.fontSize=angrySize;
}
```

You may think that that's all there is to it, but one important detail remains: assigning default values to the `angryColor` and `angrySize` properties if no values are assigned in the HTML document. To do that, you create a function that initializes the variables and then attach that function to the behavior's `onload` event. Here is an example of a `<public:attach>` tag that assigns a function named `event_onload` to the `onload` event:

```
<public:attach event="onload"
    for="window" onevent="initProperties()" />
```

The `initProperties()` function should assign a default value to each property only if the property value is null, like this:

```
function initProperties() {
   if (angryColor==null)
     angryColor="red";
   if (angrySize==null)
     angrySize=48;
}
```

The code in Listing 20-5 shows the complete HTC file, this one named `angry3.htc`, with the changes necessary to expose the `angryColor` and `angrySize` properties.

Listing 20-5	The angry3.htc Script

```
<public:component>
<public:property name="angryColor" />
<public:property name="angrySize" />
<public:attach event="onmouseover"
    onevent="Angry()" />
<public:attach event="onmouseout"
    onevent="CalmDown()" />
<public:attach event="onload"
    for="window" onevent="initProperties()" />

<script language="JScript">

var savedColor, savedSize

function Angry() {
  savedColor = style.color;
  savedSize = style.fontSize;
  style.color = angryColor;
  style.fontSize = angrySize;
}

function CalmDown() {
  style.color = savedColor;
  style.fontSize = savedSize;
}

function initProperties() {
  if (angryColor==null)
    angryColor="red";
  if (angrySize==null)
    angrySize=48;
}

</script>

</public:component>
```

The beauty of behavior properties is that after you have assigned a behavior to an HTML element, you can use the behavior's properties as if they were attributes of the HTML element's tag. For example, the following HTML snippet shows how to set the angryColor to yellow so that the text changes to yellow instead of red:

```
<style>
  .angry {behavior: url(angry3.htc)}
</style>
  .
  .
  .
<h1 class=angry angryColor="yellow">
Don't Make Me Angry!
</h1>
```

Notice how angryColor is used as if it is an attribute for the <H1> tag.

Exposing methods

DHTML behaviors can also expose methods that can be called from other script components on the page. For example, the Angry behavior that I describe throughout this chapter may expose its Angry and CalmDown functions as methods. Then you can connect the Angry behavior to a text element of a Web page and have other elements of the page direct that text element to become angry or to calm down by invoking its Angry or CalmDown methods.

Figure 20-1 shows a Web page that contains a text element ("Don't Make Me Angry!") and the Get Angry and Calm Down buttons. The text exhibits the Angry behavior, changing its size to 48 point and its color to red when the user moves the mouse pointer over the text and reverting to normal when the user moves the mouse pointer away. To demonstrate how methods can be used, the text also responds to the buttons. When the user clicks the Get Angry button, the Get Angry button invokes the text element's Angry method, which in turn changes the text size to 48 and color to red. Clicking the Calm Down button invokes the text element's CalmDown method, which restores the text to its previous size and color.

Listing 20-6 contains the HTML for the page shown in Figure 20-1.

Listing 20-6	Using Behavior Methods

```
<html>
<head>
<title>Welcome!</title>
<style>
  .angry {behavior: url(angry4.htc)}
</style>
</head>
```

```
<body>
<h1 id=head1 class=angry>
Don't Make Me Angry!
</h1>
<form name='myform'>
  <input name='button1' type='button'
    value='Get Angry'>
  <script language='JScript' for='button1'
  event='onclick'>
    head1.Angry();
  </script>
  <input name='button2' type='button'
    value='Calm Down'>
  <script language='JScript' for='button2'
  event='onclick'>
    head1.CalmDown();
  </script>
</form>
</body>
<html>
```

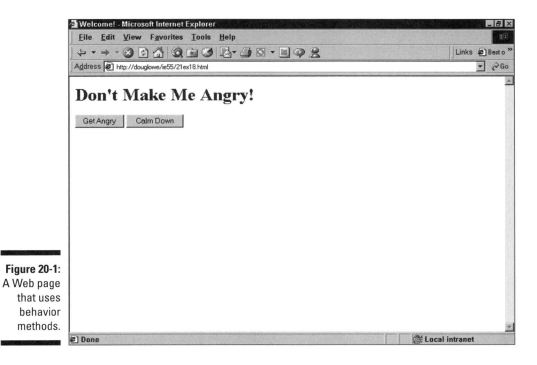

Figure 20-1:
A Web page
that uses
behavior
methods.

The `<style>` section creates a class named `angry` that uses the `angry4.htc` behavior, which is presented later in this section. Then in the `<body>` section, the `<h1>` tag that formats the "Don't Make Me Angry!" text uses the `angry` class. In addition, the `<h1>` tag uses an id attribute so that the tag can be accessed by other elements.

The `<form>` block creates the two buttons. The key to how these buttons operate is in the `<script>` blocks that follow each button. The scripts are attached to the `onclick` event for each button. For the first button, the script consists of the following line:

```
head1.Angry();
```

This line invokes the `Angry` method for the `head1` element, which causes the `head1` element's size and color to change.

To invoke the `CalmDown` method, the script for the second button uses this line:

```
head1.CalmDown();
```

This line causes the text to revert to its previous setting.

To expose a behavior function as a method, you use a `<public:method>` tag, as in these examples:

```
<public:method name="Angry"/>
<public:method name="CalmDown"/>
```

These two additions are all that is necessary to expose the `Angry()` and `CalmDown()` functions as methods. However, exposing these functions as methods forces you to make another change to the behavior script: The behavior must now keep track of the status of its text element. In other words, the `Angry()` function should apply the angry text size and color only if the text is not already angry, and the `CalmDown()` function should restore the text size and color only if the text is in its angry state.

To keep track of the state of the text element, add a variable named `isAngry`, like this:

```
var isAngry=0;
```

Then modify the `Angry()` and `CalmDown()` functions as follows:

```
function Angry() {
  if ( ! isAngry) {
    savedColor = style.color;
    savedSize = style.fontSize;
    style.color = angryColor;
    style.fontSize = angrySize;
```

```
      isAngry = true;
   }
}

function CalmDown() {
   if (isAngry) {
      style.color = savedColor;
      style.fontSize = savedSize;
      isAngry = false;
   }
}
```

Each function begins by testing the status of the `isAngry` variable and ends by setting `isAngry`.

Listing 20-7 shows the new HTC file, named `angry4.htc`, with its methods exposed.

Listing 20-7   **The angry4.htc Script**

```
<public:component>
<public:property name="angryColor" />
<public:property name="angrySize" />
<public:method name="Angry" />
<public:method name="CalmDown" />
<public:attach event="onmouseover"
    onevent="Angry()" />
<public:attach event="onmouseout"
    onevent="CalmDown()" />
<public:attach event="onload"
    for="window" onevent="initProperties()" />

<script language="JScript">

var savedColor, savedSize;
var isAngry;

function Angry() {
   if ( ! isAngry) {
      savedColor = style.color;
      savedSize = style.fontSize;
      style.color = angryColor;
      style.fontSize = angrySize;
      isAngry = true;
   }
}

function CalmDown() {
   if (isAngry) {
```

(continued)

Listing 20-7 *(continued)*   **The angry4.htc Script**

```
      style.color = savedColor;
     style.fontSize = savedSize;
      isAngry = false;
    }
}

function initProperties() {
  if (angryColor==null)
    angryColor="red";
  if (angrySize==null)
    angrySize=48;
}

</script>

</public:component>
```

Exposing events

You can also create behaviors that have their own custom events. For example, suppose that you want to provide the Angry behavior with events that are triggered whenever the text becomes angry or calms down. To do that, you can implement two custom events, named onAngry and onCalmDown. Any HTML document that uses the Angry behavior can then attach scripts to the onAngry and onCalmDown events.

To create a custom event, you add a <public:event> tag to at the beginning of the HTC file, as in these examples:

```
<public:event name="onAngry" id="idAngry"/>
<public:event name="onCalmDown" id="idCalmDown"/>
```

The <public:event> tag creates an object for each event. The name attribute gives the name that your HTML file will use to handle the event, and the id attribute gives the name your script will use to refer to the event object.

To actually trigger an event, you invoke the fire method for the event object. For example, to fire the onAngry event, include the following line in the Angry() function:

```
idAngry.fire();
```

Listing 20-8 shows a version of the angry behavior, named angry5.htc, that includes the onAngry and onCalmDown events. For simplicity, this version of the Angry behavior does not implement the angryColor or angrySize properties or the Angry or CalmDown methods.

Listing 20-8	The angry5.htc Script

```
<public:component>
<public:event name="onAngry" id="idAngry" />
<public:event name="onCalmDown id="idCalmDown" />
<public:attach event="onmouseover"
    onevent="Angry()" />
<public:attach event="onmouseout"
    onevent="CalmDown()" />
/>

<script language="JScript">

var savedColor, savedSize;
var isAngry;

function Angry() {
  savedColor = style.color;
  savedSize = style.fontSize;
  style.color = "Red";
  style.fontSize = "36pt";
  idAngry.fire();
}

function CalmDown() {
  style.color = savedColor;
  style.fontSize = savedSize;
  idCalmDown.fire();
}

</script>

</public:component>
```

To handle a custom event in HTML, you can use the custom event name as an attribute in the tag that applies the behavior. For example, here is an HTML document that displays an alert box when the onAngry event is raised:

```
</html>

<head>
<title>Welcome!</title>
<style>
  .angry {behavior: url(angry5.htc)}
</style>
</head>

<body>
<h1 id=head1 class=angry
    onAngry="alert('Now you did it!')" >
```

(continued)

```
Don't Make Me Angry!
</h1>

</body>

</html>
```

Figure 20-2 shows what appears when the user moves the mouse over the "Don't Make Me Angry!" text.

Figure 20-2:
An alert box
triggered by
a custom
event.

But Wait, There's More

In this chapter, I only scratch the surface of what is possible with DHTML behaviors. For example, I haven't shown how you can use behaviors to add or remove content from the Web page to create effects such as collapsible outlines, which reveal or hide subheadings when the user clicks a heading. And I haven't even mentioned that behaviors can be implemented as Java or C++ programs rather than scripts.

For complete information about DHTML behaviors, check out Microsoft's Internet Explorer Developer Center at msdn.microsoft.com/ie.

Chapter 21

Still More New DHTML Features for Web Developers

***

In This Chapter

▶ Creating HTC ViewLink components

▶ Creating editable text fields

▶ Creating sideways text

▶ Creating drop caps and first-line effects

▶ Zooming in on text and images

***

Dynamic HTML (DHTML) behaviors, which are discussed in Chapter 20, are the most highly touted new feature of Internet Explorer for Web developers. But with each new release of Internet Explorer, Microsoft manages to pile on a few other interesting features that are also worth knowing about. This chapter serves as a brief introduction to some of the most useful of these new features. For complete information about the new developer features of Internet Explorer 5.5, check out the Internet Explorer Developer Center at msdn.microsoft.com/ie.

Creating ViewLink Components

ViewLink, one of several new features in Internet Explorer 5.5, lets you create software components using Dynamic HTML. In Chapter 20, you find information about how you can use HTML component (HTC) files to create element behaviors, which separate the scripts needed to implement behaviors, such as rollover mouse effects, from the HTML used to create the content for a Web page. ViewLink takes the separation of a behavior from the main HTML document one step further by allowing the behavior to actually display its own information on the main HTML page.

As an example, in this section I show you how to create a ViewLink component that creates a simple button bar that changes background color when the user points the mouse at each button on the bar. The ViewLink component implements a tag named Button, which has a property named ButtonName. The ViewLink component displays the text you supply in the ButtonName property with a silver background, but changes the background color to yellow when you point the mouse at the button. In addition, the ViewLink component changes the mouse pointer to a hand to let the user know that he or she can click the button.

To keep things simple, the Button ViewLink component doesn't do anything if the user clicks the button. You can figure out how to do make the component actually do something in response to a button click for extra credit.

Listing 21-1 contains the complete HTC file (button1.htc) for the Button ViewLink component.

Listing 21-1   **The button1.htc Script**

```
<public:component tagName="button">
  <public:defaults viewLinkContent />
  <public:property name="ButtonName">
  <public:attach event="oncontentready"
         onevent="Init()"/>
  <public:attach event="onmouseover"
         onevent="MouseOver()"/>
  <public:attach event="onmouseout"
         onevent="MouseOut()"/>
</public:component>

<script language="JScript">
function Init() {
  document.body.innerHTML = " "
    + ButtonName + " ";
  document.body.style.background = "Silver";
}

function MouseOver() {
  document.body.style.background = "Yellow";
  document.body.style.cursor = "Hand";
}

function MouseOut() {
  document.body.style.background = "Silver";
  document.body.style.cursor = "Default";
}
</script>

<body>
</body>
```

The following paragraphs summarize the key parts of the `button1.htc` file:

- ✔ The `<public:component>` tag in the first line establishes that the file is an HTC component and indicates that the custom tag name for the component is `button`.

- ✔ The second line is a `<public:defaults>` tag, which is required for ViewLink components. This tag gives the ViewLink component the ability to display information on the main HTML page.

- ✔ The `<public:property>` tag creates the `ButtonName` property, which is used to display the text for the button.

- ✔ The three `<public:attach>` tags set up event handlers for the `oncontentready`, `onmouseover`, and `onmouseout` events. These events are handled by the `Init()`, `MouseOver()`, and `MouseOut()` functions.

- ✔ In the `Init()` function, the `innerHTML` property for the component's `document.body` object is set to the value of the `ButtonName` property, with non-breaking spaces before and after. In addition, the background color is set to Silver.

- ✔ In the `MouseOver` function, the background color is set to Yellow, and the cursor is changed to a hand.

- ✔ In the `MouseOut` function, the background color is set back to Silver, and the cursor is changed back to its default.

Listing 21-2 contains an HTML file that uses the Button ViewLink component to create a button bar with four buttons named File, Edit, View, and Help.

Listing 21-2   Using the Button ViewLink component

```
<html xmlns:btn>
<head>
  <?import namespace="btn"
      implementation="button1.htc">
</head>

<body>

Check out this way cool button bar:
<p>
<btn:button ButtonName="File"/>
<btn:button ButtonName="Edit"/>
<btn:button ButtonName="View"/>
<btn:button ButtonName="Help"/>

</body>
</html>
```

The following paragraphs highlight the key points to notice in this HTML file:

- ✔ The `<html>` tag includes an `xmlns` attribute to create an XML name-space for the custom tag that the Button ViewLink component implements.

- ✔ The `<?import>` tag specifies that `button1.htc` is required to provide the implementation for the `btn` namespace.

- ✔ Each of the `<btn:button>` tags creates a button on the button bar, using the name indicated in the `ButtonName` property.

Figure 21-1 shows how this HTML file appears when displayed.

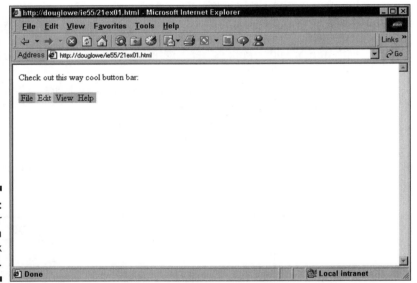

Figure 21-1:
A button bar
created with
a ViewLink
component.

As you might guess, ViewLink components can be much more complex than this simple example would lead you to believe. For more information about ViewLink, see Microsoft's documentation at `msdn.microsoft.com/workshop`.

Edit This!

Internet Explorer 5.5 includes a new attribute called `ContentEditable`, which lets you create editable text regions on an HTML page without resorting to form fields. You can use the `ContentEditable` attribute with any tag that encloses text, such as `<p>`, `<h1>`, `<div>`, and `<span>`.

The `ContentEditable` attribute can have one of three values: `true` makes the text editable, `false` makes the text not editable, and `inherit` causes the text to inherit the `ContentEditable` setting from its parent element.

The example in Listing 21-3 shows you how to create a simple editable text field. To demonstrate how to retrieve and use the edited text, the example includes a form button that displays the edited text in an alert box when the user clicks the button.

Listing 21-3	Using an Editable Text Field

```
<body>

You can edit the following text:

<span id="span1" style="background: yellow"
    ContentEditable="true">
Replace this text with your own.
</span>

<p>

<form name="myform">
 <input name="button1" type="button" value="Show Text">
 <script language="JScript"
     for="button1" event="onclick">
   alert(span1.innerText)
 </script>
</form>

</body>
```

In the example in Listing 21-3, the editable text field is marked by a `<span>` tag that includes the `ContentEditable` attribute and an `id` attribute. The script that is attached to the `onclick` event for the button simply displays the `innerText` value for the span.

Figure 21-2 shows how this page works. Here, I edited the text field by adding "OK, I think I will." Then, I clicked the Show Text button to display the alert box. As you can see, the text I typed in the editable field appears in the alert box.

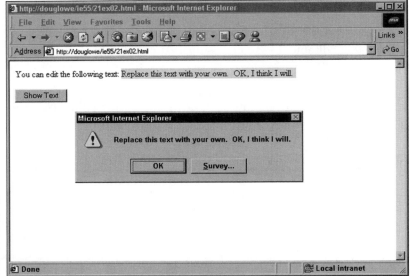

Figure 21-2:
Using an
editable text
field.

Writing Sideways with the writing-mode Attribute

Internet Explorer 5.5 includes a new style attribute named `writing-mode`, which you can use on tags that contain text to control the direction in which Internet Explorer writes the text. You can set the `writing-mode` property to one of two values: `lr-tb` tells Internet Explorer to write the text from left to right and top to bottom, as English and other Roman-based languages are written; `tb-rl` writes the text top to bottom and right to left, as in East Asian languages. If you use `tb-rl` with Roman-style fonts (such as Times New Roman and Arial), the letters are also flipped 90 degrees.

To see how the `writing-mode` property works, have a look at the example in Listing 21-4.

Listing 21-4	Writing Text Sideways

```
<div style="font: 36pt Arial; position: absolute;
            left: 0px; top: 0px; height: 5in;
            writing-mode: tb-rl;
            background-color: bisque">
This is sideways </div>

<div style="position: absolute; left: 0.75in;
            top: 0px">
<P><P>
All work and no play makes Jack a dull boy.
All work and no play makes Jack a dull boy.
All work and no play makes Jack a dull boy.
All work and no play makes Jack a dull boy.
All work and no play makes Jack a dull boy.
All work and no play makes Jack a dull boy.
All work and no play makes Jack a dull boy.
All work and no play makes Jack a dull boy.
</div>
```

The example in Listing 21-4 uses two `<div>` tags to set up a page layout that has a vertical sidebar at the left edge of the page with normally formatted text in the center. The `<div>` tag for the vertical sidebar specifies `writing-mode: tb-rl` in the `style` attribute to display its text sideways — that is, top to bottom, right to left. Figure 21-3 shows how this page appears when displayed by Internet Explorer 5.5.

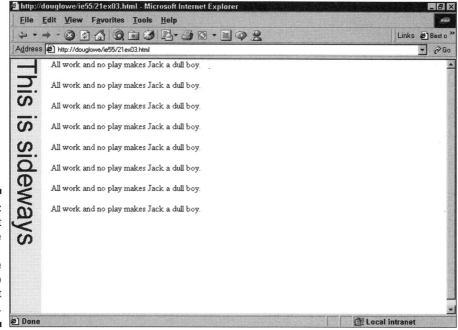

Figure 21-3:
A page that uses the `writing-mode` style attribute to display text sideways.

Creating Drop Caps and Other Effects

Internet Explorer 5.5 supports two new HTML style elements — `first-letter` and `first-line` — that let you apply special formatting to the first letter of a text element and to the first line of a text element. (Technically, `first-letter` and `first-line` are known as *pseudo-elements*.) You can use these new style elements for effects such as a large drop cap for the first letter of a paragraph and all capital letters for the first line of a paragraph, as shown in Figure 21-4.

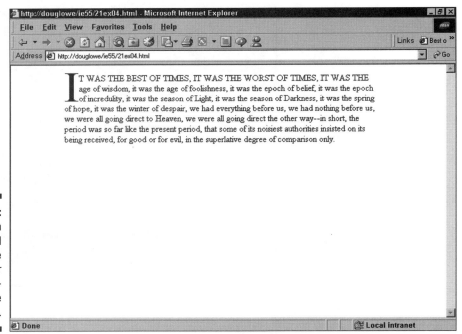

Figure 21-4:
A paragraph formatted with a large first letter and all capitals for the first line.

To use the `first-letter` or `first-line` style elements, create a style class for the tag you want to use to format the text, typically `<p>`. Then, use `first-letter` and `first-line` to specify the formatting, like this:

```
<style>
    p.firstgraf:first-letter {font-size: 500%;
        float: left}
    p.firstgraf:first-line {text-transform: uppercase}
</style>
```

In this example, `first-letter` specifies that the first letter of the paragraph should use a font that is five times as large as the paragraph's base font and should be positioned to the left of the rest of the text. first-line specifies that the text for the first line of the paragraph should be formatted with all capital letters.

To apply these elements to a paragraph, just use the class attribute in the <p> tag, naming the class you created (in the example, firstgraf).

Listing 21-5 contains the HTML I used to create the paragraph shown in Figure 21-4.

Listing 21-5	Using the first-letter and first-line Styles

```
<style>
   p.firstgraf:first-letter {font-size: 500%;
      float: left}
   p.firstgraf:first-line {text-transform: uppercase}
</style>

<div style="position: absolute; left: 1in; right: 1in">
<p class="firstgraf">
It was the best of times, it was the worst of times,
it was the age of wisdom, it was the age of
foolishness, it was the epoch of belief, it was
the epoch of incredulity, it was the season of Light,
it was the season of Darkness, it was the spring of
hope, it was the winter of despair, we had everything
before us, we had nothing before us, we were all going
direct to Heaven, we were all going direct the other
way--in short, the period was so far like the present
period, that some of its noisiest authorities insisted
on its being received, for good or for evil, in the
superlative degree of comparison only.
</p>
</div>
```

Zooming In

Another new formatting attribute introduced for Internet Explorer 5.5 is zoom, which lets you set the zoom factor for any HTML element — be it a bit of text, an image, or an entire page. You can include the zoom attribute on just about any HTML tag, and you can set the zoom attribute via a script if you want.

The zoom attribute can have one of three values:

- ✔ normal indicates that the element should be displayed at its regular size.
- ✔ number uses a number to indicate a zoom factor. Normal size is 1.0. Anything less than 1.0 is smaller than normal; greater than 1.0 is larger than normal.

✔ percent uses a number followed by a percent sign to indicate a zoom percentage. 100% is normal size.

Here are some examples of tags that use the zoom attribute:

```
<p zoom='normal'>
<div zoom='1.5'>
<body zoom='50%'>
```

The zoom attribute provides a convenient way to increase the size of text for a mouse rollover effect. For example, the following tag creates a rollover effect that doubles the size of the element when the user moves the mouse over the element:

```
<p onmouseover="this.style.zoom='200%'"
   onmouseout="this.style.zoom='normal'">
Don't make me angry!
</p>
```

The advantage of using this method rather than changing the font size is that the zoom attribute works for images as well as text elements.

But Wait, There's More!

All in all, Internet Explorer 5.5 introduces more than 200 new DHTML objects, properties, methods, and events. In this chapter, I cover just a few of them. Here are a some of the other interesting new DHTML features:

✔ **HTML+TIME:** Previous versions of Internet Explorer have supported timed animations, but Internet Explorer 5.5 introduces many new timing elements that let you create simple animations for your Web page. You can have elements appear and disappear at certain intervals or move across the page following simple or complex paths, and you can use special effects to transition from one element to another.

✔ **Colored scroll bars:** You can now control the color of various aspects of scroll bars using attributes such as scrollbarArrowColor, scrollbarFaceColor, and scrollbarBaseColor.

✔ **Pop-ups:** Internet Explorer 5.5 introduces a new type of window that you can use for dialog boxes, messages and alerts, or to display pop-up menus, tips, or annoying advertisements.

✔ **Printing controls:** Several new properties and methods have been introduced to give you more control over how Web pages are printed. For example, a new printPage method lets you send any HTML element to a printer.

For information about these new DHTML features, check out the Internet Explorer Developer Center at msdn.microsoft.com/ie.

Part VI
The Part of Tens

The 5th Wave   By Rich Tennant

"What I'm looking for are dynamic Web applications and content, not Web innuendoes and intent."

In this part . . .

*I*f you keep this book in the bathroom (where it rightfully belongs), the chapters in this part are the ones destined to gain the most readership. Each of these chapters offers up ten (more or less) things that are worth knowing about various aspects of using Internet Explorer.

Without further ado, here they are, direct from the home office in Fresno, California. . . .

Chapter 22

Ten Tips for Using Internet Explorer Efficiently

In This Chapter

▶ Creating a custom start page

▶ Using Favorites to call up your favorite Web sites

▶ Using the Links toolbar to get to your favorites sites even quicker

▶ Creating desktop shortcuts for Web pages

▶ Clicking in unusual places

▶ Searching efficiently

▶ Living with annoying advertisement windows

▶ Typing dot-com addresses quickly

▶ Improving Internet Explorer with other software

*T*he Internet can be a fun place to explore. But because it's so big, losing your way is easy. Fortunately, Internet Explorer 5.5 is filled with nifty little tricks that can make your Internet explorations more fruitful. The tips presented in this chapter can help you explore the Internet more efficiently so that you won't get lost in the woods. Many of these tips are covered elsewhere in this book; I gathered them here together merely for your convenience, at no extra charge.

Customizing Your Start Page

By default, Internet Explorer 5.5 configures itself to use www.msn.com as its start page. The msn.com home page is a great place to start your explorations of the Internet. But the best thing about the msn.com page is that you can customize it to show the information you are most interested in. By personalizing msn.com, you can get stock quotes, news headlines on the subjects that interests you, sports scores, movie reviews, and other useful information all on one page, so you don't have to waste time surfing through page after page to find the information you need.

To personalize the msn.com start page, click the <u>Change Content</u> link. You can choose the content items that you want to add to your personalized home page.

If you'd rather switch to an altogether different start page, you can do that, too. Choose <u>T</u>ools⇨Internet <u>O</u>ptions, click the General tab, and then change the home page Address field to the address of any page you want to use for your start page.

For more information, see Chapter 13.

Stashing Goodies in the Favorites Menu

Internet Explorer's Favorites menu lets you gather up your favorite Web pages into a single location so that you can get to them easily. If you find yourself visiting a Web page frequently, add it to the Favorites menu so that you can go to that page directly from any other Web page. For example, if you like to visit Dummies.com to find out what the latest *For Dummies* books are, add Dummies.com to your Favorites menu. You can go directly to the Dummies.com page at any time simply by choosing Dummies.com from the Favorites menu.

To add an item to your Favorites menu, follow these steps:

1. **Go to the page that you want to add to your Favorites menu.**

2. **Choose F<u>a</u>vorites⇨<u>A</u>dd to Favorites.**

   Doing so brings up the Add Favorite dialog box.

3. **If you don't like the description of the page listed in the <u>N</u>ame text box, you can type a new description.**

4. **Click the OK button.**

For more information about working with Favorites, see Chapter 5.

Customizing Your Links Toolbar

An even faster way to access the pages that you use most is to add them to your Links toolbar. The Links toolbar, located at the top of the Internet Explorer window, contains buttons that let you go to frequently used Web pages with a single click of the mouse.

When you first install Internet Explorer, the Links toolbar includes links to Web sites that Microsoft thinks you should visit often, such as Microsoft's own corporate Web site, Microsoft's Windows Web site, and other Microsoft sites. But you can easily add your own sites to the Links toolbar. Just follow these steps:

1. **Go to the page that you want to add to your Links toolbar.**
2. **Drag the page icon from the Address bar to the Links toolbar.**

   This step is a little tricky. The page icon appears right next to the Web page address in the Address toolbar. Point the mouse at this icon, and then press and hold the left mouse button. Next, move the mouse to the position on the Links toolbar where you want the link to appear. When you release the mouse button, a button for the page appears.

To remove a link from the Links toolbar, right-click the link, and then choose the Delete command.

For more information about customizing the Links toolbar, refer to Chapter 5.

Creating Desktop Shortcuts

Yet another way to go quickly to a Web page that you use frequently is to create a desktop shortcut for the page. You can call up the page at any time by double-clicking the shortcut on your desktop.

To create a desktop shortcut, follow these steps:

1. **Go to the page that you want to create a shortcut for.**
2. **Right-click in an empty portion of the page and choose the Create Shortcut command.**

   Doing so brings up a dialog box informing you that a shortcut will be created.

   If the Create Shortcut command doesn't appear in the menu, right-click somewhere else on the page. The Create Shortcut command won't appear if you right-click a link, picture, or other object on the page.

3. **Click the OK button.**

   The shortcut is created on your desktop.

Be careful about creating too many desktop shortcuts. If you create too many shortcuts, your desktop can become cluttered.

Discovering Weird Places to Click

The Internet is a mousy place. You can click your way through link after link to get wherever you want to go. However, there are more places to click than you are probably aware of. In many cases, the links on a page are not as obvious as you would hope. Move the mouse pointer over different areas of the page to find out. If the mouse pointer changes to a hand, you've found a hidden link.

Another way to exercise your mouse skills is to try right-clicking various objects on Web pages. Right-clicking an object on a page summons a pop-up menu of commands that apply to the object. For example, right-click a picture on a Web page to get a menu of commands that lets you save the picture to a file, print the picture, or use the picture as your Windows desktop wallpaper.

Finally, try working out the mouse on Internet Explorer's toolbars. You can use your mouse to rearrange the location of the toolbars by dragging the toolbar handle (the vertical bar located at the left edge of each toolbar). You can customize your toolbars by right-clicking between the buttons of any toolbar to bring up a pop-up menu that lists customization options. And don't miss the little extension arrows that appear at the right edge of the toolbars. Click these arrows to reveal additional toolbar buttons.

Searching Tips

When you need to look something up on the Internet, you can turn to one of the Internet's many search services, such as Yahoo!, Lycos, AltaVista, or Microsoft's own MSN Search. Unfortunately, if you don't use these search services wisely, you can spend hours looking for something without ever finding it.

Here are some tips for using Internet Explorer's search features efficiently:

  ✔ Use the Search bar. It enables you to display search results in a separate pane on the left side of the Internet Explorer window while viewing Web pages at the same time.

  ✔ Choose your search keywords carefully. If you search for broad terms like "Animals" or "History," you'll get — as Carl Sagan would have said — billions and billions of results to sift through. If your search words are too narrow, you won't get any results. It's usually best to start with search words that you think may be too narrow, and then move to more general words if you don't get the results you want. The Internet is a huge place, and you'll be surprised by how many results you get from searches that you may at first think are too specific. (For example, I recently searched for "Bald starship captain" and got 283 results, most of them correctly identifying Patrick Stewart from *Star Trek: The Next Generation*.)

✔ Use the advanced search page available on most search services rather than the search text box found on search service's home pages. The advanced search pages let you use advanced search features to help you make more efficient searches, such as searching for pages that contain all of the words that you typed in the search field or any of the words that you typed in the search field. You can also search for pages that contain two words in close proximity to one another.

✔ Don't give up if you don't find the information you're looking for right away. If one search service doesn't turn up the page you need, try the same search using another service.

✔ To access search services quickly without having to wade through the search pane, add a link to the search service to your Links toolbar.

✔ When you do find a Web page that is interesting, add it to your Favorites menu so that you won't have to trudge through a complicated search to find the page again later.

Dealing with Those Annoying Ad Windows

Many Web pages have an annoying habit of popping up advertisements in separate windows. Eventually, your entire desktop can become cluttered with little ad windows. You can dismiss an ad window by clicking the window's Close button, but sometimes the windows keep popping back up.

Here's a little trick that sometimes suppresses those annoying windows that insist on reappearing after you dismiss them: Instead of closing the persistent window, minimize it. The window is sent to your taskbar, where it remains until you leave the site. If the window remains on your taskbar after you leave the site, you can safely close it.

Typing Web Addresses the Easy Way

If you've been using the Internet for awhile, you probably have the keystrokes for `www.` and `.com` ingrained in the motor-memory of your fingers. If you're tired of typing these keystrokes for just about every Web page you visit, you'll be happy to know that you can leave them off when you use Internet Explorer.

Just type the middle portion of the Web address — the part that comes between www. and .com, and press Ctrl+Enter instead of just Enter to go to the Web site. When you press Ctrl+Enter, Internet Explorer automatically adds www. to the beginning and .com to the end of the Web address.

Using Other Software to Improve Internet Explorer

Although Internet Explorer is a great Web browser, you can get even more out of the Internet by using other software to add features that Internet Explorer doesn't offer. The following are several types of programs you can use along with Internet Explorer:

✔ Internet security programs can make your Internet excursions safer by preventing hackers and other unscrupulous nuts from sneaking in to your computer while you are online. Two of the best security programs are BlackICE Defender (www.networkice.com) and Norton Internet Security from Symantec (www.symantec.com). Both security programs cost about $50.

✔ Cookie managers help you control the proliferation of cookies — little files that many Web sites leave behind on your computer. Some cookies are necessary. For example, online stores that let you add items to a shopping cart before you check out place cookies on your computer to keep track of which items you have selected. Other cookies are questionable. Some are put there to keep track of what Web sites you visit or to gather personal information about you. A cookie manager program can alert you to cookies being stored on your computer and can selectively remove cookies that you don't want to keep. Some of the more popular cookie managers are Cookie Crusher (www.thelimitsoft. com), Cookie Pal (www.kburra.com), and Cookie Cruncher (www. rbaworld.com).

✔ Bookmark managers make it easier to manage Favorites and convert between Internet Explorer Favorites and Navigator bookmarks.

✔ Hotbar (www.hotbar.com) is a free Internet Explorer enhancement that lets you change the look of your browser by installing colored backgrounds for the toolbars and menus.

Chapter 23

Ten Things That Sometimes Go Wrong

In This Chapter

▶ Finding that you don't have Internet Explorer

▶ Missing out on a modem connection

▶ Forgetting your password

▶ Getting strange messages about unexpected errors

▶ Being unable to find Internet Explorer

▶ Losing a file that you know you downloaded

▶ Getting cut off from the Internet in the middle of a big download

▶ Forgetting where to find your favorite Web page

*A*ctually, it's probably accurate to say that more like 10,000 things *can* go wrong, but this chapter describes some (okay, so I list nine, not ten — but who's counting) of the things that often get out of kilter.

I Don't Have Internet Explorer!

No problem. Internet Explorer 5.5 is available from many sources, and it's free. If you have any type of access to the Internet, you can find Internet Explorer 5.5 at the Microsoft Web site, located at the following URL:

```
www.microsoft.com/ie
```

If you don't have access to the Internet or you don't want to contend with a horrendously long download (it can take hours), you can purchase Internet Explorer 5.5 at your local computer store for a modest charge.

I Can't Connect to the Internet!

You double-click the Internet Explorer icon, the Connection Manager dialog box appears, and you type in your name and password, but you can't get any further. For some reason, you are unable to connect to the Internet. Arghhhhh!

Many, *many* things could be wrong. Here are a few general troubleshooting procedures that can help you solve the problem or at least narrow down the possibilities:

✔ Make sure that the phone cable is securely connected to the telephone wall jack and to the correct jack on the back of the modem. Phone cables sometimes jar loose. They go bad sometimes, too, so replacing the cable may solve the problem. If you're not sure which jack is the correct one, consult the manual that came with the modem.

✔ Make sure that the modem is not in use by another program, such as a fax program or the Windows Hyperterminal program.

✔ Make sure that your teenager isn't talking on a phone that shares the same phone line as the modem. (With three teenage daughters, this happens often at my house.)

✔ Try calling your Internet access number on a regular phone to see if it answers. If you get a busy signal or if it just rings on and on, something may be wrong with the local access number. Try again later, and call your Internet service provider's customer service department if the problem persists.

✔ Double-check the phone number in the Connection Manager dialog box. If your Internet service provider supplies an alternate phone number, try that one instead.

If you just installed the modem or if the modem never has worked right, you should make sure that the modem is configured to use the proper Communications Port within your computer. To change the port setting, follow these steps:

1. **Click the Start button on the taskbar and choose Settings⇨Control Panel.**

2. **Double-click the Modems icon.**

3. **Click the Properties button.**

4. **Change the Port setting for the modem.**

5. **Click OK twice.**

6. **Try dialing in again.**

Sometimes, removing and reinstalling the modem within Windows solves the problem. If all else fails, try this:

1. **Click the Start button on the taskbar and choose Settings➪Control Panel.**
2. **Double-click the Modems icon.**
3. **Click the modem to select it and then click the Remove button.**
4. **Click Add.**
5. **Follow the Install a New Modem wizard to reinstall the modem.**

I Forgot My Password!

Didn't I tell you to write it down and keep it in a safe place? Sigh. If you really did forget your password and you didn't write it down anywhere, you have to call your Internet service provider for assistance. If you can convince the person on the other end of the line that you really are who you say you are, he or she can reset your password for you.

Now, to avoid this kind of time-consuming mess, write down your password and store it in a secure location. Here's a list of several not-so-secure places to hide your password:

- In a desk drawer, in a file folder labeled *Not My Internet Password*
- On a magnet stuck to the refrigerator (No one, including you, will ever be able to pick it out from all the other junk stuck up there.)
- On the inside cover of this book, in Pig Latin so that no one can understand it
- Carved on the back of a park bench
- On the wall in a public rest room
- Tattooed on your left buttock, backward so that you can read it in a mirror

I Got an Unexpected Error Message!

Sometimes, when you try to follow a link to a cool Web page or you type a URL yourself and press Enter, instead of getting the page you expected, you face a dialog box with a message that looks something like this:

```
Internet Explorer cannot open the Internet site
         http://www.whatever.com
A connection with the server could not be established.
```

Sometimes no dialog box appears, but instead of the page you're looking for, you just get a page with some bland text that says something like:

```
HTTP/1.0 404 Object Not Found
```

These error messages and others like them mean that your Internet Explorer couldn't find the page that you tried to access. Several possible explanations may account for this error:

- ✔ You typed the URL incorrectly. Maybe it should have been www. whoever.com instead of www.whatever.com.

- ✔ The page you're trying to display may no longer exist. The person who created the page may have removed it.

- ✔ The page may have been moved to a new address. Sometimes you get a message telling you about the new address, sometimes not.

- ✔ The Web site that hosts the page may be having technical trouble. Try again later.

- ✔ The page may be just too darn popular, which causes the server to be busy. Hit the refresh button a couple of times. If that doesn't work, try again later.

The Internet Explorer Window Disappeared!

You know that you are signed in to the Internet, but you can't seem to find Internet Explorer anywhere. The window has mysteriously vanished!

Here are a few things to check before giving up in despair:

- ✔ Find the taskbar, that Windows thingy that usually lurks down at the bottom of your screen. The taskbar has a button for every program that's running. If you find the Internet Explorer button in the taskbar, clicking it should bring the window to the front. (You may have to move your mouse all the way to the bottom edge of the screen to make the taskbar appear. Also, if you moved your taskbar, it may be on the top, left, or right edge of the screen rather than at the bottom.)

- ✔ If no Internet Explorer window appears in the taskbar, you may have closed Internet Explorer but remained connected to the Internet. To make Internet Explorer come alive again, click the Internet Explorer icon in the taskbar or click the Start button and choose Internet Explorer from the Programs menu. Because you're already connected to the Internet, you don't have to reconnect.

✔ You may have been disconnected from the Internet for one reason or another. Normally when that happens, a dialog box appears, informing you that you have been disconnected and offering to reconnect. If no dialog box appears, you can reconnect by clicking Start, choosing Settings⇨Dial-Up Networking, and then double-clicking the icon for your Internet connection.

You can tell whether you're connected to the Internet by looking for the little connection icon in the corner of the taskbar next to the clock; it looks like two little computers strung together with kite string. If the icon is present, you're connected. If the icon is missing, you're not.

I Can't Find a File I Downloaded!

Don't worry. The file is probably around; you're just not looking in the right place. Internet Explorer offers a Save As dialog box that you must complete before downloading a file, so presumably you know where the file has been saved. However, you can all-too-easily click OK without really looking at this dialog box when it appears.

Fortunately, all you have to do is choose File⇨Save As to recall the Save As dialog box, which by default opens the same folder the dialog box was opened to last. Just check the Save In field at the top of the dialog box to find out the folder where you saved your file.

If you can't remember the name of the file you downloaded, here's a trick that may help you find it:

1. **Open a My Computer window for the folder in which you saved the file.**

   Click My Computer and then navigate your way through your drives and folders until you come to the one where you saved the file.

2. **Choose View⇨Details and make sure that your toolbar is visible.**

3. **Choose View⇨Arrange Icons⇨By Date.**

   The list of files is sorted into date sequence, with the newest files appearing at the top of the list.

4. **Look at the files at the top of the list.**

   With luck, one of these files rings a bell.

I Was Disconnected in the Middle of a Two-Hour Download!

Wow. Tough break. Unfortunately, the Internet doesn't have any way to restart a big download, picking up where you left off. The only solution is to download the entire file again.

Don't blame me — I'm just the messenger.

I Can't Find That Cool Web Page I Saw Yesterday!

I've faced this problem myself. The Web is such a large place that you can easily stumble into a page you really like and then not be able to find it again later.

If you can't seem to retrace your steps, you may still have a record of where you were. Click the History button to display links to all the pages you recently visited. With some luck, you can find the page in the History folder.

To avoid the frustration of misplacing the Web sites you love, use the Favorites⇨Add to Favorites command anytime that you come across a Web page you think you may want to visit again. That way, you can always find the page again by choosing it from the Favorites menu. If you later decide that the page isn't so great after all, you can always delete it from Favorites.

I've Started a Nuclear War!

If you're minding your own business, enjoying a nice game of Global Thermonuclear War at www.wargames.com, and you suddenly hear air-raid sirens and see mushroom clouds on the horizon, don't panic. See if you can interest the computer in a nice game of chess instead.

Just kidding. Nothing you do can start a nuclear war from the Internet. Experienced computer hackers have been trying to start nuclear wars on the Internet for years, and no one has succeeded . . . at least not yet.

Chapter 24

Ten Safety Tips for Kids on the Net

In This Chapter

▶ Safety tips for kids and their parents

▶ Ways to help keep the Internet a safe place for everyone

The Internet is an inherently risky place for kids (and adults, too). Along with pictures of Neil Armstrong on the moon, your kids can just as easily find images that you probably don't want them to see. And although chatting online can be fun and enlightening, it can also be unhealthy and possibly even dangerous.

This chapter lists ten important safety tips that parents should drill into their kids' heads before they allow them to go online.

I really don't want to be an alarmist here. Overall, the Internet is a pretty wholesome place. Don't be afraid to let your kids venture out online, but don't let them go it alone, either. Make sure that they understand the ground rules.

Don't Believe That People Really Are Who They Say They Are

When you sign up with an Internet service provider, you can type anything you want for your user ID. And no one makes you tell the truth in e-mail, newsgroups, or chats. Just because someone claims to be a 16-year-old female is not reason enough to believe it. That person can be a 12-year-old boy, a 17-year-old girl, or a 35-year-old pervert.

Never Give Out Your Address, Phone Number, Real Last Name, or Credit Card Number

If you're not sure why Rule No. 2 exists, see Rule No. 1.

Never Pretend to Be Someone You're Not

The flip side of not believing who someone says he or she is is that other people may believe that you are who you say you are. If you are 13 years old and claim to be 17, you're inviting trouble.

We all like to gloss over our weaknesses. When I'm online, I don't generally draw attention to the fact that a substantial portion of my hair is gone and I'm a bit pudgy around the waistline (well, okay, I'm a *lot* pudgy around the waistline). But I don't represent myself as a super athlete or a rock star, either. Just be yourself.

Save Inappropriate Postings to a File So That You Can Show Them to an Adult

If someone sends you inappropriate e-mail — not just something that makes you feel angry or upset, but something that seems downright inappropriate — choose File⇨Save As to save the message as a file. Then show it to an adult.

If Someone Says Something Inappropriate to You in a Chat, Save the Chat Log

If someone is vulgar or offensive in an online chat, save the chat log to a file. Then show it to an adult. In MSN Messenger, you can save the chat to a file by choosing File⇨Save.

Watch Your Language

The Internet isn't censored. In fact, it can be a pretty rough place. Crude language abounds, especially on Usenet and in chat rooms. But that doesn't mean that you have to contribute to the endless flow of colorful metaphors. Watch your language while chatting online or posting messages.

Don't Obsess

The Internet can be fun, but there's more to life than going online. The best friendships are the ones in which you actually spend time in the presence of other people. If you find yourself spending hour upon hour online, maybe you should cut back a bit.

Report Inappropriate Behavior to an Adult

If something seems really amiss in your Internet experience — for example, if you think someone is harassing you beyond what should be normal or if someone asks you questions that make you uncomfortable — tell an adult.

You can also complain by sending e-mail to the administrator of the perpetrator's Internet service provider. If the perp is clever, you may not be able to figure out his or her true e-mail address. But you often can. If you receive harassing mail from idiot@jerk.com, try sending a complaint to postmaster@jerk.com.

If You Feel Uncomfortable, Leave

Don't stick around in a chat session if you feel uncomfortable. Just leave.

Similarly, don't bother to reply to inappropriate e-mail messages or newsgroup articles.

Parents, Be Involved with Your Kids' Online Activities

Don't let your kids run loose on the Internet! Get involved with what they are doing. You don't have to monitor them every moment they are online. Just be interested in what they're doing, what friends they have made over the network, what they like, and what they don't like. Ask them to show you around their favorite Internet pages.

Appendix A

Glossary

● ●

activeX: The Microsoft Web-based object technology that enables intelligent objects to be embedded in Web documents to create interactive pages.

ActiveX control: An ActiveX object that can be embedded in a Web page. Most ActiveX controls are user-interface gadgets, such as list boxes and command buttons, but some provide behind-the-scenes functions, such as timers.

Address Book: A file that stores the Internet e-mail addresses of the people with whom you correspond regularly. Outlook Express maintains an Address Book for your e-mail.

AFK: *Away from keyboard,* an abbreviation commonly used when chatting. See also *IRC*.

America Online: A popular online information service that also provides Internet access. America Online is often referred to as *AOL*. To send e-mail to an AOL user, address the message to the user's America Online name followed by the domain name (@aol.com). For example, if the user's AOL name is Barney, send an e-mail message to Barney@aol.com.

anonymous FTP: An FTP site that allows access to anyone, without requiring an account.

AOL: See *America Online*.

applet: A program written in the Java language and embedded in an HTML document. An applet runs automatically whenever someone views the Web page that contains the applet.

ARPANET: The very first incarnation of the Internet, built by the Department of Defense during the Summer of Love.

article: A message posted to a Usenet newsgroup.

ASCII: The standard character set for most computers. Internet newsgroups are *ASCII-only,* meaning that they can support only text-based messages.

attach: Sending a file along with an e-mail message or newsgroup article. Internet Explorer automatically encodes and decodes attachments.

attachment: A file attached to an e-mail message or a newsgroup article.

AutoComplete: A mostly useful but sometimes annoying feature of Internet Explorer that anticipates what you are trying to type and tries to complete your typing before you finish. AutoComplete works in the Address bar and in form fields.

AVI: The Microsoft standard for video files that can be viewed in Windows. AVI is one of the more popular video formats on the Web, but other formats, such as QuickTime and MPEG are also widely used.

bandwidth: The amount of information that can flow through a network connection. Bandwidth is to computer networks what pipe diameter is to plumbing: The bigger the pipe, the more water allowed through.

baud: See *bits per second*. (Actually, a technical difference does exist between *baud* and *bits per second,* but only people with pocket protectors and taped glasses care.)

binary file: A non-ASCII file, such as a computer program, a picture, a sound, or a video.

BITNET: A large network connecting colleges and universities in North America and Europe through the Internet. BITNET mailing lists are presented as Usenet newsgroups under the `bit` hierarchy.

bits per second (bps): A measure of how fast your modem can transmit or receive information between your computer and a remote computer, such as your Internet service provider. You won't be happy browsing the Internet using anything less than a 28,800 bps modem (commonly referred to as a *28.8 modem*). Note that the term *Kbps* is often used to designate thousands of bits per second. Thus, 28,800 bps and 28.8 Kbps are equivalent.

BRB: *Be right back,* an abbreviation commonly used when chatting. See also *IRC*.

browser: A program, such as Internet Explorer, that you can use to access and view the World Wide Web. Internet Explorer is, at its core, a browser.

cable modem: A high-speed Internet connection that is always connected to the Internet and works outrageously faster than a dial-up connection.

cache: An area of your computer's hard disk used to store data recently downloaded from the network so the data can be redisplayed quickly.

cappuccino: An Italian coffee drink that blends espresso, steamed milk, foam, and (if you're lucky) a dash of cinnamon. Not to be confused with *Java*.

Certificate: An online form of identification that gives one computer assurance that the other computer is who it claims to be. Certificates are a common form of security on the Internet.

CGI: *Common Gateway Interface.* A method of programming Web sites, mostly used to handle online forms. CGI uses script programs that run on the server computer, as opposed to Java or VBScript programs, which run on client computers.

chat: See *IRC*.

chat room: A place where two or more Internet users gather online to hold a conversation. See also *IRC*.

chat server: An Internet server that hosts a chat.

Chaucer: A dead English dude who didn't spell very well.

compressed file: A file that's been processed by a special *compression program* that reduces the amount of disk space required to store the file. If you download the file to your computer, you must decompress the file using a program, such as WinZip or PKUNZIP before you can use it.

CompuServe: A popular online service that provides Internet access. To send Internet mail to a CompuServe member, address the mail to the user's screen name followed by `cs.com`, as in `Gopher@cs.com`. (Some CompuServe users have CompuServe Classic accounts, which use a numeric user ID composed of two groups of numbers separated by a comma. To send mail to a CompuServe Classic user, address the mail to the numeric user ID followed by `@compuserve.com`. However, use a period instead of a comma in the user ID. For example, if the user's ID is `55555,1234`, send e-mail to `55555.1234@compuserve.com`. You have to use the period because Internet e-mail standards don't allow for commas in e-mail addresses.)

Cone of Silence: A top-secret security device employed by agents of CONTROL to prevent spies from KAOS from eavesdropping on sensitive conversations.

connect time: The amount of time you're connected to the Internet or your online service. Internet service providers that limit your monthly connect time or charge you by the hour are going the way of the dodo bird. However, some providers automatically disconnect you if you stay connected but don't do anything for a certain length of time.

Connection Manager: A gizmo that comes with Internet Explorer to take care of dialing in to your Internet service provider and logging you on to the Internet.

Content Advisor: An Internet Explorer feature that lets you block Web sites based on their ratings. See also *rating*.

cookie: A file that a Web server stores on your computer. The most common use for cookies is to customize the way a Web page appears when you view it. For example, customizable Web pages such as www.msn.com use cookies to store your viewing preferences so that the next time you visit that Web page, only the elements that you request are displayed.

cyberspace: An avant-garde term used to refer to the Internet.

decode: The process of reconstructing a binary file that was encoded using the uuencode scheme, used in e-mail and newsgroups. Outlook Express automatically decodes encoded files.

decompression: The process of restoring compressed files to their original states. Decompression is usually accomplished with a program, such as WinZip and PKUNZIP. (You can download the shareware version of PKUNZIP at www.pkware.com.)

decryption: See *Tales from Decrypt.* Just kidding. Decryption is the process of unscrambling a message that has been encrypted (scrambled so that only the intended recipient can read it). See also *encryption*.

dial-up connection: An Internet connection that uses a modem and a telephone line to connect to the Internet. Faster alternatives include *cable modems, DSL,* and *ISDN*.

dial-up script: A special file that contains the instructions used to log you in to your ISP so that you can connect to the Internet.

"Dixie": A happy little tune that you can whistle while you are waiting for a Web page to finish downloading.

DNS: *Domain Name Server.* The system that enables us to use almost intelligible names, such as www.microsoft.com, rather than completely incomprehensible addresses, such as 254.120.0.74.

domain: The last portion of an Internet address (also known as the *top-level domain*), which indicates whether the address belongs to a company (com), an educational institution (edu), a government agency (gov), a military organization (mil), or another organization (org).

domain name: The address of an Internet site, which generally includes the organization domain name followed by the top-level domain, as in `www.janethatesbill.com`.

download: Copying a file from another computer to your computer via a modem.

DSL: *Digital Subscriber Line.* A high-speed connection that, like a cable modem connection, is always connected to the Internet and runs much faster than a dial-up connection.

Dynamic behavior: A feature of Internet Explorer 5.5 that lets you associate a script with a Web page element.

Dynamic HTML: An advanced type of HTML that is supported by Internet Explorer and that enables you to create Web pages in which every element on the page (text and graphics alike) can be dynamically changed as the user interacts with the page.

e-mail: *Electronic mail,* an Internet service that enables you to send and receive messages to and from other Internet users.

emoticon: Another word for a *smiley* — an expressive face you can create with nothing more than a few keystrokes and some imagination. :-)

encode: A method of converting a *binary file* to ASCII text, which can be sent by Internet e-mail or posted to an Internet newsgroup. When displayed, encoded information looks like a stream of random characters. But when you run the encoded message through a decoder program, the original binary file is reconstructed. Outlook Express automatically encodes and decodes messages, so you don't have to worry about using a separate program for this purpose.

encryption: Scrambling a message so that no one can read it, except, of course, the intended recipient, who must *decrypt* the message before reading it.

ETLA: *Extended three-letter acronym.* A four-letter acronym.

event: In Dynamic HTML, a user action (such as moving the mouse) that can be handled by a VBScript or JScript program. See also ***Dynamic HTML***.

Explorer bar: The left one-third or so of the Internet Explorer main window, which Internet Explorer periodically uses to display a special toolbar when you click the Search, History, or Favorites button.

FAQ: A *frequently asked questions* file. Contains answers to the most commonly asked questions. Always check to see if a FAQ file exists for a forum or Usenet newsgroup before asking basic questions. (If you post a question on an Internet newsgroup and the answer is in the FAQ, expect to be flamed for sure.)

Favorites: A collection of Web page addresses that you visit frequently. Internet Explorer enables you to store your favorite Web addresses in a special folder so that you can recall them quickly.

File Transfer Protocol (FTP): A system that allows the transfer of program and data files over the Internet.

flame: A painfully brutal response to a dumb posting on an Internet newsgroup. (On some newsgroups, just having aol.com in your Internet address is enough to get flamed.)

freeware: Software that you can download and use without paying a fee.

FrontPage Express: A WYSVRWYG (what-you-see-vaguely-resembles-what-you-get) HTML editor that comes with Internet Explorer.

FTP: See *File Transfer Protocol.*

FTP site: An Internet server that has a library of files available for downloading with FTP. Internet Explorer lets you browse FTP sites as if the sites were folders on your own hard drive.

GIF: *Graphic Interchange Format.* A popular format for picture files. The GIF format uses an efficient compression technique that results in less data loss and higher quality graphics than other formats, such as PCX.

History bar: A place where you can sip a martini while discussing the Civil War. Just kidding. Actually, it is a variant of the Explorer bar, which lists pages you have visited recently so that you can conveniently return to them.

home page: (1) The introductory page at a Web site; sometimes refers to the entire Web site. (2) The first page displayed by Internet Explorer when you start it. By default, the home page is set to www.msn.com, but you can change the home page to any Web page you want.

host computer: A computer to which you can connect via the Internet.

HTML: *Hypertext Markup Language.* A system of special tags used to create pages for the World Wide Web.

HTTP: *Hypertext Transfer Protocol.* The protocol used to transmit HTML documents over the Internet.

hyperlink: A bit of text or a graphic in a Web page that you can click to retrieve another Web page. The new Web page may be on the same Web server as the original page, or it may be on an entirely different Web server halfway around the globe.

hypermedia: A variation of hypertext in which hyperlinks can be graphics, sounds, or videos as well as text. The World Wide Web is based on hypermedia, but the term *hypertext* is often loosely used instead.

hypertext: A system in which documents are linked to one another by text links. When the user clicks on a text link, the document referred to by the link is displayed. See also ***hypermedia***.

IBM: A big computer company.

ICRA: *Internet Content Rating Association,* the organization that developed and oversees the use of Internet ratings.

Information Superhighway: Al Gore's pet name for the Internet.

instant message: An Internet feature that lets you exchange messages with other Internet users in real time, like an online phone conversation but using text instead of voice. See ***MSN Messenger***.

Internet: A vast worldwide collection of networked computers — the largest computer network in the world.

Internet address: A complete address used to send e-mail to someone over the Internet. Your Internet address is your user ID plus the host name of your Internet ISP's. For example, if your user ID is `JClampett` and your ISP's host name is `beverly.hills.com,` your Internet address is `JClampett@beverly.hills.com.`

Internet Connection Wizard: A program that comes with Internet Explorer to help you get connected to the Internet.

Internet Explorer: The Microsoft program for browsing the Internet.

Internet Relay Chat: See *IRC*.

Internet service provider: Also known as an *ISP*. A company that provides access to the Internet.

IP: *Internet Protocol.* The data transmission protocol that enables networks to exchange messages; serves as the foundation for communications over the Internet.

IRC: *Internet Relay Chat.* A system that enables you to carry on live conversations (known as *chats*) with other Internet users.

ISDN: A digital telephone line that can transmit data at up to 128 Kbps. For most people, a cable modem or DSL connection is better.

ISP: See *Internet service provider*.

Java: An object-oriented programming language created and designed by Sun Microsystems to be used on the World Wide Web. Java is one way to add sound, animation, and interactivity to Web pages. Although Internet Explorer supports Java, Microsoft prefers that you use VBScript instead.

JavaScript: A scripting language used with Netscape Navigator that enables Web-page authors to embed Java programs in HTML documents. *JScript* is the Internet Explorer version of JavaScript.

JPEG: *Joint Photographic Experts Group*. A popular format for picture files. JPEG uses a compression technique that greatly reduces a graphic's file size but results in some loss of resolution. For photographic images, this loss is usually not noticeable. Because of its small file sizes, JPEG is a popular graphics format for the Internet.

JScript: The Microsoft implementation of JavaScript for use with Internet Explorer.

KB: An abbreviation for *kilobyte* (1,024 bytes).

Kbps: A measure of a modem's speed in thousands of bits per second. Two common modem speeds are 28.8 Kbps and 56 Kbps.

LAN: See *local area network*.

link: See *hyperlink*.

Links toolbar: A special Internet Explorer toolbar that lets you quickly access a handful of the sites you visit most frequently.

Linux: A free version of UNIX that is used on many Web servers throughout the world.

LISTSERV: A server program used for mailing lists, which are basically e-mail versions of newsgroups. See also *mailing list*.

local area network: Also referred to as a *LAN*. Two or more computers that are connected to one another to form a network. A LAN enables the computers to share resources, such as disk drives and printers. A LAN is usually located within a relatively small area, such as in a building or on a campus.

LOL: *Laughing out loud*. A common abbreviation used to express mirth or joy when chatting on MSN Messenger, in e-mail messages, or in newsgroup articles.

lurk: To read articles in a newsgroup without contributing your own postings. Lurking is one of the few approved forms of eavesdropping. Lurking for a while in a newsgroup before posting your own articles is the polite thing to do.

mailing group: A list of e-mail addresses. You can send mail to everyone on the list by specifying the list name.

mailing list: An e-mail version of a newsgroup. Any messages sent to the mailing list server are automatically sent to each person who has subscribed to the list.

MB: *Megabyte.* Roughly a million bytes.

message rule: An Outlook Express feature that lets you automatically delete messages that you don't want to read or move certain types of messages to other folders besides your inbox.

Microsoft: The largest software company in the world, at least for now. Among other things, Microsoft is the maker of Windows and the Microsoft Office suite, which includes Word, Excel, PowerPoint, and Access. Oh, and I almost forgot — Internet Explorer, too.

MIME: *Multipurpose Internet mail extensions.* One of the standard methods for attaching binary files to e-mail messages and newsgroup articles. See also **uuencode**.

modem: A device that enables your computer to connect with other computers over a phone line. Most modems are *internal* — they're housed within the computer's cabinet. *External* modems are contained in their own boxes and must be connected to the back of the computer via a serial cable.

moderated newsgroup: A newsgroup whose postings are controlled by a moderator, which helps to ensure that articles in the newsgroup follow the guidelines established by the moderator.

MPEG: *Motion Picture Experts Group.* A standard for compressing video images based on the popular JPEG standard used for still images. Internet Explorer includes built-in support for MPEG videos.

MSN: The Microsoft Network, a commercial online service. A few years ago, Microsoft thought MSN would become the center of the online universe. Now, MSN is little more than a glorified Internet service provider.

MSN Messenger: An instant messaging program that lets users exchange messages with one another in real time, kind of like a phone call but using text instead of voice.

NetMeeting: A program that comes with Internet Explorer 5.5 and enables you to have online meetings with other Internet users.

Netscape: The company that makes the popular *Netscape Navigator* browser software for the Internet. Internet Explorer and Navigator are currently duking it out for the title of "Best Web Browser."

Network Wizards: An organization that monitors the growth of the Internet. Check out its Web page at www.nw.com to find out how big the Internet really is.

news server: A host computer that stores newsgroup articles. You must connect to a news server to access newsgroups; your Internet service provider probably has a server to which you can connect. Microsoft uses its own news servers for its product support newsgroups.

newsgroup: An Internet bulletin board area where you can post messages, called *articles,* about a particular topic and read articles posted by other Internet users. Thousands of different newsgroups are out there, covering just about every conceivable subject. You can access newsgroups with Outlook Express.

object model: An important aspect of Dynamic HTML that enables scripts written in VBScript or JScript to access any element of an HTML page. See also ***Dynamic HTML***.

OIC: *Oh, I see.* A commonly used abbreviation in chats or e-mail messages.

online: Connecting your computer to a network, to an online service provider, or to the Internet.

Outlook Express: A scaled-back version of the Microsoft Outlook program that comes with Internet Explorer 5.5. (You can get the full Outlook program with Microsoft Office 2000.)

Personal Web Server: A program that comes with newer versions of Windows and lets you turn your computer into a Web server.

PKZIP: A popular shareware program used to compress files or to expand compressed files. You can get your copy at www.pkware.com.

PMJI: *Pardon me for jumping in.* A commonly used abbreviation in newsgroup articles.

posting: Adding an article to a newsgroup.

PPP: *Point to Point Protocol.* The protocol that enables you to access Internet services with Internet Explorer.

protocol: A set of conventions that govern communications between computers in a network.

public domain: Computer software or other information that is available free of charge. See also ***shareware***.

QuickTime: A video format popularized by Apple for its Macintosh computers. Internet Explorer provides built-in support for QuickTime movies, so you don't need separate software to view QuickTime files.

rating: A voluntary system of rating the content of Internet sites, similar to the ratings used for movies and television. Internet Explorer lets you block Web sites based on their ratings.

ROFL: *Rolling on the floor laughing.* A common abbreviation used in chats, newsgroup articles, and e-mail messages. You may see variations, such as ROFLPP and ROFLMAO. Figure those out yourself — this is a family book.

RSAC: *Recreational Software Advisory Council,* the organization that developed and oversees the use of Internet ratings. Now known as the Internet Content Rating Association (ICRA).

script: A type of program that you can embed in an HTML document. Internet Explorer allows scripts that are written in one of two languages: VBScript and JScript.

Search Assistant: An Internet Explorer feature that helps you look for various types of information on the Internet, such as Web pages, e-mail addresses, or encyclopedia articles.

Search bar: A special toolbar that appears in the left one-third or so of the Internet Explorer main window when you click the Search button. See also *Explorer bar*.

Secure Sockets Layer: *SSL.* The preferred method of security for sending confidential information, such as credit card numbers, over the Internet.

server: A computer or computer program that provides services to other computers or programs on the Internet or on a local area network. Specific types of Internet servers include news servers, mail servers, FTP servers, and Web servers.

service provider: See *Internet service provider*.

shareware: A software program that you can download and try — free of charge. The program is not free, however. If you like the program and continue to use it, you are obligated to send in a modest registration fee. See also *public domain*.

shortcut: An icon that can represent a link to a location on the Internet. You can place shortcuts just about anywhere, including on your desktop, in a Windows folder, or even in a document.

signature: A fancy block of text that some users routinely place at the end of their e-mail messages and newsgroup articles. Outlook Express lets you use signatures. See also ***stationery***.

SLIP: *Serial Line Internet Protocol.* A method for accessing the Web, now largely replaced by PPP connections.

smiley: A smiley face or other *emoticon* created from keyboard characters and used to convey emotions in otherwise emotionless e-mail messages or newsgroup postings. Some examples include

:-)	Feelin' happy
:-D	Super-duper happy
8^)	Smiling Orphan Annie (Leapin' lizards!)
;-)	Conspiratorial wink
:-o	You surprise me
:-(	So sad
:-|	Apathetic

spam: Unsolicited e-mail or newsgroup postings that do not relate to the topic of the newsgroup. Spam is the electronic equivalent of junk mail.

SSL: See ***Secure Sockets Layer***.

stationery: An Outlook Express feature that lets you add a background graphic, a signature, and a font style to your e-mail messages and newsgroup postings.

style: In HTML, a style is a special type of element that provides formatting information for other HTML elements.

taskbar: A Windows feature that displays icons for all open windows, a clock, and the Start button, which you use to run programs. Normally, the taskbar appears at the bottom of the screen, but it can be repositioned at any edge of the screen you prefer. If the taskbar is not visible, try moving the mouse to the very bottom of the screen or to the left, right, or top edge of the screen.

TCP/IP: *Transmission Control Protocol/Internet Protocol.* The basic set of conventions that the Internet uses to enable different types of computers to communicate with one another.

Telnet: A protocol that enables you to log in to a remote computer as if you were actually using a terminal attached to that remote computer.

TIFF: *Tagged Image File Format.* A format for picture files. TIFF files are large compared with other formats, such as JPEG and GIF, but they preserve all of the original image's quality. Because of their large size, TIFF files aren't all that popular on the Internet.

thread: An exchange of articles in a newsgroup. Specifically, an original article, all of its replies, all the replies to replies, and so on.

TLA: *Three-letter acronym.* Ever notice how just about all computer terms can be reduced to a three-letter acronym? It all started with IBM. Now, there's URL, AOL, CGI, and who knows what else. I guess I shouldn't complain; this book is being published by IDG Books.

Uniform Resource Locator: Also known as a *URL.* A method of specifying the address of any resource available on the Internet, used when browsing the Internet. For example, the URL of IDG Books Worldwide, Inc., is `www.idg-books.com`.

UNIX: A computer operating system that is popular among Internet users. The Internet was developed by UNIX users, which is why much of the Internet has a UNIX look and feel — especially when you leave the World Wide Web and venture into older parts of the Internet, such as FTP sites.

upload: Copying a file from your computer to the Internet.

URL: See *Uniform Resource Locator.*

Usenet: A network of Internet newsgroups that contains many of the more popular newsgroups. You can access Usenet from Outlook Express, which comes free with Internet Explorer.

uuencode: A method of attaching binary files, such as programs or documents, to e-mail messages and newsgroup articles. The other method is called *MIME.*

VBScript: A version of Visual Basic that enables you to create programs that can be embedded in HTML documents.

virus: An evil computer program that slips into your computer undetected, tries to spread itself to other computers, and may eventually do something bad like trash your hard disk. Because Internet Explorer doesn't include built-in virus detection, I suggest that you consider using one of the many virus-protection programs available if you're worried about catching an electronic virus.

Visual J++: The Microsoft Java compiler and development environment that programmers can use to create ActiveX controls in their Web pages.

Web: See *World Wide Web*.

Web browser: A program that can find pages on the World Wide Web and display them on your home computer. Internet Explorer is an example of a Web browser.

Web host: A computer that stores Web pages that can be accessed over the World Wide Web. See also *Web server*.

Web page: An HTML document available for display on the World Wide Web. The document may contain links to other documents located on the same server or on other Web servers.

Web Publishing Wizard: A program that comes with Internet Explorer that makes it easy to post HTML documents that you have created to a Web server.

Web server: A server computer that stores HTML documents so that they can be accessed on the World Wide Web.

wide area network: Commonly called *WAN*. A computer network that spans a large area, such as an entire campus, or perhaps a network that links branches of a company in several cities.

Windows Millennium Edition: The newest version of the Microsoft Windows operating system, also known as *Windows ME*. Windows ME (along with its predecessors, Windows 98 and Windows 95) is the main operating system for Internet Explorer, although versions of Internet Explorer exist for Windows NT, Windows 3.1, and Macintosh computers.

WinSock: Short for *Windows Sockets*. The standard by which Windows programs are able to communicate with TCP/IP and the Internet. Fortunately, you don't have to know anything about WinSock to use it. In fact, you don't even have to know you're using it at all.

WinZip: A Windows version of the popular PKZIP compression program.

World Wide Web: Abbreviated *WWW* and referred to simply as *the Web*. This relatively new part of the Internet displays information using fancy graphics. The Web is based on *links,* which enable Web surfers to travel quickly from one Web server to another.

XML: *eXtensible Markup Language*. A definition of the rules used to create markup languages, such as HTML.

zipped file: A file that has been compressed using the PKZIP or WinZip program.

Index

• Numbers & Symbols •

\ (backslash), 246
^ (caret), 246/
"" (double quotes), 245
/ (forward slash), 46
- (hyphen), 300
< (less-than sign), 246
+ (plus sign), 193
? (question mark), 67

• A •

About Internet Explorer command, 28
About Internet Explorer dialog box, 28
access control, 210
  Approved Sites feature for, 229, 230
  banning or allowing access to specific
    sites, 229, 230
  Internet ratings and, 221–224
Accessibility button, 209
accessibility options, 209, 212
Account Information page, 154
Accounts command, 160
Accounts tab, 192
Active Desktop
  basic description of, 29
  installing, 34
ActiveX controls, 347
Add a Contact dialog box, 170
Add Favorite dialog box, 78, 80, 81,
    86, 90, 332
Add Files button, 183
Add Signatures to All Outgoing Messages
    option, 142
Add to Favorites command, 78
Add/Remove Programs dialog box, 168
Add/Remove Software button, 241
Address bar, 43, 213
Address Book
  basic description of, 347
  entries in, changing/deleting, 123

  folders, working with, 123–125
  Hotmail and, 165
  mailing groups, 144, 145, 147
  sending a message to someone in, 122
Address Book button, 121
Address Book command, 121
Address Book dialog box, 123
Address box, 47, 48
  searching from, 67
  typing a question mark in, 67
Address toolbar, 43, 84
  basic description of, 202
  customizing, 203
Adobe GoLive, 258
Adobe PageMill, 259
Advanced button, 286
Advanced options, 212–213
Advanced options dialog box, 213
Advanced tab, 207, 212
advertisements, 335
AIM (AOL Instant Messenger), 17, 167, 168
All Messages option, 197
Allow Control button, 184
AltaVista Web site, 69
Amazon.com Web site, 233
Angry method, 314
Angry() function, 314, 316
angry1.htc script, 306
angry2.htc script, 308, 309
angry3.htc script, 310, 311
angry4.htc, 315
angryColor property, 310
angrySize property, 310
animations, 328
AOL (America Online), 6, 19, 24
  basic description of, 24
  e-mail addresses, 111
  rates, 24, 27
  software, 27
  Web hosting services, 258
Appear Offline status settings, 175
Apply Stationery command, 137

Approved Sites feature, 229, 230
Approved Sites tab, 229
Arial font, 301
ARPANET, 11, 12
Arrange Icons command, 341
ASCII (American Standard Code for
    Information Interchange), 348
AT&T WorldNet Service, 26
Attach button, 114
Attach File button, 113
attachments, 114
  adding, 113, 114
  basic description of, 113
  message rules and, 130
  saving, 118, 196
  size of, 114
  tips for sending, 114
  used in newsgroups, 196
AutoComplete, 47, 212, 348
Automatically Put People I Reply to in My
    Address Book option, 121
Autosearch, 67
Available Toolbar Buttons list, 205
Away status setting, 175

• *B* •

Back button, 44, 50, 53
background attribute, 300
Background Image option, 280
backslash (\), 246
Baroudi, Carol, 3
baud rates, 21
Bcc command, 110
Be Right Back status setting, 175
Bebak, Arthur, 253
behaviors
  applying, 306–307
  basic description of, 293, 294
  creating, 304–305
  creating custom tags with, 307–309
  events and, 316–318
  methods and, 312, 314
  properties for, 309–312
  reusing, 295

  styles and, 295–302
  understanding, 294–295
Best of the Web, 83
binary files, 187, 196
Biographical Information section, 268
bionet newsgroups, 187
bit newsgroups, 187
bitmap format, 58
bitnet, 187, 348
biz newsgroups, 187
BlackICE Defender, 336
blind carbon copies, of e-mail, 110
Block Senders list, 134
blockquote tag, 299
body tag, 296, 302
bookmarks, 77, 336
bps (bits per second), 21
Browse button, 139
Browse Files button, 284
Browse Folders button, 285
Buena Vista Internet Group, 71
bulleted lists, 116, 274
Bulleted tab, 274
Business & Careers category, 216, 218
Business Items folder, 128
Business tab, 121
business Web sites, 255
Business Week, 74
Busy status setting, 175
Button ViewLink component, 320–322
ButtonName property, 320–322
buttons
  adding, 204, 205
  DHTML and, 296, 312, 314
  size settings for, 206
  on the Standard Buttons toolbar, 204, 205
By E-mail Address option, 172

• *C* •

C drive icon, 60
cable access, 22–23
caches, 52
Calm Down button, 312
CalmDown method, 312, 314

CalmDown() function, 314
capitalization, 300
carbon copies, of e-mail, 110
Career options, 207
caret (^), 246
Carnegie Mellon University, 72
carriage-return character, 245
Cascading Style Sheets (CSS), 295
case sensitivity, 300
CBS Events, 216
CBS News, 216
CBS Sportsline, 216
CD-ROMs, 29–30
censorship, 16
Century Schoolbook font, 299
certificates, 232, 237
Certificates button, 237
certification authority, 237
CGI (Common Gateway Interface), 349
Change button, 113
Change Content button, 217
Change Content link, 332
Change Password button, 229
Change To box, 113
Channel Guide, 83
channels, listings of, 83
Charles Schwab, 216
chat
  access control and, 224
  Microsoft NetMeeting features for, 179–180
  NetMeeting, 176
Chat button, 179
Check Names button, 112
children
  chat and, 344, 345
  safety tips for, 343–346
class attribute, 327
Clear History button, 209
Close button, 50, 52, 61, 265
Close command, 61
CNN (Cable News Network), 216
color
  background, for stationery, 139
  DHTML and, 298, 300, 303, 305, 310–311
  link, 209

printers, 213
  scroll bars and, 328
  text, 116, 272, 305, 311
color attribute, 300
Colors button, 209
Combine and Decode command, 196
Comments and Suggestions section, 268
comp newsgroups, 187
Compose tab, 141
compression, 114, 349
CompuServe, 19, 24, 27
  basic description of, 25
  e-mail addresses, 111
  rates, 25
Computer Name field, 291
Computing & Web category, 216
Computing Central, 216
Cone of Silence, 231
Configure button, 248
Congress, Internet legislation, 16
Connect button, 40
Connected dialog box, 62
Connection Manager dialog box, 34, 338
Connections options, 211
Connections tab, 207, 211
Contact Information section, 268
Contacts Currently Online section, 173
Contacts folder, 123, 124
Contacts Not Online section, 173
Content Advisor, 210
  activating, 224–227
  banning or allowing access to specific
    sites with, 229–230
  basic description of, 221
  unrated sites and, 228–229
Content Advisor dialog box, 225, 229
Content options dialog box, 224, 225
Content tab, 207, 210, 224, 228
ContentEditable attribute, 323
Contents tab, 96
Control Panel, 168, 291
Cookie Cruncher, 336
Cookie Crusher, 336
cookies, 336, 350
Copy button, 204

Copy to Folder command, 130
copying URLs, 48
copyrights, 58
Create Folder button, 81
Create Folder dialog box, 129
Create Hyperlink dialog box, 275
Create New button, 138
Create Shortcut command, 333
Create Supervisor Password dialog box, 226
Creating Web Pages For Dummies, 4th Edition (Smith and Beback), 253
credit card information, 232, 235, 344
Current Projects section, 268
Current Toolbar Buttons list, 205
customer surveys, 255
Customize button, 66
Customize Search Settings page, 66, 67
Customize Toolbar dialog box, 204–206
Cut button, 204
cybercafés, 20

● *D* ●

Daily Diversions category, 216
decoding techniques, 196
Decrease Text Size button, 272
Deja.com Web site, 194
delay command, 243
Delete button, 82
Delete command, 87, 333
Delete Contact command, 172
Delete Files button, 208
Deleted Items folder, 128, 134
deleting
  Address Book entries, 123
  contacts, 172
  e-mail, 118, 164
  folders, 82
  History folder files, 209
  links, 86, 87
  message rules, 134
  temporary files, 208
Description text box, 133
desktop shortcuts, creating, 333
Details button, 262
Details command, 341

DHTML (Dynamic HTML)
  basic description of, 293, 294
  behaviors, creating, 304–307
  behaviors, creating custom tags with, 307–309
  behaviors, understanding, 294–295
  `ContentEditable` attribute and, 323
  custom tags and, 303
  new features for, 328
  object model, 356
  properties, methods, and events, 309–311, 314, 316, 317
  pseudo-elements and, 326
  styles and, 295–303
  ViewLink components and, 319–322
  `writing-mode` attribute and, 324
  `zoom` attribute and, 327–328
Dial-up Connection dialog box, 40, 91
Dial-Up Scripting tool, 241
dial-up scripts, 41, 239–240
  attaching, to a dial-up connection, 246–249
  commands for, 242, 244–245
  creating, 241–242
Disable Ratings button, 227
Disconnect button, 62, 204
Discovery Channel, 216
Discuss button, 45
Disney, 71
Display button, 100
Display field, 120
Display Newsgroups Which Contain text box, 190
Display Results button, 262
`div` tag, 302, 325
DNS server address, 30
domain names, 256, 257
Don't Synchronize option, 197
Dornfest, Asha, 253
double quotes (""), 245
Download More button, 141
downloading
  attachments, 197
  basic description of, 351
  files, 59–60
  FrontPage Express, 262–265

getting disconnected during, 342
graphics, 53
Internet Explorer, 28–29
locating files after, 341
MSN Messenger, 168
newsgroup content, 190, 197
security and, 232
stationery, 141
synchronizing Web pages through, 89, 92, 93
use of the term, 59
Drafts folder, 128, 165
drop caps, 326, 327
DSL (Digital Subscriber Line), 22, 23, 40
Dummies.com Web site, 332
Dynamic HTML For Dummies, 2nd Edition (Hyman), 294

• E •

E-mail & Chat category, 216
E-mail Server Names page, 161
e-mail
  accounts, synchronizing, 125
  addressing, 111
  advantages of, 107
  attachments, 113, 114, 118
  basic description of, 14, 107, 108
  blind carbon copies of, 110
  carbon copies of, 110
  deleting, 118, 164
  forwarding, 118
  free, 20, 109
  HTML format for, 115, 116
  ISPs and, 24
  offline access to, 149
  printing, 118
  reading, 164
  receiving, 117
  replying to, 118
  screening unwanted, 130–134
  security features, 149–150
  sending, 109–111
  signatures, 142–143

software, 15
spell checking, 112
e-mail addresses
  Address Book for, 119–125
  configuring your Internet connection and, 30, 34
  finding, with Internet search services, 143, 144
  Hotmail, 154, 155, 157
  posting, on Web sites, 254
Edit button, 45
Edit Hyperlink dialog box, 276
Edit menu
  Find command, 61, 143
  Horizontal Line Properties command, 277
embedded style sheets, 301, 309
emoticons, 358
Employee Information section, 268
Enable button, 225
encapsulation, 295
Encoding button, 204
encoding techniques, 196
endproc command, 243
Enter Network Password dialog box, 287
Entertainment category, 216
Eraser tool, 181
error messages, 339
Ethernet interface cards, 23
Ethernet ports, 23
EuroSeek Web site, 70
events, 296–298, 305
Excite Web site, 70
Exit command, 181
Expedia, 216
Explorer bar, 44, 51, 52

• F •

Family.com, 216
FAQs (Frequently Asked Questions), 102, 255
Favorites bar, 44
Favorites button, 44, 82

Favorites menu
  accessing Web sites from, 79
  Add to Favorites command, 78
  adding Web pages to, 78, 332
  basic description of, 77
  folders, using, 80
  offline browsing and, 90–91
  Organize Favorites command, 81
  organizing links on, 81–82
  Synchronize command, 93
Favorites tab, 96, 99–100
fax transmissions, 21
Federal Express, 14
File Download dialog box, 59–60
File menu
  Close command, 61
  Delete Contact command, 172
  Exit command, 181
  Import and Export command, 82
  New Contact command, 121
  New Folder command, 123
  New Group command, 145
  Offline command, 91
  Print command, 54
  Print Preview command, 55
  Save As command, 57
File Name field, 57
File Transfer command, 183
File Transfer dialog box, 183
File Transfer Protocol (FTP), 6
filenames
  entering, 57
  for saved graphics, 58
  for saved Web pages, 57
files
  compression of, 114, 349
  downloading, 59–60
Filled Ellipse tool, 182
Filled Rectangle tool, 182
Filter & Sort button, 262
filtering e-mail, 130–134
financial information, 216
Find a Picture category, 64
Find command, 61

Find dialog box, 61
Find in Newsgroups category, 64
Find Now button, 144
Find People dialog box, 143, 144
Find Someone window, 177
First Amendment, 16
First field, 120
first-letter style element, 326, 327
first-line style element, 326, 327
flamed, use of the term, 195
Folder Properties dialog box, 125
folders
  Address Book, 123–125
  creating, 80, 81, 128
  deleting, 82
  moving, 82
  moving messages between, 129
  organizing e-mail in, 127–129
  organizing links in, 80–82
  renaming, 82
Folders and Groups command, 125
Folders button, 204
Font dialog box, 272–273
Font Size drop-down list, 272
font-family attribute, 300, 301
fonts
  customizing, 56, 209
  HTML and, 115
  selecting, 272–273
  size of, 56, 116, 209, 271
  stationery, 139
  styles and, 299, 301, 307
Fonts button, 209
font-size attribute, 300, 302
Forbes, 216
Format menu
  Appy Stationery command, 137
  Rich Text (HTML) command, 115
Fortune, 74
Forward button, 44, 50, 118
forward slash (/), 46
Fox News, 216
Fox Sports, 216

frames, 55
free e-mail, 20, 84, 109
free Internet access, 20
free Web hosting services, 257
Frequently Asked Questions (FAQs), 6
Fresno State softball team Web site, 90
From field, 160
FrontPage, 258, 259, 261, 286
FrontPage 2000 For Dummies
    (Dornfest), 253
FrontPage Express, 259
  basic description of, 261
  creating links with, 275
  formatting text with, 271, 273–274
  inserting graphics with, 276–281
  installing, 261–265
  Personal Home Page Wizard, 267–269, 271
  starting, 266
  viewing HTML source code with, 281–282
FTP (File Transfer Protocol)
  basic description of, 17
  uploading Web pages with, 286–287
Full Screen button, 204
full-screen view, 53

Gaming Zone (MSN), 216
General tab, 206, 207, 209, 228
GeoCities Web site, 258
Get Angry button, 312
Global Thermonuclear War, 342
Go button, 43
GO.com Web site, 71
Golf For Dummies (McCord), 201
GoTo.com Web site, 65, 71
graphics
  adding, to Web sites, 276–281
  attachments as, 119
  background, 280
  copyrights and, 58
  DHTML and, 296, 302
  downloading, 53
  finding, on the Web, 278

links consisting of, 48–49
  saving, 58
  Web site, 254
  which server as backgrounds for
    stationery, 139
Group Name text box, 145

hard disk space, 60
head tag, 298, 301
Headers Only option, 198
headings, 271, 299, 301, 302
Health category, 216
health information, 216
help, 6
  accessing, 95
  familiarizing yourself with, 96
  Hotmail, 165
  index, 98
  online resources, 102
  Personal Web Server and, 290
  scanning the contents of, 97
  Windows Millennium, 101, 102
Help dialog box, 99
Help menu
  About Internet Explorer command, 28
  Help Topics command, 95
Help toolbar, 98
Help Topics command, 95
Highlighter tool, 181
History bar, 50–52
History button, 44, 50, 342
history folder, 50, 209
hits
  basic description of, 65
  number of, displayed by search
    services, 65
Hoffman, Paul, 13
Home and Real Estate category, 216
Home button, 44, 51
home pages, 6
  adding your own links to, 216
  basic description of, 13, 253

home pages *(continued)*
customizing, 217–219
going to, 44, 51
personal, 254
settings for, 208, 214
Home tab, 121
HomeAdvisor (MSN), 216
Horizontal Line Properties command, 277
horizontal lines, 276, 277
host addresses, 46
host names, 10
hot keys, 3
Hotbar, 336
HotDog Professional, 259
Hotmail, 20, 84, 109
accounts, configuring Outlook Express to use, 160, 161, 163
accounts, signing up for, 152–155, 157–159
basic description of, 151
directories, 155
Inbox Protector, 157
MSN Messenger and, 170, 172
reasons to use, 151, 152
using, from the Web, 163–165
Hotmail icon, 159
Hotmail Web site, 109
href attribute, 302
HTC files, 304–305, 308, 319–321
HTML(Hypertext Markup Language)
components, 304
DHTML and, 294
files, saving, 58
formatting for e-mail, 115, 116
object model, 300
source code, viewing, 281, 282
HTML 4 For Dummies, 2nd Edition (Tittel and Pitts), 253
HTML command, 281
HTML formatting toolbar, 115
html tag, 303, 322
HTTP (Hypertext Transfer Protocol), 45, 46, 161, 212, 286
Hyman, Michael I., 294
Hyperterminal, 338
hyphen (-), 300

• I •

Icon Options control, 206
icons
indicating secure connections, 234
used in this book, 6
ICRA (Internet Content Rating Association), 353
ICRA Web site, 223
id attribute, 300
iframe tag, 302
Ignore All button, 113
Ignore button, 113
Image dialog box, 278
image maps, 49
IMAP accounts, 125
img tag, 296, 302
Import and Export command, 82
Inbox, 117, 125
Inbox folder, 128, 165
Inbox icon, 117
Inbox Protector page, 157
Include Message in Reply option, 194
Include Subfolders check box, 285
Increase Text Size button, 272
Index tab, 96, 98
Information Superhighway, 10
Infoseek Web site, 72
Init() function, 321
initProperties() function, 310
inline styles, 302
innerHTML property, 321
Insert Attachment dialog box, 113
Insert Image button, 278
Insert menu, Signature command, 143
Install a New Modem wizard, 339
Install Confirmation dialog box, 265
installation
configuring your Internet connection, 30–34
custom, 29
disks, 30
Internet Explorer, 28–29
Instant Message dialog box, 173
Instant Message window, 174

instant messaging
  basic description of, 17–18
  offline notifications, 175
  receiving messages, 174
  sending messages, 173, 174
  setting up, 168
  software for, 18
  using, 167–170, 172
Integrated Services Digital Network
  (ISDN), 6
Internet
  access setup, 20, 21, 23–27
  basic description of, 9–11
  diverse services offered by, 12–14, 16, 17
  free access to, 20
  invention of, 11, 12
Internet Accounts dialog box, 162
Internet Address field, 286
Internet Connection Wizard, 30–34, 160,
  161
Internet Content Rating Association
  (ICRA), 222, 223
Internet Directories page, 155
Internet Domain Survey, 10
Internet E-mail Address page, 160, 161
Internet Explorer Developer Center, 319, 328
Internet Explorer icon, 28, 34, 39
The Internet For Dummies, 7th Edition
  (Levine, Baroudi, and Young), 3
Internet Mail Logon page, 161
Internet Options command, 206
Internet Options dialog box, 206–214, 224
Internet White Pages directory, 155
Internet zone, 235
intrinsic events, 296–298
IP (Internet Protocol), 11, 30, 35
IRC (Internet Relay Chat), 18
isAngry variable, 315
ISDN (Integrated Services Ditigal
  Network), 22
ISPs
  basic description of, 20, 23, 256
  deleting of e-mail from servers by, 125
  hosting services offered by, 256–257
  Hotmail and, 152
  information from, configuring your
    Internet connection and, 30, 31

  newsgroups and, 186
  rates, 27, 62
  services provided by, 23
  types of, 26, 27

JavaScript, 354
JPEG (Joint Photographic Expert Group)
  format, 58
JScript, 294, 296, 300, 354, 356

keyboard shortcuts, 2
kids
  chat and, 344, 345
  safety tips for, 343–346

LAN (local area networks), 20
Language button, 209
languages, foreign, 209
Last field, 120
Launch Internet Explorer Browser icon, 39
Launch Outlook Express button, 108, 188
less-than sign (<), 246
Levine, John R., 3
Library of Congress Web site, 278
Line tool, 181
line-feed character, 245
link tag, 301
linked style sheets, 301–302
links
  basic description of, 13
  color of, 48, 209
  creating, 275
  customizing your home page with, 216
  deleting, 86, 87
  following, 48, 49
  graphical, 48, 49
  returning to, 50
Links folder, 86

Links to the Past link, 49
Links toolbar, 43, 83, 85, 86
  basic description of, 202
  customizing, 203, 332, 335
List Properties dialog box, 274
local information, 216, 217
Local intranet zone, 235
Lock Contents tool, 182
Lock icon, 234, 235
logging off
  basic description of, 62
  commands for, 62
logon
  automatic, 41
  basic description of, 39–41
  offline browsing features which use, 93
  scripts, 239–242, 244, 245, 247–249
Logon option, 93
logos, 58
Look Up a Word category, 64
Lycos Web site, 72

• *M* •

Macromedia Dreamweaver 3, 258
Mail and News command, 108, 188
Mail button, 44, 108, 110
Mail check box, 138
Mail icon, 188
mail servers, 125
mailing groups, 144–146
mailing lists, 187
Make a New Connection Wizard, 211
Make Available Offline check box, 78
Make Available Offline option, 78, 90
Map Drive button, 204
margins, 139, 140
marquees, 279
Maximize button, 40, 266
Mayo Clinic, 216
McCord, Gary, 201
MediaOne, 186
Members list box, 146
menu bars, 43
Merriam-Webster, 216

Merrill Lynch, 216
Message menu
  Combine and Decode command, 196
  New Message command, 109
  New Message Using command, 137
message rules, 130, 131, 133, 134
Message Rules command, 131
Message Rules dialog box, 132, 134
Messenger button, 45
methods, 312, 314
microphones, 176, 179
Microsoft Content Replication System
    (CRS), 286
Microsoft Home Publishing Web site, 141
Microsoft NetMeeting
  basic description of, 18, 176
  features, list of, 176
Microsoft Network, The, 19, 24
  basic description of, 25
  e-mail addresses, 111
  rates, 25, 27
  Web browsers and, 27
Microsoft Office 2000, 15
Microsoft Outlook, 108
  basic description of, 15
Microsoft public newsgroups, 188
Microsoft TechNet, 216
Microsoft Visual InterDev, 258
Microsoft VM options, 213
Microsoft Web site, 47, 84, 102
Microsoft Word, 58
Middle field, 120
MILNET, 11
misc newsgroups, 187
Modem Properties dialog box, 249
modems
  basic description of, 21, 355
  configuring your Internet connection
    and, 31, 249
  fax support for, 21
  installing/reinstalling, 339
  port settings for, 338
  shopping for, 21
  speed of, 21
  terminology for, 21
  troubleshooting, 338, 339

Modems icon, 338
moderated newsgroups, 185, 186
motion picture ratings, 221, 222
mouse rollover effects, 328
MouseOut function, 321
mouseover effect, 298, 299
MouseOver function, 321
Move Down button, 197, 206
Move Handle, 203
Move to Folder button, 82
Move to Folder command, 130
Move Up button, 197, 206
MSN Home Pages Web site, 258
MSN Messenger
  basic description of, 18, 167
  contact lists, 169–172
  offline notifications, 175
  receiving instant messages with, 174
  running, 169
  saving chat files in, 344
  sending instant messages with, 173–174
  setting up, 168–170, 172
  starting, 45
  status settings, 175
  using, 167, 168
MSN Messenger command, 169
MSN Messenger icon, 168, 169
MSN Search Web site, 74
msn.com Web site, 214–216, 218, 219,
    331, 332
MSNBC, 216
MSNBC Entertainment, 216
MSNBC Health, 216
MSNBC Sports, 216
MTV, 216
multimedia, 213
Murphy's Law, 53
My Computer, 29, 60, 341
My Documents folder, 57

• N •

Name field, 78, 90
Name tab, 120
Name text box, 78

namespaces, 303, 308, 322
National Park Service Web site, 49, 53
National Science Foundation (NSF), 12
navigation
  following links, 48, 49
  going to specific pages, 47, 48
  returning to links, 50
  using the History feature, 50, 51
NETCOM, 26
NetMeeting
  chat feature, 179, 180
  placing calls with, 177, 179
  sending files with, 176, 182, 183
  setting up, 211
  sharing applications with, 176, 184
  Whiteboard feature, 176, 180–182
Netscape Communicator, 13
Netscape Communicator 4.5 For Dummies
    (Hoffman), 13
Netscape Navigator browser
  basic description of, 13
  Hotmail and, 152
  importing links from, 82
  learning more about, 13
Network dialog box, 291
Network icon, 291
Network Solutions Web site, 257
Network Wizards, 10
Network Wizards Web site, 10
New Account Setup command, 152
New Contact command, 121
New Folder button, 80
New Folder command, 123
New Group command, 145
New Mail button, 109, 163
New Mail Rule dialog box, 132, 133
New Message command, 109
New Message dialog box, 109, 110, 122, 163
New Message Rule dialog box, 133
New Message Using command, 137
New Message window, 136
New Messages Only option, 198
New Page dialog box, 267
New Post button, 195

News category, 216
news headlines, 216
news newsgroups, 187
news servers, 30, 34, 186, 188
  deleting of older newsgroup postings
    by, 194
  newsgroup listings on, 189, 190
  setting up, 189
  using multiple, 192
News tab, 192
newsgroups
  accessing, 188–190
  attachments found in, 196
  basic description of, 15–16, 185–186
  categories of, 187
  ISPs and, 24
  Microsoft, 188
  moderated, 185, 186
  names of, 187
  offensive content in, 186
  offline access for, 197
  printing articles from, 193
  reading articles in, 193
  reading threads in, 192
  regional, 187
  replying to articles in, 194
  saving articles from, 193
  subscriptions to, 191
  switching to and from articles in, 193
  types of, 185, 186
  unmoderated, 186
  writing articles for, 195
Newsgroups button, 192
normal value, 327
Northern Light Web site, 74
Norton Internet Security from
    Symantec, 336
Notepad, 241
NSFNET, 12
Number of Copies setting, 54
number value, 327
numbered lists, 116, 274
Numbered tab, 274

• O •

offline browsing feature
  making pages available with, 90, 91
  synchronizing Web pages with, 89, 92, 93
  viewing Web pages with, 91, 92
Offline command, 91
Offline mode, 92
On Idle option, 93
On the Phone status setting, 175
onAngry event, 316, 317
onblur event, 297
onCalmDown event, 316
onclick event, 296, 297
ondblclick event, 297
onfocus event, 297
onkeydown event, 297
onkeypress event, 297
onkeyup event, 297
online services
  advantages of, 26
  basic description of, 24, 25
  changing role of, 27
  rates, 25, 26
Online status setting, 175
onload event, 297
onmousedown event, 297
onmousemove event, 297
onmouseout event, 297, 298, 305
onmouseover event, 297
onmouseup event, 297
onunload event, 297
Open dialog box, 248
Options command, 138
Options dialog box, 137, 138, 140–142
Options page, 165
Organize Favorites command, 81
Organize Favorites dialog box, 81, 82, 86, 91
Out to Lunch status setting, 175
Outbox folder, 128
Outlook Express
  Address Book, 119–124, 125
  basic description of, 15
  changing identities with, 147, 148
  checking for e-mail with, 109

configuration of, 34, 211
finding e-mail addressses on the Internet
  with, 143, 144
folders, using, 127–129
HTML formatting with, 115, 116
mailing groups, 144–146
newsgroup access with, 16, 188–193,
  195–197
offline mode, 149
receiving e-mail with, 117
screening unwanted mail with, 130–134
security features, 149, 150
sending attachments with, 113, 114
sending e-mail with, 109–111
signatures, 142, 143
spell checking messages with, 112
starting, 108, 109
stationery, 135–140
using Hotmail accounts with, 160,
  161, 163

● *P* ●

Page Properties dialog box, 280, 281
Page Title text box, 269
Page URL text box, 269
paragraphs, 299, 307, 326, 327
Parent Soup, 216
Passport service, 170, 171
Password field, 154
passwords
  changing, 229
  configuring your connection and, 30, 33
  Content Advisor and, 226, 227, 229
  forgetting your, 339
  Hotmail, 154, 162
  logon and, 40
  logon scripts and, 240, 241, 243, 245
  supervisor, 226, 229
  tips for picking, 227
  uploading Web pages and, 287
Paste button, 204
pasting URLs, 48
Pen tool, 181
percent value, 328

personal certificates, 237
Personal Finance category, 216
Personal Home Page Wizard, 267– 269, 271
Personal Interests section, 268
Personal Items folder, 128
Personal Web Manager, 290, 291
Personal Web Manager dialog box, 291
Personal Web Server
  accessing Web pages on, 291
  basic description of, 289
  publishing Web pages with, 291
  starting, 290
Personalize page, 219
Pitts, Natanya, 253
PKUNZIP, 349
PKZIP, 360
plus sign (+), 193
pop-ups, 328
pornography, 16, 222
portals, 214
PPP (Point-to-Point Protocol), 35
Prevent Control button, 184
Prevention's Healthy Ideas, 216
Print button, 45, 55
Print command, 54
Print dialog box, 54, 55
Print Frames option, 55
Print Preview, 55
Print Preview button, 205
Print Preview command, 55
printing
  basic description of, 54, 55
  controls, 328
  e-mail, 118
  newsgroup articles, 193
  number of copies setting for, 54
  options, 213
  Web pages, 54, 55, 328
  Whiteboard drawings, 181
printPage method, 328
procmain command, 243, 244
Product Updates link, 262
Profile Information page, 153
Programs tab, 207, 211, 212

Properties button, 338
Properties command, 125, 247
Properties dialog box, 121, 145, 146, 247, 248
pseudo-elements, 326
public libraries, 20

• *Q* •

question mark (?), 67
Question Mark icon, 95
QuickTime, 357

• *R* •

Radio & Video category, 216
radio broadcasts, 216
Radio toolbar
  basic description of, 202
Rathbone, Andy, 3
ratings
  limitations of, 224
  numbers for, meaning of, 222
  settings for, 224–226
  unrated sites and, 224, 228, 229
Read Mail option, 108
Read News command, 188
Read News link, 189, 191
Real button, 45
real-estate information, 216
Real.com Web site, 45, 84
RealPlayer, 84
rec newsgroups, 187
Reference category, 216
refresh action, 44, 52, 53
Refresh button, 44
Region and Time Zone page, 153
regional newsgroups, 187
rel attribute, 302
Related button, 205
Remote Pointer tool, 182
Remove button, 100
Rename button, 82
Reply to All button, 118
Reply to Group button, 194

resource names, 46
Restricted sites zone, 235
Retype Password field, 154
Reuters News, 72
Rich Text (HTML) command, 115
right-clicking, 334
RSAC rating system, 222–226
Rule Description text box, 132, 133
Run This Program from Its Current Location option, 60
Run This Program from the Internet option, 60

• *S* •

Sausage Software, 259
Save As command, 57
Save As dialog box, 57, 58, 60, 118, 341
Save button, 58
Save Picture As command, 58
Save This Program to Disk option, 59, 60
savedColor variable, 305
savedSize variable, 305
saving
  attachments, 196
  chat files, 344
  e-mail attachments, 118
  graphics, 58
  inappropriate postings, 344
  newsgroup articles, 193
  scripts, 242
  Web pages, 57, 271
Scheduled option, 93
sci newsgroups, 187
Scripting tab, 247
scripts
  basic description of, 295–298, 300
  functions and, 298, 299
  HTML tag for, 296
scroll bars, 44, 328
scrolling marquees, 279
Search bar, 44, 334
  accessing, 64
  basic description of, 63–65
  customizing, 66, 67

tips for using, 66
using search services from, 68–72, 74, 75
Search button, 44, 63
search engines
  accessing, 68
  basic description of, 68, 334, 335
  list of, 68–76
Search for a Contact option, 172
Search tab, 96, 99
Search text box, 170
security, 6
  basic issues, 232, 233
  certifying your, 237
  downloading and, 232
  e-mail and, 149, 150
  levels, 219
  options, 206, 209, 213, 219, 238
  software, 336
  SSL, 232,–235
  viewing Web sites and, 233
  zones, 233, 235, 236
Security tab, 206, 209, 219
Select a Directory drop-down list, 177
Select Area tool, 182
Select Background Image dialog box, 281
Select Group Members dialog box, 145
Select Recipients dialog box, 122, 125
Select Stationery dialog box, 135, 136, 138
Select Window tool, 182
Selector tool, 181
Send button, 110
Send tab, 121, 194
Sent Items folder, 128
Sent Messages folder, 165
Separator option, 205
Serial Line Internet Protocol (SLIP), 6
Set As Wallpaper command, 58
Set Up a Newsgroups Account link, 189
Settings button, 197, 208
Setup Hotmail Account Wizard, 152, 153
Setup program, 29
Sharing command, 184
Shopping category, 216
shortcuts, creating, 333
Show Text button, 324

Show TOC button, 278
Sidewalk City Guide, 216
Signature command, 143
signatures
  basic description of, 142
  creating, 142, 143
  creating multiple, 143
Signatures list box, 143
Signatures tab, 142
site certificates, 237
Size button, 56, 57, 204
SLIP (Serial Line Internet Protocol), 35
smileys, 358
Smith, Bud, 253
soc newsgroups, 187
Software folder, 265
Solitaire, 173
source code, viewing, 281, 282
span tag, 302
Special Styles tab, 273
Specific Search Item text box, 262
spell checking, 112, 195
Spelling command, 112
spiders, 69
Sports category, 216
sports news, 216
SSL (Secure Sockets Layer), 232–234
Standard Buttons toolbar, 43, 44, 50
  adding buttons to, 204, 205
  basic description of, 202
  customizing, 203–205
Standard toolbar, 64, 82
Stanford University, 75
stationery
  basic description of, 135
  creating, 138–140
  creating messages with, 135–137
  setting default, 137, 138
  used for newsgroup articles, 196
Stationery Setup Wizard, 138–140
status bars, 44
Stop button, 44, 53, 290
strings, 245
style attribute, 302
Style drop-down list, 271

style sheets
  basic description of, 299
  embedded, 301, 309
  inline styles and, 302
  linked, 301, 302
style tag, 301
styles, 271, 295–302, 326, 327
Subject field, 110, 114
Subscribe button, 191
Subscribed tab, 192
subscriptions
  newsgroup, 191
  use of the term, for the offline browsing
    feature, 89
Summary tab, 120
Supervisor Can Type a Password to Allow
    Users to View Restricted Content
    option, 229
Supreme Court, Internet legislation ruling, 16
Synchronization Settings dialog box, 93
Synchronize Account button, 198
Synchronize All command, 125
Synchronize command, 92
Synchronize dialog box, 92
synchronizing e-mail accounts, 125
synchronizing newsgroups, 197
synchronizing Web pages, 89, 92, 93

• T •

talk newsgroups, 187
taskbar, 340
technical support, 6, 102
  provided by ISPs, 24
  provided by online services, 26
telephone lines, 20, 22, 338
telephone numbers, for Internet access,
    30, 32
templates, 258, 268
temporary files, 208
text
  adding, to Whiteboard drawings, 181
  aligning, 116, 273
  color, 116, 272, 305, 311
  file format, 58
  finding, 61

indenting, 273
  scrolling marquees, 279
  styles, 271
Text Color button, 272
Text Options control, 206
Text Size command, 56
Text tool, 181
threads
  basic description of, 192
  collapsing, 193
  reading, 192
timing elements, 328
title bars, 43
Tittel, Ed, 253
To Join This Conversation option, 174
Today on MSN category, 216
toolbars
  arranging, 203
  basic description of, 201, 202
  buttons on, 201
  customizing, 204–206, 334, 336
  hiding/displaying, 202, 203
Toolbars command, 56, 202
Toolbars menu, 202
Tools menu
  Accounts command, 160, 192
  Address Book command, 121
  File Transfer command, 183
  Internet Options command, 206
  Mail and News command, 108, 188
  Message Rules command, 131
  MSN Messenger command, 169
  New Account Setup command, 152
  Options command, 138
  Sharing command, 184
  Spelling command, 112
  Synchronize All command, 125
  Synchronize command, 92
  Whiteboard command, 180
transmit command, 243, 245
Trash Can folder, 165
travel information, 216
troubleshooting, 6, 101
Trusted sites zone, 235
TurnItOn function, 299
Type Specific Words dialog box, 132

• *U* •

Unfilled Ellipse tool, 182
Unfilled Rectangle tool, 182
UNIX, 257
unmoderated newsgroups, 186
Unsynchronize tool, 182
Up button, 204
Update button, 67
upgrades
  Internet Explorer, 29, 30
  Windows operating system, 20
URLs
  AutoComplete feature for, 47
  basic description of, 45, 46
  copying/pasting, 48
  display of, in the Address bar, 43
  entering, 45, 47, 335, 340
  examples of, 46
  formatting of, in this book, 3
  going to specific, 47, 48
  parts of, 45
Use Current button, 208, 214
Usenet
  basic description of, 186
  newsgroup names, 187
  servers, 186
Usenet newsgroups, 16
user IDs, 40
Users Can See Sites That Have No Rating
  check box, 228

• *V* •

VBScript, 300, 356, 359
video communications, 176, 179
View menu
  Arrange Icons command, 341
  Bcc command, 110
  Details command, 341
  Folder and Groups command, 125
  HTML command, 281
  Text Size command, 56
  Toolbars command, 56, 202

ViewLink components, 319–322
viruses, 119, 359
Visual Basic (Microsoft), 296

• *W* •

`waitfor` command, 243, 244
Wall Street Journal, The, 74
wallpaper settings, 58
War Games Web site, 342
Web browsers
  basic description of, 13
  online services and, 27
  provided by ISPs, 24
  types of, 13
Web pages, 6
  basic description of, 12, 13, 253
  creating, 215, 253–258
  deciding what to put on, 254, 255
  going to specific, 47, 48
  hosting services for, 256, 257
  refreshing, 52, 53
  saving, 57
  size of, 12
  synchronizing, 89, 92, 93
Web Publishing Wizard
  starting, 284
  updating Web files with, 289
  using, 283–291
Web servers
  basic description of, 13, 255
  getting space on, for your Web page,
    255–257
  uploading Web pages to, 283, 284, 286,
    287, 289, 290, 291
Web sites, 6
  basic description of, 13, 253
  restricted, 235
  secure viewing of, 233
  special interest, 254
  trusted, 235
WebCourier page, 158
Whiteboard, 176, 180–182
Whiteboard command, 180

windows
  expanding/collapsing elements of, 43
  finding lost, 340, 341
  hiding/displaying elements of, 44, 52
  parts of, 42, 43, 44
  sizing/resizing, 40
Windows 2000 (Microsoft), 20, 30, 257
Windows 95 (Microsoft), 241
Windows 98 (Microsoft), 30, 241
Windows 98 For Dummies (Rathbone), 3
Windows Explorer, 123
Windows folder, 58
Windows Hyperterminal, 338
Windows Millennium Edition (Microsoft),
      20, 168, 176, 241, 262
  help system, 101, 102
  troubleshooters, 101, 102
Windows NT (Microsoft), 257
Windows Paint, 176, 181
Windows Setup, 262
Windows Update, 30, 84, 262, 264
WinZip, 114, 349, 360
WinZip Web site, 114
Wired, 216
Work Offline button, 91

World Wide Web, 6
  basic description of, 12, 13, 360
  HTML and, 115
writing-mode property, 324, 325
WU Corporate Catalog, 262

XML (eXtensible Markup Language), 303
xmlns attribute, 303, 322

Yahoo! Web site, 75, 258, 278
Young, Margaret Levine, 3
Your Links category, 216

zip codes, 216, 217
zones, security, 233, 235, 236
zoom attribute, 327
Zoom tool, 182

Notes

Notes

Notes

Notes

Notes

Notes

YOUR ONLINE RESOURCE

WWW.DUMMIES.COM

Discover Dummies Online!

The Dummies Web Site is your fun and friendly online resource for the latest information about *For Dummies*® books and your favorite topics. The Web site is the place to communicate with us, exchange ideas with other *For Dummies* readers, chat with authors, and have fun!

Ten Fun and Useful Things You Can Do at www.dummies.com

1. Win free *For Dummies* books and more!
2. Register your book and be entered in a prize drawing.
3. Meet your favorite authors through the IDG Books Worldwide Author Chat Series.
4. Exchange helpful information with other *For Dummies* readers.
5. Discover other great *For Dummies* books you must have!
6. Purchase Dummieswear® exclusively from our Web site.
7. Buy *For Dummies* books online.
8. Talk to us. Make comments, ask questions, get answers!
9. Download free software.
10. Find additional useful resources from authors.

Link directly to these ten fun and useful things at
http://www.dummies.com/10useful

For other technology titles from IDG Books Worldwide, go to
www.idgbooks.com

Not on the Web yet? It's easy to get started with *Dummies 101*®: *The Internet For Windows® 98* or *The Internet For Dummies*® at local retailers everywhere.

Find other *For Dummies* books on these topics:
Business • Career • Databases • Food & Beverage • Games • Gardening • Graphics • Hardware
Health & Fitness • Internet and the World Wide Web • Networking • Office Suites
Operating Systems • Personal Finance • Pets • Programming • Recreation • Sports
Spreadsheets • Teacher Resources • Test Prep • Word Processing

IDG BOOKS WORLDWIDE BOOK REGISTRATION

Register This Book and Win!

We want to hear from you!

Visit **http://my2cents.dummies.com** to register this book and tell us how you liked it!

- ✔ Get entered in our monthly prize giveaway.

- ✔ Give us feedback about this book — tell us what you like best, what you like least, or maybe what you'd like to ask the author and us to change!

- ✔ Let us know any other *For Dummies®* topics that interest you.

Your feedback helps us determine what books to publish, tells us what coverage to add as we revise our books, and lets us know whether we're meeting your needs as a *For Dummies* reader. You're our most valuable resource, and what you have to say is important to us!

Not on the Web yet? It's easy to get started with *Dummies 101®: The Internet For Windows® 98* or *The Internet For Dummies®* at local retailers everywhere.

Or let us know what you think by sending us a letter at the following address:

For Dummies Book Registration
Dummies Press
10475 Crosspoint Blvd.
Indianapolis, IN 46256

...FOR DUMMIES™

BESTSELLING
BOOK SERIES